Camp Sites

Post 45 Florence Dore and Michael Szalay, Editors
Post•45 Group, Editorial Committee

Camp Sites

Sex, Politics, and Academic Style in Postwar America

Michael Trask

Stanford University Press
Stanford, California

Stanford University Press
Stanford, California

Printed in the United States of America on acid-free, archival-quality paper

Library of Congress Cataloging-in-Publication Data

Trask, Michael, 1967– author.
 Camp sites : sex, politics, and academic style in postwar America / Michael Trask.
  pages cm. — (Post 45)
 Includes bibliographical references and index.
 ISBN 978-0-8047-8440-5 (cloth: alk. paper) - ISBN 978-0-8047-8441-2 (pbk: alk. paper)
  1. American literature—20th century—History and criticism. 2. Homosexuality and literature—United States—History—20th century. 3. Politics and literature—United States—History—20th century. 4. Literature and society—United States—History—20th century. 5. Camp (Style)—United States—History—20th century. 6. Politics and culture—United States—History—20th century. 7. Universities and colleges—Political aspects—United States—History—20th century. 8. United States—Social life and customs—1945–1970. I. Title. II. Series: Post 45.
 PS225.T73 2013
 810.9'3587392—dc23
                    2012050735

Typeset by Bruce Lundquist in 10/15 Minion

For Stephen, who makes life go best

Contents

Acknowledgments

I am grateful to Beth Hewitt and Jared Gardner, whose thorough attention to the various drafts of this book has made its final incarnation even possible. I am lucky that the best readers I know are also my best friends. Tony Scott has commented on many of the pages that follow; his example inspires and grounds my own thinking. At crucial stages of this book's gestation, Jonathan Kramnick has provided advice as humane and sound as his friendship.

I have been unusually blessed in my friends and colleagues at the University of Kentucky, and I'd like to thank them for creating a community in which I feel I have thrived for the last decade. Brandy Anderson, Stefan Bird-Pollan, Virginia Blum, Jeff Clymer, Andy Doolen, Janet Eldred, Pearl James, Peter Kalliney, Karen Rignall, Ellen Rosenman, and Leon Sachs in particular have made life and work in Lexington a pleasure verging on the idyllic. Gordon Hutner and Alan Nadel have been supporters of this project for a long time, and I am grateful to both for encouraging me at important turns in the book's evolution. Nancy Armstrong and Tom Otten make the world a better place for thinking people everywhere.

The Post•45 series editors, Michael Szalay and Florence Dore, have shepherded this book through publication with splendid good humor and a considerateness for which I'll long be in their debt. I am just as obliged to the press readers for their transformative reports and to Stanford's supremely capable acquisitions editor, Emily-Jane Cohen.

Parts of Chapters 2 and 5 appeared in "In the Bathroom with Mary McCarthy: Theatricality, Deviance, and the Postwar Commitment to Realism," *Criticism* 49.1 (Winter 2007): 7–33. Part of Chapter 4 appeared as "Patricia Highsmith's Method," *American Literary History* 22.3 (Fall 2010): 584–614.

4

Abbreviations

A	Goffman, *Asylums*
"AC"	Riesman, "The Academic Career"
BB	McCarthy, *A Bolt from the Blue and Other Essays*
C	Cleto, *Camp: Queer Aesthetics and the Performing Subject*
CE	Ellison, *The Collected Essays of Ralph Ellison*
EL	Goffman, *The Presentation of Self in Everyday Life*
FW	Varnum, *Fencing with Words*
IR	Goffman, *Interaction Ritual*
LC	Riesman, *The Lonely Crowd*
LL	Nabokov, *Lectures on Literature*
OC	McCarthy, *On the Contrary*
PS	Mailer, *The Prisoner of Sex*
"PSR"	Riesman, "Permissiveness and Sex Roles"
PW	Highsmith, *Plotting and Writing Suspense Fiction*
S	Goffman, *Stigma*
"SA"	Gray, "Stanislavski and America"
SO	Nabokov, *Strong Opinions*
TS	Bloom and Breines, *"Takin' It to the Streets"*
VG	Jay and Young, *Out of the Closets: Voices of Gay Liberation*
WA	Kameny, *We Are Everywhere*

Introduction

Camp Sites tracks the career of the ironic social style that both shaped the liberal consensus in Cold War America and furnished a prime target for those who sought to dismantle that consensus in the era of the New Social Movements. The book's governing antithesis seems to rehearse a familiar grudge match: in this corner, an establishment liberalism; in that corner, an activism arising in and through the New Left. However, the differences between the conformist Fifties and the dissident Sixties are much less substantive than we have been encouraged to assume. Heeding the curiously central role that a vision of closeted homosexuality played in the cultural politics of the postwar United States, I lay out the shift from a representation of queer sexuality as the abject other of mainstream liberal culture to an image of queer sexuality as the statist enemy of the counterculture and the New Left. I demonstrate that the New Left's critique of establishment liberalism drew with surprising frequency on Cold War culture's wide repertoire of homophobic suppositions. By focusing on the New Left insistence that institutions be normatively authentic, that they live up to their professed missions, I also show why the New Social Movements had such difficulty with the queers whom they could neither quite welcome nor quite expel from their midst. The equation radicals forged between authenticity and a meaningful life rendered gay culture's uncommitted and artificial persons beyond redemption, even if such figures would serve a role in defining countercultural commitment by their negative example.

That Sixties radicals coveted authenticity and denounced artifice is hardly news. Yet attending to camp will allow us to chart the rise and fall of liberalism's ironic style by other means. This book explores the parallel between camp's strategies of improvisation and the various postwar university disciplines that together fostered what I call an "epistemology of make-believe." "One of the most effective and fruitful ways to develop scenarios and aid the imagination," the Cold War nuclear strategist Herman Kahn writes in *Thinking about the Un-thinkable* (1962), "is by an artificial role-playing type of exercise."[1] Kahn belonged to a cohort of systems analysts who understood the games they devised as a matter of life and death and had no qualms about submitting themselves as players in the simulated environments they concocted. This vogue for self-experimentation bears more than passing resemblance to what Susan Sontag calls "the theatricalization of experience embodied in the camp sensibility."[2] From B. F. Skinner's behaviorism to Erving Goffman's dramaturgical account of social life to the New Critics' disdain for literalist reading, midcentury academic disciplines placed the theatrical, the synthetic, the artificial, and the constructed at the heart of their research programs.

As Kahn's example vividly shows, the appreciation for contrived experience accompanied the rise of a novel conception of politics in Cold War America. This era not only gave voice to the notion that politics existed outside the parameters of official government institutions but also fostered the assumption that politics was something one was more or less always performing. For reasons detailed in the first chapter, this duet of assumptions was strongly anchored in the postwar university, whose personnel spent a good deal of time reflecting on the politicization of their institution—indeed, reflecting in general on the contingency of that institution. In the broad institutional support it granted to a flexible take on reality, postwar school culture gravitated toward the account of knowledge that John Dewey, the twentieth century's foremost pragmatist as well as its most prominent educational theorist, dubbed "instrumentalism." It is through his presiding example that we can see how closely the pragmatic educational mandate in postwar society followed on the heels of the esteem accorded to what I call the "syllabus of experience." Under Dewey's auspices, educators pursued a curricular revision whose goal was both to elevate experience as a category of interpretation and to sever experience from claims to self-evidence.

"Instrumental logic," as Lawrence Frank maintained in a 1950 gloss on Dewey's thought, consisted in elucidating what Frank called the "circular processes which produce personalities who in turn maintain the culture."[3] The college's role in the research and development of such "circular," context-dependent subjectivity rendered it an inevitable target for the New Social Movements. The student Left's favorite allegation was that the university, through its insistence on rote performances whose substance and meaning everyone was taught to disbelieve, tutored its clientele in the lessons of an inauthentic life. To speak of the Fifties as a "consensus culture" is to recognize what was really a consensus of make-believe, less in the sense that such consensus was imaginary than in the sense that make-believe was something whose value diverse thinkers could all agree on. In the postwar ideal of social order, persons were compelled by no regulatory agency more onerous than their agreement to behave as if an institution had a constraining effect on their actions that no one honored except in the breach.

This antifoundational temperament, in which the sole mandate was to feign an institutional loyalty that few were naïve enough to heed, revealed an uncomfortable resemblance between the liberal's endorsement of collusive playacting and the less savory versions of such notions in the subculture of closeted queer life. The latter's denizens were as adept as the professors in navigating institutions whose rules they pretended to observe as a pretext for electing roles outside those prescribed by those institutions. In the figure of the closet queen, the New Left had a ready-to-hand template with which to format its critique of the professoriat. Based on what appeared to be a shared attitude toward the provisional nature of institutional roles, the homosexual and the college professor came together frequently in the New Left imagination, and it was no strain on the radical mind to enroll the queer's bad character as a way of holding the faculty in contempt. *Camp Sites* devotes much attention to the cunning dialectical vagaries of what David Johnson has called "the lavender scare," the prolonged moment of homosexual panic that helped to cement, long after its Fifties heyday, an enduring equation between the closet and bureaucratic personhood.[4] In renouncing the Cold War establishment, the New Left assimilated the inauthentic liberal to the effeminate perverts whose bad habits liberals had themselves treated as the abject foil to the academic style.

The term "liberalism" in this book refers to a conceptual framework whose modern origins are traceable to utilitarianism by way of John Stuart Mill, on the one hand, and American pragmatism by way of Dewey, on the other. I am the first to admit that this is a selective genealogy (particularly since it leaves America's Lockean pedigree by the wayside), but it has the advantage of highlighting the fact that midcentury American liberals renovated their political theory by combining utilitarian consequentialism and pragmatist antifoundationalism into what Charles Taylor calls "procedural liberalism."[5] This is a mouthful of "isms," a fact that renders slightly ironic the point I mean to draw from this combination, which is the tendency of such procedural liberalism to announce its bona fides by renouncing isms, a disavowal that post-war American intellectuals enshrined as the "end of ideology." Propelled by the thermals of the utilitarian and pragmatist traditions, midcentury liberals imagined themselves carried above the fray of doctrinal belief. Moreover, they enhanced this self-image not only by massively widening the scope of what counted as orthodoxy but also by giving a certain intellectual heft to what the political theorist Robert McCloskey referred to as "the American preoccupation with process as contrasted with substance."[6] What I mean to stress is less the content of liberalism, or even its method, than the social style to which that lineage gives rise: a *personality* (to invoke a term of art favored among postwar intellectuals) for whom all positions are mere formalities, opportunities from which to choose when necessary to make what McCloskey calls "*ad hoc* adjustments to circumstances as they arise."[7]

In defining politics as "adjustment," McCloskey makes clear how much the postwar liberal establishment had come to tailor its thought to the pragmatist view of things, an outlook captured in William James's assertion, in 1907, that "all our theories are *instrumental,* are mental modes of *adaptation* to reality."[8] In the consolidation of midcentury liberalism, what comes to prominence is a political framework grounded on *stylistics,* a kind of political etiquette whose "manners are as various and flexible," according to James, as those of pragmatism itself.[9] And what recedes from view is a political framework grounded on *ethics,* on the appeal to what a democracy ought to be, what normative aims it should have, and what qualities might guarantee or advance those aims. The result, as Chapters 1 and 2 spell out in detail, is a shift from a liberalism founded on positive beliefs to a liberalism founded on a suspension of disbelief worthy of its Coleridgean forebear. These chapters describe how the penchant for construing the proper epistemological relation to the knowable world as strategic make-believe not only lays claim to the social field in and around the university but also promotes a personality congenial to that setting: what Taylor calls the "buffered identity" of the "secular age," a figure both "disengaged" and "disciplined" (indeed, whose self-discipline amounts to disengagement), a self whose relation to modernity is predicated on "minimal conformity" to the "code" of its prevailing institutions.[10]

While we are used to seeing the pre-Sixties moment in the grip of a by-now-clichéd conformism, we rarely observe the frequency with which Fifties thinkers understood this particular social ill as equipped with its own autoimmune response, detectable in Taylor's provocative notion of "minimal conformity." "The implication," Taylor says of the early modern buffered identity in a gloss that applies in part to midcentury liberalism, "is that there is some global option possible to 'believe,' which is here being wisely and bravely refused, presumably involving unnecessary, gratuitous, unfounded beliefs, about things that the buffered identity happily considers external and ignorable."[11] Taylor is describing the modern cultural logic whereby "buffered" persons, so long as they pay what they understand as the barest of deference to institutional legitimacy (his example is church membership), can be pulled into an institution's orbit yet disencumbered of the obligation—or spared the indignity—of being, to use the postwar liberal's pejorative, "true believers." In fact, however, this is at best an approximation of the midcentury liberal situation. For the liberal personality on the rise after World War II was not only keenly suspicious of "unfounded beliefs" but also willing to give any belief the benefit of the doubt provided that it could be shown to have demonstrable utility. Taylor's buffered identity, inhabiting a world where lay and religious forces vie for dominance, makes a separate peace with faith in which the world is divided into real and "unnecessary" beliefs. Postwar liberals by contrast don't see any beliefs as necessary. But by the same token, neither do they see any beliefs as unnecessary. More accurately, because postwar liberals did not identify themselves with their beliefs, they imagined themselves as capable of donning and shedding beliefs as needed in order to work toward best outcomes.

In this respect, it is worth emphasizing that the most pronounced feature of the liberal personality whose social style I extrapolate in the following pages is its stringent antiessentialism, its disinclination to sacrifice the versatility of an ecumenical mind-set for the consolation to be had by identifying with a movement or orthodoxy whose promise of certitude ultimately delivers the self into bondage. In the essay "How to Anchor Liberalism" (1948), Dewey produces an argument that somewhat contradicts his title, since the essay's goal is to assert the need to avoid all anchors on the assumption that they are merely traps in disguise. Foremost among these fallacious groundings is "individualism," or the claim that an individual is separable from his or her context and attachable to a particular identity, however exalted or sacrosanct—for "nothing can be gained," Dewey concludes, "by inserting the words 'moral' or, worse yet, 'spiritual' before *individual*."[12] This is not to say that Dewey failed to appreciate the value of such terms. But the emphasis was on their tactical advantage rather than their ability to reveal a truth about personhood. What is "required," Dewey maintains, "is less talk about the individual and much more study of specific social conditions."[13]

Dewey's "concatenism," as Sidney Ratner noted in a 1950 essay, was inseparable from his "contextualism."[14] If persons were the sum of their circumstances, the latter included for Dewey the indicatively modern social arrangement that theorists from Bourdieu to Giddens call "reflexivity." Like most fortifications in the world of strong institutions, the institution of autocritique is more or less compulsory, disciplining moderns into endless reappraisals of the "social conditions" in which they are inscribed. Reflexivity forces us to be participant-observers of our own modernity. Downplaying such coerciveness, Dewey was notoriously optimistic about the link between self-criticism and self-determination. As Sheldon Wolin notes, Dewey believed that helping persons find the means "to revise their own experiences" was the goal of "political education," which "was not a separate undertaking distinguishable from education proper."[15]

To be sure, the recursive skepticism that extended from Dewey's instrumentalism into postwar liberal circles met with a fair share of skepticism itself. Leo Strauss, whose views on liberalism's nihilistic tendencies furnish a keystone in the edifice of modern conservatism, argued that the academic liberal's disdain for "values," which he treated as "nothing but objects of desire," revealed not a salutary repudiation of fanaticism but an indecent mania in its own right. "A man for whom every stimulus is a value or who cannot help giving in to every desire" is, according to Strauss, "a defective man."[16] He doesn't have values so much as perversions. Long before Strauss summoned the specter of liberal decadence at the end of the 1960s, liberalism's defenders were exercised by the ease with which their opponents laid tracks between their centrist politics and the louche outer boroughs of deviance. In his 1953 article "Some Present-Day Critics of Liberalism," F. W. Coker observed the willingness of the titular detractors to cast their critique in the language of degeneracy, a tendency that derived from the charge that liberals had no "strong moral convictions." The impulse to link liberals to corruption was indeed one to which even Coker himself surrenders when he notes that "tolerance," liberalism's great standard, "may degenerate into indifference and irresponsibility."[17]And though it would be anachronistic to claim that liberal "tolerance" extended in the early Cold War decades to what Alfred Gross called the "strangers in our midst," the title of his 1962 book on homosexuality, it is less of a stretch to suggest that the lack of recognition accorded to the homosexual by the Cold War liberal was at least partly a function of the uncomfortable resemblance, faintly hinted at in essays like Coker's, between the liberal and the homosexual on various fronts.

Dewey's "contextualism," for example, bears a notable likeness to camp's own framing devices: "Camp is character," Philip Core announces, "limited to context."[18] Just as its contextualism confirms postwar liberalism as a resolutely empiricist undertaking, so camp might likewise be understood as an essay in radical empiricism because camp followers are in the position of never fully accepting as certain the evidence in front of them. Camp might be seen as the evil twin of the pragmatist stance that saturated academic life in the mid-twentieth century, for camp takes pragmatism's slogan, "whatever works," and turns it inside out. Camp's slogan might be "whatever doesn't work." Whereas pragmatism is frequently charged with preferring a certain smoothness (often taken for lack of friction) in the transformation of ideas into action, camp's great vice is its devotion to those things that get stuck in place or cannot circulate efficiently or with ease of use, objects that camp mocks but refuses to surrender. Camp's perverse logic seems analogous to the postwar liberal's account of belief: beliefs are what you publicly pretend to have while privately admitting their emptiness. Belief is a formal structure purified of content. For camp, however, there is no hollowing out of content. It is a mistake to regard camp as a "formalist" aesthetic. Because camp revels in the gap between form and content, it is wholly invested in the obstinacy of content. As a result, camp goes only so far along the path the Cold War liberal breaks. It remains wed to content in an era when the inclination is to distance oneself from content. But camp also rejects the content that matters to Sixties radicals in their revolt against the pragmatists of the American technocracy. For even as it fetishizes content, camp refuses to recognize any content as authentic.

If its pleasures depend on the irreducible disconnect between how a thing appears and what it is supposed to mean, this is no doubt because the gay people who have cultivated camp have paid inordinate attention to the way their existence simulates a real identity without being wholly delivered over to certitude. The provisionality that formed an aspirational cornerstone of postwar liberalism was for the postwar homosexual simply a fact of life. "However 'natural' his inversion may seem to him," Robert Masters writes in *The Homosexual Revolution* (1962), "no homosexual can avoid being haunted by the possibility that his condition is the result of a chemical imbalance, a glandular abnormality, or of arrested emotional development resulting from environmental factors."[19] And the gay studies pioneer Harold Beaver has noted that the "conceptual schema of homosexuality can never be *proved*."[20] For Masters, spouting the common wisdom of his era, the homosexual's "feeling of natural-ness" is really "based . . . on the negative belief (or hope) that science is not going to be able to do anything to prevent or 'cure' sexual inversion" (226). It is not an empirical judgment, then, but a *resistance* to empirical evidence that convinces the homosexual of his nature. Deprived of the liberal's skepticism, the homosexual makes do with wishful thinking.

Such constant questioning of homosexuality—unchanging essence or modifiable condition?—confirms the view prevalent in Masters's book and throughout the culture in which it appeared that the "vacillation between reality and unreality is an almost universal characteristic of American homosexuals" (63). I have noted that a certain suspension between belief and disbelief, which locates the self in the gray area of *making believe*, was crucial to the larger paradigm shift in higher education and liberal discourse during the postwar period. The task of affirming this subjunctive mood among liberals rested in no small measure on misrecognizing the link between procedural liberalism and the camp mode by disavowing the latter's ability to keep the space of make-believe in focus or to keep its highly fungible categories stable or discrete. Despite their formidable irony, or so Masters concludes, homosexuals are continually slipping into fantasy. Unequipped with the respect for "process" that redeemed the liberal's disrespect for "substance," the homosexual's antifoundationalism was merely a flight of fancy.

In the liberal mind, camp followers became so hopelessly beholden to surfaces that they were incapable of taking advantage of the opportunistic gap between appearance and depth, the gap in which realpolitik unfolded. The noteworthy thing about what Masters calls the "problem of perspective" within "the homophile movement" (62), however, was how widely shared his account of the queer's perspectival limitations was among members of that movement itself. Thus, in *The Homosexual in America*, the 1951 book regarded as the inaugural text of the postwar "homophile movement," Donald Webster Cory describes the "camp" contingent in a gay bar who "can more aptly be compared to actors, seeking to imitate, yet not at all believing that they are play-acting." These figures not only suffer from a "problem of perspective" but also infect everyone around them with the same condition: "After a few hours with groups of this sort, there is hardly a homosexual unable to say *Joan* for *Joe*, *Roberta* for *Robert*, although with some trepidation . . . perhaps even mocking himself: 'She's nice,' referring to a male entertainer."[21]

The self-aware "mocking" Cory describes among the camp followers would appear to undermine the characterization of the barflies as beholden to their performances as though they were not playacting. Cory, we might say, does not diagnose so much as enact the "problem of perspective" that Masters understands as endemic to the homosexual's plight. What is at issue in reactions like those of Masters and Cory to the ostensible delusions of the queen is not the status of the camp follower's attitude toward reality but precisely the status of the polarized gender system whose binary oppositions the camp mode insistently slackens. It is important to be clear on this point, since it routinely gets lost in the critical discussion of camp from Sontag onward. The problem is not that the gay man aims to pass for a woman but that he strives for a state of suspended animation in which he passes as neither a man nor a woman. According to Cory, just as the campy queen's swish is "not quite like the movements of either men or women" (123), so it is the swish himself, as Masters notes, "with his falsetto voice and limp wrist, bleached hair, and carefully plucked eyebrows . . . who comes to mind when the average citizen thinks of 'fairies,' or 'faggots' or 'queers'" (160).

Given that "to behave effeminately is to *camp*," as Cory defines it, and that "the person who is effeminate is called a *camp*" (112), it is important to supplement our notion of the queer's provisional or subjunctive attitude with an easily forgotten datum: for the duration of the history of homosexuality, the queer stands between reality and unreality as between gender essences. This truism about homosexual "intermediacy" is worth foregrounding because it helps illuminate the bright line between the liberal style of strategic make-believe and the camp sensibility to which it bears comparison. If the liberal has to reckon with the fact that many people believe things he doesn't credit except in the midst of a procedural process, the camp homosexual must confront a far more stubborn faith-based community. Though some people might be convinced that "freedom," as Dewey's disciple Milton Konvitz asserted, "does not inhere in persons," apparently no one can be made to believe that gender doesn't.[22]

Then, too, it is the immemorial linkage between effeminacy and camp that points to the other clear line of demarcation between the liberal and the fairy. The midcentury liberal defended his position between foundational values and utilitarian considerations as the fulcrum of a renovated masculinity, a manhood that combined "tough-minded" pragmatism with a sensitivity to nuance and a distance from all isms. But even if the homophile movement "declared that the only *ism* in which it had any interest was Americanism" (68), according to Masters, its members were no more capable of producing the liberal's agnosticism than of reproducing his gender bona fides as other than a shabby imitation. While the campy queen may be an abomination, "the horror of an individual," as Cory puts it, "who can never be what he was not made to be" (130), the straitlaced gay man who passes for normal is just fooling himself: "Anyone with both feet planted firmly on the ground of the larger American reality would know," Masters concludes, that homosexuality "by its very nature is extreme and radical" (62).

The alignment of camp with the liberal style of opportunistic make-believe, then, appears undone by the fact that homosexuals finally succumb to what postwar liberals defined as the most intractable issue facing their culture: an overweening faith in an identity that, to make matters worse, no one in "the larger American reality" was willing to grant them as "real." This is what leads Alfred Gross to argue that "the most successfully adjusted homosexual is the best hypocrite . . . he can possibly be," someone in thrall to the "hope that the actor will play his part so well that, sooner or later, actor and role become one."[23] As Cory and Gross demonstrate, a striking feature of the "homophile" discourse of the pre-Stonewall age is that its participants shared with their straight-world counterparts a dread of the unreality that spread out from the ground zero of the camp follower's social orbit.

Gross's book provides an object lesson in how such dread operates. This defrocked Anglican priest–turned–social worker among New York's gay men rushes headlong into the realm of enchantment in a claim about the alleged "unreality" of the gay demimonde itself. "It is a strange world—the homosexual's," Gross writes.

> At its portals sit the three weird sisters, brewing their devilish draught of fears. Those who enter must quaff a cup of the witches' potion. And it is a strong brew indeed. Some say it tastes like nectar; others call it strong poison. Nor can anyone tell when it will take effect. Some may go through life without ever having to pay for their drink; others may suffer a tragic experience within minutes after passing through the doors. (138)

Given that he "looks askance" (132) at "the most exhibitionistic of 'fairies'" (131), who "bring disgrace on every homosexual" (132), Gross does not help his case much by inventing a narrative of gay life that depends on fairy tales themselves. Yet even as such ironies are the very stuff of camp appreciation, it is the latter that for Gross does the most damage to the homophile cause precisely because the camp follower wallows in—rather than rectifies—the dissonance he embraces. What makes the fairy's self-display appalling is that, fully knowing it is an act, he nonetheless insists on carrying it off as though it were otherwise. In the hands of the camp follower, the liberal's strategic make-believe becomes a form of bad faith.

For Gross and other homophiles, in other words, the camp follower is like Dewey's ideal liberal, both immersed in circumstances and aware of their limits. But unlike the liberal, the camp follower does not treat those limits as subject to change through the solvent power of education. He treats them only to a fatalistic derision. If Gross thus condemns the "escape into fantasy" among some homosexuals as a shameless "irresponsibility" for which all are then held accountable (149), he does so because homosexuality is indelibly tattooed with the sign of overattachment. Here is William S. Burroughs describing a dream in a 1954 letter to Allen Ginsberg in which "a fatuous fairy . . . pounces on every word with obscene double entendre. Beneath this camp, I can feel incredible evil." Unlike Susan Sontag, who sees camp as "a tender feeling" (292), Burroughs treats the "fatuous fairy" "like some loathsome insect [that] was clinging to my body.[24] Burroughs sees camp as threatening an unwelcome attachment to effeminacy rather than affording what Sontag calls a "necessary detachment" (285), a refusal of "extreme states of feeling" (287).

Given her preference for camp as noninvolvement, Sontag, not surprisingly, also seeks to neutralize camp of its most rebarbative feature, its swish factor, by substituting the rather sanitized word "androgynous" for camp's much more contentious gender trouble (279). This neutralization accompanies the equally pronounced effort in "Notes on Camp" to make the camp mode "a way of looking at things" rather than a kind of performance (277). Yet if the goal of legitimizing camp obliges Sontag to demote its rankest element, an aggressively sissified presentation verging on exhibitionism, it remains unclear whether the mode so legitimated can continue to be called "camp." However much one might like to define it as "a certain sensibility," Richard Dyer notes in "It's Being So Camp As Keeps Us Going" (1977), it cannot be denied that "camping" just *is* "mincing and screaming" (*C*, 110). By raising this issue, I am not particularly interested in the charge that Sontag defends a view of camp as, to use her word, "depoliticized" (277). I am, however, interested in the many post-Stonewall commentators who have felt the need to derive a politics from camp based on what they take to be its dominant feature: a manifestation of sensibility (progressive) or an attention-grabbing performance (reactionary). Burroughs's "fatuous fairy" prefigures the bête noire faced by the gay liberationist aiming to disunite gay identity and camp self-presentation. For camp has long functioned as a wedge issue within gay liberation precisely because many liberationists have sought to promote their "sensibility" (their taste in object choice) over a self-presentation (effeminate men, masculine women) from which their "way of looking at things" is insistently presumed to stand apart.

In "The Cinema of Camp" (1978), Jack Babuscio thus sees camp as a means to "promote solidarity and a greater sense of identification within our community" because it infuses "the gay sensibility" with "a heightened awareness of certain human complications of feeling that spring from the fact of social oppression" (*C*, 118). Compare Babuscio's version of camp as consciousness raising to the retrograde version that Andrew Britton describes in "For Interpretation: Notes against Camp" (1979): "Camp strives to give an objective presence to an imaginary construction of bourgeois psychology" (*C*, 138). For Britton, camp not only reeks of "complicity" with the larger culture's efforts to keep "the ways of being gay" "extraordinarily limited" but also (and more damningly) amounts to "little more than being 'one of the boys' by pink limelight" (*C*, 142). Camp in Britton's view is not a sensibility. It is a form of acting out. Yet while Britton writes his polemic in opposition to Babuscio, his charge that camp is "mere play" is not really far removed from Babuscio's effort to recuperate a "subversive" (*C*, 128) camp from its "often exaggerated" performances (122), since those theatrics bespeak an excess that tips, for Babuscio and Britton both, into meaninglessness.

Despite the critique often leveled at Sontag, then, even gay activists who have looked to camp for its political utility tend to favor her "attenuated" camp of apperception (277), which has the virtue of parsing normative culture's incongruities, over the "exaggerated" camp of performance, which "runs the risk," Babuscio argues, "of being considered not serious at all" (*C*, 128). Procedural liberalism has often been vulnerable to the charge that it is just an *act* so not a valid politics. Because it is continually mindful of what Sontag calls "the metaphor of life as theater" (280), camp has likewise been accused of denying political change on terms that resonate with those leveled at liberalism, especially from the Left and especially during the 1960s. Both postwar liberalism and postwar camp are distillations of the antagonist at which radicals took aim: a culture of command performances in which we are all unwittingly taking nonstop direction from a steady stream of unseen auteurs.

In a 1957 essay that analyzes the postwar liberal's "Machiavellian" style, Andrew Hacker observes that "the new men . . . are admired only for the duration of the popular appeal which they evoke for their personal performances."[25] Such "pragmatic" figures begin with a keen sense of their precarious existence in the public sphere: "The new men are not anything as individuals. All they possess are their wits."[26] Who could be more sympathetic to the anxiety occasioned by such a crowd-sourced existence than the campy barflies who are only as good as their last jokes? Though its *politics of performance* aligns liberalism with camp, my point is not that camp is liberalism in drag but that camp makes it hard to infer from it a politics because it discomfits our vexatious political presumption (inherited from Sixties radicals, who took it over from establishment liberals) that attitudes *are* politics. Since camp is often seen as nothing *but* an attitude, one that revels in its own inefficacy, it appears to run counter to the effort to tie political change to consciousness raising, the radical's preferred form of activism. Camp, like poetry in Auden's infamous phrase, "makes nothing happen."[27] But this is less because the camp follower is in need of a consciousness upgrade than because attitudes in themselves can never count for the sort of political interventions we like to think they furnish.

Then, too, to say that camp does not quite support a political agenda is not to say that it does not serve *any* tactical use. Part of this book's goal is to make interpretive hay of the slightly paradoxical fact that camp, a style that exults in its own pointlessness, draws a number of acolytes to its cause well beyond the ranks of the gay men who form its obvious demographic. That cause is by and large a mode of distinction that, as Bourdieu points out, is hard to separate from snobbism. (When Sontag defines camp as "how to be a dandy in the age of mass culture" [288], she means to say that camp is not a demotic sensibility.) While it may not be accurate to say that camp's reference group is amorphous, it is nonetheless undeniable that the sensibility that attaches to camp is never precisely embodied in gay male identity, although it routinely comes to rest there. For this reason, writers like Patricia Highsmith, Sontag, and Mary McCarthy can "take on" the camp sensibility, either by surrogating camp archness (in Highsmith's case), displacing its gay stakeholders (in Sontag's), or outmaneuvering them in the game of bitchy putdowns (in McCarthy's). For all these figures, the embrace of a camp slyness served a biographically demonstrable need for deflection in their public self-fashioning: Highsmith was an expatriate queer woman who sought a higher brow level than her readers or critics were willing to give her; Sontag was lesbian in orientation though not in print; and McCarthy enjoyed a promiscuous sex life worthy of the most well-traveled gay man even as she presented herself as a booster of monogamy. All these figures stood to benefit from camp's policy of cognitive dissonance.

The point of highlighting camp's mobility in these terms, or among such incongruous camp followers, is not to detach it from its empirical context—which it would be a mistake in any event to reduce to gay male identity—but rather to suggest that the context that matters most is the alibi-ridden, impression-managed social space of a pre-Stonewall world that absorbs not only gay men but all comers in the logic of a closet culture. We might say that the continual derogation of camp as a gay male prerogative itself signals a strategic detachment on the part of those who exploit camp's wily and worldly logic while disowning its unsavory (sentimental, trivial, or effeminate) associations. Given that camp functions as something between a privileged form of perceptiveness and an offensive showiness, it encourages a social strategy the goal of which is always to outwit everyone else. And no one appeared easier to best in the game of ironic one-upmanship than the gay man whose social failings were just barely sheltered from exposure by his own camp subterfuges. But to grasp why such a strategy should have made its way into the period's most lively writing requires us to take note of the premium the culture placed on knowingness prior to the advent of the New Left.

Chapter 1 of *Camp Sites* charts the advent of the novel civic character modeled in and by the postwar university. I argue that school culture's advocacy of a healthy respect for counterfactuals permeated off-campus society to reshape liberal subjectivity in the era of the national security state. The chapter spells out the rise of pretense as a currency the college tendered to the nation for use in the Cold War project of civil defense and then turns to the surprising intersections among military analysts, social scientists, and humanists with regard to the epistemology of make-believe. I conclude with a reading of Ralph Ellison's *Invisible Man* that situates the novel in the context of the campus intellectual's preference for both strategic irony and experiential knowledge. I argue that, in his extended critique of the academic style, Ellison resorts to a theme that proved recurrently appealing as the Cold War consensus gave way to the New Left Sixties: the casting of the postwar academic as a pervert.

Chapter 2 examines the contestation of academic authority by looking at novelists who rewrite the university's hegemony as a fantasy of self-aggrandizement. I analyze the midcentury college as the site of an innovative utopian experiment in which selfhood becomes a subject fit for perpetual examination and revision. I then consider the threat to both realism and democratic process that off-campus intellectuals locate in postwar school culture in general and the humanities in particular. The chapter examines two canonical campus novels whose authors charge the rise of experiential reading and instrumentalist pedagogy with crimes ranging from perjury (Mary McCarthy's *Groves of Academe* [1951]) to pedophilia (Vladimir Nabokov's *Pale Fire* [1962]).

Chapter 3 begins by revisiting Berkeley's Free Speech Movement to show how the student Left traded in the subjunctive mood favored by its teachers for an indicative mood that sanctified overstatement. I argue that this shift in idiom derived from the New Left assumption that the "system" it targeted, from the school to the government, practiced forms of subterfuge and nondisclosure that were indistinct from the stratagems of the Cold War closet and its habitués. The chapter then considers how the New Left's politics of authenticity resulted in a strange cross-pollination between gay liberation and the counterculture. I show that just as gay liberationists formed their project in uneasy accord with the goals of New Left identity politics, so figures like Norman Mailer, E. L. Doctorow, and Huey Newton imagined a countercultural narrative that borrowed its basic plot from gay liberation: what I call "coming out straight."

Chapter 4 looks at midcentury culture's competing accounts of "performance," perhaps the most vexing term in the postwar critical lexicon. I contrast the dramaturgical view of society espoused by a diverse range of sociologists affiliated with symbolic interactionism (for whom the commitment to social life as stagecraft rendered authenticity moot) with the antitheatrical naturalism championed by teachers of Method acting (for whom the revolt against reactive performances rendered authenticity necessary). I then read Patricia Highsmith's *The Talented Mr. Ripley* (1955) as a text caught up in the crosscurrents of these opposing views of performance. With his powers of mimicry and his keen awareness of how others see him, Highsmith's title character not only appears tailor-made for a Method stage but also exemplifies the costs and benefits of the relentless impression management brought to light by midcentury sociology.

Chapter 5 assesses the impact of dramaturgical social theory on Sixties-era queer social scientists who, making use of the postwar sociology of deviance, reject the limiting presumptions of expressive authenticity. I read work by Laud Humphreys and Esther Newton alongside Kurt Vonnegut's *Slaughterhouse Five* (1969), a novel that channels its antiwar commitments through a critique of social-scientific impersonality. I then consider the omission of symbolic inter-actionism from the work of Judith Butler, whose account of gender and per-formativity feels as though it should be in dialogue with Erving Goffman. I suggest that the key to this silence lies in the incommensurateness of Goffman's and Butler's attitudes toward the political work that consciousness can do. The chapter ends with an analysis of what I call "mean camp," an aesthetic category whose fantasy of consciousness lowering plays havoc with the redistribution of sentience in the post-Sixties climate of deep ecology and other movements grounded in consciousness raising and its gestalt of transformation.

Chapter 6 takes up the problem of consciousness raising again by arguing that this emancipationist strategy is impossible to separate from the postwar commitment to meritocracy, which is inextricable from what business gurus call "high performance." The chapter begins by considering the "parafeminist" moment of the 1950s and early 1960s, when the expert discourse of frigidity, which distilled that national epidemic to a conflict between control and spon-taneity, helped engineer an account of meritorious womanhood whose exem-plary practitioners were Helen Gurley Brown and Jacqueline Susann. Then I address some touchstones of women's liberation: Joan Didion's *Play It As It Lays* (1970), Sylvia Plath's *The Bell Jar* (1963), and Erica Jong's *Fear of Flying* (1973). I argue that far from condemning the asylum, Didion and Plath use it to renew certain promises of establishment liberalism. Finally, I explain how Jong's novel reveals a commitment to a new and improved meritocracy that values what I call "performance at a distance," in which the labors of the creative elite are de-tached from identities and organizations and become self-rewarding.

As these synopses indicate, *Camp Sites* covers a lot of ground between a fairly narrow pair of historical bookends (roughly 1945 to 1975). Its strong sense of inclusiveness has dictated what might appear to be a hermeneutic shell game; the book insistently shuffles diverse cultural players into idiosyncratic (though not unwarranted) contexts. Scrambling the cognitive map of a period in order to extract its overriding "logic" is the standard move in New Historicist practice; and the book's apparent embrace of a method now held in some disrepute may smack of recidivism. Neglecting to distinguish what goes on at the RAND Corporation from what transpires in English 101, combining unlikely figures without heeding the differences in their brow level, lavishing too much attention on too little of the past, *Camp Sites* might be accused of practicing what it preaches: it not only analyzes camp but also takes a camp view of things. Or perhaps its perceived loyalty to New Historicism is itself a species of camp insofar as its author strives, with the zeal of a show queen pining for Broadway's golden age, to revive a methodological has-been that his outré devotions serve only to zombify. What hopefully spares the book from such conjectures, or at least their dismissive intent, is that *Camp Sites* aims for an extensive revision of what the camp view of things is.

1 The Schooling of America

A Consensus of Make-Believe

In the late 1940s, the federal government established a commission to puzzle through a dilemma that preoccupied the crafters of the national security state in the aftermath of Hiroshima and Nagasaki: the tendency of the atomic threat to induce either paralysis or panic. Presuming that the trauma inflicted by the idea of the bomb would prove no less disabling than the force from a detonation, Project East River (as the commission was named) encouraged citizen-survivors to maintain an open-minded skepticism with regard to the otherwise self-evident specter of annihilation. To use the phrase coined by Irving Janis in *Air War and Emotional Stress* (1951), civil defense depended on "emotional inoculation," and the best way to inject this psychological booster shot was through drills that served as dress rehearsals of the postnuclear apocalypse.[1] "As in combat training," the Project East River report argued, "every approach toward realism in the training situations will be a gain inasmuch as it guarantees greater transfer of the learned responses to the situation of real danger."[2]

By this logic, undergoing mock-ups of catastrophe would so inure persons to the real thing that in the event of a bona fide thermonuclear exchange, "learned response" would take over the panic reflex and "return" "the individual to rationality."[3] In emphasizing potential scenarios and in habituating citizens to a condition of make-believe, the report gives to "realism" some novel connotations. This is the realism of the behaviorist, for example, who imagines that reality is flexible enough to be reconditioned as the controlling agent sees fit. Alternatively it suggests the realism of the stage actor who, through sheer force of will, subdues his own personality in the effort to suspend disbelief in a script on which his very survival is now understood to depend. Finally, it suggests the "simulation aesthetic," to use Sharon Ghamari-Tabrizi's term, that would come to dominate the RAND Corporation in the 1950s.[4] That fledgling think tank made its mark on postwar policy making by aggressively promoting "realism" on what Bruce Kuklick calls a "nonempirical basis."[5]

In the writing of the history of post-1945 America, few things have invited as much finger wagging as the effort to make the nuclear arsenal appear continuous with conventional technologies of warfare. My point in revisiting this particular folly is to draw attention to the oblique but crucial role played in the postwar regime of emotion management by the school system here represented by the professors who constituted Project East River—or, as its chartered body was otherwise known, Associated Universities, Inc.[6] Under the aegis of civil defense, the architects of the national security state enlisted academics to import into the body politic the counterintuitive "detachment" increasingly characteristic of postwar school culture. What the nation's educators were imagined to contribute to the public good was a social style rooted in the sort of make-believe that Project East River encouraged.[7] The potential of this social style to effect alternative visions by inverting the terms of naïve empiricism emerged as one of the chief dividends of the postwar college campus. It was also an enduring one, judging by Don DeLillo's choice to make a series of "simulated" disaster scenarios, orchestrated by the SIMUVAC lackeys who roam the streets of College-on-the-Hill, an integral subplot of *White Noise* (1985).[8] Long before DeLillo satirized the college as a breeding ground for imaginary crisis management, postwar thinkers seized upon school culture's penchant for improvisational reality.

To say that the Cold War university collaborated in the project of emotion management by way of its openness to conditionals is to run the risk of hollowness that attaches to any general claim about that institution. As Theodore Caplow and Reece McGee wrote in *The Academic Marketplace* (1958), "It is easy to agree that the purpose of a factory is production" but "not at all easy . . . to determine the fundamental purposes of a university."[9] Yet as Caplow and McGee's book itself demonstrates, the resistance to specifying what the university did was accompanied throughout the postwar decade by a massive escalation in the industry dedicated to worrying that very purpose. Academics' discovery of the problematic status of the university occasioned a discursive watershed in the 1950s, and the torrent of publications on this hitherto uncontroversial subject routinely marshaled a self-distancing skepticism akin to the structure of disbelief in the Project East River report. Accustomed to a steady flow of monographs that take as their subject the university in crisis, we may scarcely realize that it was not ever thus. Self-criticism was not quite a novelty in school culture before 1950, but neither had it been the habitual distraction it would become during the Eisenhower era. One task in this chapter is to pursue the implications of this autocritical gesture.

A related task is to articulate some of the less overt or official features of the academic style that nurtured it, features that rarely earn much attention in cultural studies of the academy even as they could be said to shape the experience of the numerous people recruited to the professoriat as well as the experience of the countless students who pass through the academic fold. By style, I mean the extracurricular manifestations of conduct and attitude that make up the university intellectuals' legacy across disciplinary and historical divides. Another name for what I have in mind is what Pierre Bourdieu calls *habitus*, the "durable, transposable dispositions," from gestures to norms of interaction, that a social group both forcefully and unknowingly reproduces across generations.[10] The essence of the academic *habitus* in Bourdieu's view is what he calls the "posture of the scholar feeling free to withdraw from the game in order to conceptualize it."[11] As outlined in an ethnographic project that extends from *Reproduction in Education, Society, and Culture* (1970, coauthored with Jean-Claude Passeron) through *Homo Academicus* (1984) to *Pascalian Meditations* (1997), Bourdieu's goal was to reattach this free-ranging "posture" to "the social foundations of the propensity to theorize."[12]

Much as my thinking is indebted to Bourdieu, I also take issue with one of his central premises: The "academic field," to use the properly Bourdieuian term, "occupies a homologous place to that of the Church" insofar as it "reproduces continually the distinction between consecrated and illegitimate works."[13] Bourdieu's focus on the school's sacral mission proves inadequate to a consideration of the American university at midcentury. For the postwar college repeatedly demonstrates its lack of interest in "consecration" or, to be precise, repeatedly subjects that task itself to critique. This is not to deny that postwar school culture sanctifies subject matter or legitimizes tradition but only to say that such curatorial labor is pursued under a nonconformist and frequently deconsecrating banner. In postwar America, the "cultural capital" to which the school "regulates access," as John Guillory puts it, is not merely the prestige associated with canonical forms of knowledge but also the prestige associated with a fundamental suspicion of such forms.[14] Along with the New Critical canon and its fetish for form, this era rallied around the hermeneutics of suspicion and its equally powerful fetish for demystification.

A better way to reconcile these seemingly opposed points in Bourdieu's work—the professoriat imagines itself detached from institutional mediation; the school functions to secure knowledge as doxa—is to note that among the objects of legitimation to which the postwar faculty consistently turns its attention is the academic discipline itself. If literary critics, for example, have been prone to imagine the boundaries of their discipline as either too porous to contain its members in a tidy unity or too soft to stand against the solid front presented by their rivals in the sciences, the reason is that they have long been in the position of never quite *believing* in the discipline of which they are (or at least used to be) lifetime members. I do not mean that they have broken faith with their discipline's ideals, as the conservative canard would have it. I mean that they proceed as if the discipline were a figment of someone's imagination. Yet this disinclination to take the profession as given finds its formative antecedents among diverse Cold War disciplines well beyond the English department.

The literature professor's makeshift sense of belonging fits into the array of ironizing strategies brought to bear in Project East River's specifically *academic* exercise in making Herman Kahn's "thinking about the unthinkable" into public policy. The postwar university does not reject belief but brackets it, turns it into a pliable faculty, a target of opportunity subject to all manner of infilling. "The question of belief or disbelief never arises when we are reading well," Cleanth Brooks claims in *The Well-Wrought Urn* (1947), because "we are willing to allow our various interests as human beings to become subordinate to the total experience."[15] The goal in reading a poem for Brooks is not to derive "propositions" but to absorb its "complexity of attitude."[16] That "attitude" shares generously in the "strategic make-believe" that Andrew Grossman sees as the bulwark of Truman-era civil defense.[17] Nor was this eminently Cold War epistemology abandoned with the end of the Cold War. It survives in Gayatri Spivak's call for "the *strategic* use of positivist essentialism in a scrupulously visible political interest," the expedient of pretending as if essences ground identities even while conceding essentialism's fictitiousness.[18] This proposal has occasioned more notoriety than it might have were critics to take a longer view of the academic *habitus* that includes Spivak as its end point. That Spivak's "political interest" is opposed to the global hegemony ratified by Cold War intellectuals should not eclipse the fact that, however nontrivial the distinction between her politics and Herman Kahn's, the goal in both cases entails a commitment to the political value of suspended disbelief.

In view of the received idea of Cold War quietism, the triumph of the research university appears to involve a paradox: a society that demanded conformism of its citizens invested massive reserves of human and economic capital in an institution that requires innovation and vigorous competition for its survival. This paradox is somewhat mitigated by the observation that the university's ascent in the 1950s included a valorization of the academic world as a structure of private self-organization. In this account, the university could be unrestrained and expansive just because it was homeostatic: a system tailored, like the ideal polity, for an optimum balance of tensions and oppositions. Then, too, the Fifties academic style turned out to be surprisingly well matched to that decade's less savory traits: its paranoia, its vigilance against threats international and domestic, and its jingoistic vision of American life as fundamentally open. The postwar American vogue for mistrust coincided almost too neatly with the hermeneutics of suspicion that emerged as the default in the university at midcentury.

It is received wisdom that the expansion of the American university occurred in response to the needs of a culture preoccupied with the uses to which science could be put for military ends. Yet by focusing on the university as the training ground for the new technocracy, this narrative slights the multiple ways the university as a whole (rather than its science departments) inserted itself into the foreground of the American national style. Nor does it seem accurate to argue, with Richard Ohmann, that "when the lines of the Cold War were firmed up, English was a pastoral retreat within the university."[19] All departments were essentially retreats in the institutional imaginary of postwar school culture, which encouraged a high level of differentiation and territoriality among the disciplines. It is not difficult to see how such a division of labor provided the blueprint for the pluralistic ideal endorsed by the architects of the Cold War consensus. In the model of the disciplines set forth in the postwar college, as in the version of liberalism set forth in opposition to fanaticism, one need not comprehend another's practices or beliefs in order to respect them. "To convert concrete issues into ideological problems, to invest them with moral color," Daniel Bell argued in defense of this agnostic tolerance, "is to invite conflicts which can only damage a society."[20]

Bell was typical of humanists and social scientists who considered it their task to lead by example in modeling the skepticism of the academic style for the nation's citizens. "Our crucial problem now and for the next decade," Howard Mumford Jones wrote in the March 1949 issue of *PMLA*, "is to master a style through which we may communicate to a reasonably intelligent general public whatever it is we have to offer."[21] "Equipped to interpret the ideals of man as recorded in his languages and literatures," Modern Language Association (MLA) president Hayward Keniston told that convention's members in 1952, "humanists" constitute "the only group that can provide us with illumined leadership in a war of ideas."[22] Consider Stanford German professor Bayard Morgan's address at the same convention, portentously titled "Unrecognized Disarmament." Language study serves the interests of national security, according to Morgan, because democracy's foes resort to subterfuges that only those skilled in critical interpretation can combat:

> One of the principal weapons of that enemy, in the Cold War now being hotly waged, is the *word* as the concealment of meaning, the lie as a substitute for truth, fiction offered as reality. To . . . act as if we could afford to ignore what our enemies, actual and potential, are thinking and saying and planning, simply to go on chewing the cud of our own inbred notions, is to perform the ostrich act and to invite the launching of an attack as unsuspected, and as unprepared for, as the one which took place on a December day that will not soon be forgotten.[23]

The most striking thing about this passage is Morgan's insistence on the literary scholar's "relevance," to borrow a term from our own disciplinary moment. It would be difficult to find a contemporary critic who rivals Morgan in foregrounding the humanist's sensibility in the advancement of the open society or endowing her credentials with the superheroic powers Morgan imagines for them. "It is not a mere figure of speech," Morgan writes, summoning precisely a figure of speech, "to say that each master of a modern foreign language supplies the state with an extra pair of mental eyes, capable of looking into an enemy's mind. . . . This kind of clairvoyance knows of no substitute whatever."[24]

Less confused about the ontology of metaphors than Morgan, but no less confident in his political acumen, Leslie Fiedler makes up for his lack of "expert knowledge in political matters" with a "sensibility trained by the newer critical methods." "It is a close reading of recent events that I should like to think that I have achieved," he writes in *An End to Innocence* (1955), "a reading that does not scant ambiguity or paradox, but tries to give to the testimony of a witness before a Senate committee or the letters of the Rosenbergs the same careful scrutiny we have learned to practice on the shorter poems of Donne."[25] Fiedler's title paid tribute to an intellectual mode popularized at the start of the 1950s with the publication of Reinhold Niebuhr's *The Irony of American History* (1952). Fore-most among the many ironies of that history, according to Niebuhr, was the discrepancy between the American's self-image as an "innocent" and his actual conduct on the world stage. "We know ourselves," he argues, "to be less inno-cent than our theories assume."[26] Opposing it not to guilt but to knowingness, Niebuhr views innocence as perilous because it causes the American to yield to the "pretensions" of "consistency" against his own better judgment. Arguing for "an interpretation of life which emphasizes the dire consequences of vain pretensions and sees them ironically refuted by actual experience," Niebuhr an-nounces: "Consciousness of an ironic situation tends to dissolve it" (168). Irony for Niebuhr is both an attribute of historical process and, more important, an awareness of that history, the viewpoint occasioned by the "ambiguity" (170) and "incongruities" (153) central to the American condition. "The final wisdom of life requires," therefore, "not the annulment of incongruity but the achieve-ment of serenity within and above it" (63).

The serenity Niebuhr lauds as the basis for the "detachment necessary for the detection of irony" (170) is one name for the "sensibility," as Fiedler calls it, privileged by the era's university personnel. And it was primarily within the university—with its status as neither quite a community nor quite an asso-ciation, neither exactly organic nor exactly anomic, and hence indicative of what Niebuhr calls "incongruity—that such an affect could flourish. "Serenity" serves Niebuhr as the rejoinder to the destructive enthusiasm of the "idealist," who "seeks to comprehend the whole realm of ends from his standpoint" (149). If the idealist can never be satisfied, the ironist can never really get upset, since idealists cannot survive without their "standpoint," but ironists for Niebuhr can take or leave theirs. More precisely, by being both "within and above" any given organization, ironists have no necessary investment in the institutional locale from which that standpoint is exerted. Whereas movements like com-munism thrive by turning their members into "prisoners of a dogmatism" (105), no one according to Niebuhr and his colleagues sees the university as other than "contingent" (149).

The university for this reason is an exemplary instance of what Niebuhr calls the "human community" as "both organism and artifact" because in it "the form of cohesion and the integration of the community have been con-sciously contrived."[27] Precisely because the university is "inconsistent inter-nally," as Clark Kerr puts it in *The Uses of the University* (1963), it has "not a single soul to call its own."[28] Yet rather than cause for alarm, the university's failure to induce loyalty turns out to be its greatest virtue, since the disinvestment of its members licenses what Kerr calls "stability of freedom" (34). "The faculty member within the big mechanism and with all his opportunities has a new sense of independence," Kerr claims, "a choice of roles and a mixture of roles to suit his taste as never before" (33). Kerr's opinion was corroborated by Alvin Gouldner's 1957 analysis of what he called academic "cosmopolitans," those college faculty who "are 'in' but not 'of' the organization" and "have little loyalty" to it.[29] The soullessness and disloyalty fostered by the multiversity lay the groundwork for a paradoxically rigorous moral purpose. Favoring private choices over collective belonging, postwar school culture's reverence for voluntarism appeared to fulfill John Dewey's promise that progressive education would serve as a conduit to liberal politics. "Only the voluntary initiative and voluntary cooperation of individuals can produce social institutions that will protect the liberties necessary for achieving development of genuine individuality," Dewey wrote in "I Believe" (1939).[30] If the university was not the only institution that could in turn "produce" the subject given to "voluntary initiative," it was surely the most pivotal. "The more . . . educated a man is," Seymour Lipset argues in *Political Man* (1960), "the more likely he is to belong to voluntary associations" and "to give democratic answers to questions concerning tolerance."[31]

Far from serving as the passive breeding ground for the military-industrial complex, the university actively helped reconstruct the beleaguered liberalism of Cold War America on a privatized footing. The university became the crucible of liberal affect, founded on a cautious nonconformism and grounded in a rhetoric of skepticism and a mood of detachment. Indeed, it was such privatization in English studies to which Wimsatt and Beardsley objected in "The Intentional Fallacy" (since "the poem belongs to the public," and criticism of it was thus a "public art") and that their objections could not finally displace.[32] In the "'liberalized' democracy" that took hold after World War II, Sheldon Wolin observes, "private freedom and interests rather than common action and shared advantages" became central tenets of political debate.[33] By the same token, McCarthy-era universities redefined academic freedom, according to Ellen Schrecker, "in institutional instead of ideological terms, as the preservation of the professional autonomy of the academy."[34] The recasting of academic freedom from a principle of inclusion to one of insularity parallels the movement from a liberalism of the public sphere to a liberalism of private life. It was the task of postwar school culture to normalize both shifts.

School Culture and the Hermeneutic Self

It would be wrong to construe Fiedler's self-proclaimed interpretive dexterity as but a harbinger of the "claim to speak authoritatively for society as a whole" that John Guillory has diagnosed as the prestige-saving gambit of the academic critic in decline.[35] We need look no further than the preface to Richard Rovere's *The Eisenhower Years* (1956) to witness the essentially commutative relation between politics and close reading in the postwar intellectual scene. "In general," Rovere asserts, "my effort has been to write about politics as much as possible in the manner of a critic making an effort, as Matthew Arnold put it, 'to see the object as in itself it really is.'"[36] But Fiedler was no Arnoldian. Like Niebuhr's, his was a hermeneutics of suspicion. The exegetical turn across a broad array of Cold War management strategies beyond the humanist classroom seems to contradict Suzanne Clark's assertion that "the critical activity of interpretive analysis itself came to seem un-American, unless it addressed the circumscribed space of a literary object."[37] This narrow view would have come as a surprise to Charles Frankel, whose book *The Democratic Prospect* (1962) espies a far more ambitious research program on its titular horizon: "The man who would now understand all the facts that are politically relevant must proceed to acquaint himself with the bottom of the ocean, the inside of Yoknapatawpha County, and the other side of the moon. What must be known is alien and complicated; knowing it requires the mastery of technical and specialized instruments and symbols."[38] Though the compulsive desire to monitor the world through interpretation originated in the realm of higher education, its disciplines would colonize the vernacular during the early Cold War.

For this reason Lipset treats "the shift away from ideology toward sociology" as the central change in postwar society.[39] "Sociology has been so popularized that its jargon has reached both market place and dinner table," Eric Larrabee observes in *The Self-Conscious Society* (1960), "and the discoverer of a new status symbol can live off it conversationally for weeks."[40] Larrabee's book took the pulse of a midcentury sociology that modeled the subject as an outsider looking in on the social world as if it were a text to be unfolded according to school culture's norms of interpretation. From David Riesman, who charted the evolution from "inner-directed" to "other-directed" individuals, to Erving

Goffman, who conceived of social agents as both participants in and observers of their own carefully constructed performances, numerous sociologists shared Fiedler's view of the self as an unencumbered close reader surveying her surroundings from the vantage of a productive alienation. For Reisman and Goffman, everyone is a New Critic, and the text to be interpreted is the social fabric in which all subjects find themselves uneasily—or paradoxically, to use New Critical parlance—both inside and outside a web of social relations that are neither fully authentic nor fully a matter of pretense or artifice.

The work of these sociologists is explored later in detail, but here I want to stress the parallel between the literary critic and the sociologist in order to observe that across the disciplines of the Fifties university, matters of hermeneutics came irrevocably to displace matters of belief. We can elaborate on this displacement by noting how often it became a source of contention in Cold War culture. The authority of the professoriat, for example, sorely taxed the patience of William F. Buckley Jr., whose *God and Man at Yale* (1951) sought to return the governance of the university to what Buckley understood as its rightful rulers, its undergraduate and alumni clientele. Yet his real quarrel was with those features of school culture—the skepticism and the aptitude for entertaining counterfactuals—that the national security state absorbed into its civil defense program. Unapologetically Catholic, Buckley argued that Yale's secular curriculum interfered with his right to believe without having his beliefs affected in the least by his education.

God and Man at Yale ushered in the long Kulturkampf mounted by the right on the academy, but like so many jeremiads in its wake it strategically misrecognized the situation it diagnosed. Though Buckley wrote against an institution that sought in his view to tamper with his beliefs, that institution in fact did not care one way or another for them. It is true that the postwar university appeared as the "culmination," in Edgar Johnson's phrase, of "the destruction in the West of the ability to believe anything," but the school did not undertake an effort to convert its clients to a secular faith.[41] Its goal was to retain the category of belief while emptying it of meaning.[42] In *The Vital Center* (1949), Arthur M. Schlesinger Jr. writes that the "thrust of the democratic faith is away from fanaticism . . . toward compromise, persuasion, and consent."[43] The crucial shift on campus was likewise from a rigorous faith to a supple one. The college was rapidly replacing what Jacques Barzun in *The Teacher in America* (1945) called "moral hokum" with an ethics of "the flexible," an ethics that taught students the value of making themselves "adaptable to different circumstances."[44]

On the other end of the political spectrum from Buckley, we find the radical writer Paul Goodman just as preoccupied as the conservative Yale alumnus with the university's socialization of its clients as citizen-subjects. In response to the overtaking of the university by the administration, Goodman's "remedy" in *The Community of Scholars* (1962) is "for bands of scholars to secede and set up where they can teach and learn on their own simple conditions."[45] While there is a bracing utopianism in Goodman's vision, it was merely the obverse of that institutional contingency toward which Niebuhr took such a sanguine view. In fact, Goodman's vaunting of mobility, whereby the professors might shrug off the yoke of their rentier administrators and regroup on greener intellectual pastures, spoke to an agitation that from the ironist's standpoint was misplaced: the professors were already free to come and go as they pleased. But the salient point here is that even critics as far outside the Cold War consensus as Goodman and Buckley must be understood to operate in response to the same overdetermination of the university that enjoined many of their peers to see in the university a ringing endorsement of the voluntarism for which midcentury liberalism stood.

Of course, Goodman's deep suspicion of liberalism led him to perceive its voluntarism as sheer illusion, a veneer for a much more insidious set of compulsions. Goodman's is an idiom of demystification. Throughout his most influential book, *Growing Up Absurd* (1956), we find a continual appeal to what he calls "the objective world," "the actual situation," "a real world," and numerous other synonyms for a reality principle he wields against the "artificial stimulation" that forms the lot of the contemporary American student.[46] The brunt of Goodman's polemic in *Growing Up Absurd* is that modern society, which is by turns "eclectic, sensational, or phony" (217), thus forces its youth to wallow in a state of permanent adolescence. It is important to distinguish the reality principle that prompts Goodman's grief over the loss of an "objective cultural standard" (177) from the principled disbelief central to postwar subjectivity. Goodman rejects the conditions that figures like Arthur Schlesinger and Daniel Bell understand as tantamount to a thriving political order. Whereas these architects of the Cold War consensus see the refusal of absolute values or objective truth as the ground for a distinctive American agency, Goodman sees the rise of artifice and pretense as obstacles that stand between persons and their self-actualization. Denouncing the performing self that Goffman would shortly make famous, Goodman writes that "its role-playing, its canned culture, its public relations, and its avoidance of risk and self-exposure are death to the spirit" (241).

Perhaps the best way to capture Goodman's simultaneous centrality and eccentricity to the formation of the Cold War academic style is to note that, however sustained his critique of the inauthentic, he answers the culturewide epidemic of false consciousness with a strenuous commitment to belief. "To give up the religious community of work is a great loss," Goodman thus argues. "Our society weakens the growing youth's conviction that there is . . . a real world rather than a system of social rules that are often indeed arbitrary" (143). Whereas Goodman disdains "role-playing" and seeks a renewal of "spirit," most of his peers regard the problem with the inauthentic in somewhat different terms. The disaffection from belief presents a middle ground between the return to authenticity that Goodman advocates and the gullible embrace of theatrical illusionism these thinkers take to be the disastrous result of a hegemonic mass culture. In keeping with the antifoundational coloring of much Fifties social thought, this middle ground is most itself when it eschews any determinate confines. It is defined instead through its habit of excluding from seriousness the two alternatives—authentic being and deluded manipulation—by treating them as versions of the same problem. Thus, Eric Hoffer writes in *The True Believer* (1951): "The association of believing and lying is not characteristic solely of children. The inability or unwillingness to see things as they are promotes both gullibility and charlatanism."[47] Hoffer turns Goodman's notion of faith as a corrective to arrested development into the thing Goodman most despises: an "imposture" (82) in which persons become the dupe of scripts that others, whether communists or Hollywood screenwriters, choose for them.

Hoffer's critique of the inauthentic both mirrors and rewrites Goodman's by locating the failure of agency not in the organization man (where Goodman sees it) but in the ranks of the dissidents with whom Goodman sides. These would-be champions of authenticity, Hoffer writes, "are made to feel that they are not their real selves but actors playing a role, and their doings a performance rather than the real thing" (71). Goodman treats acting without firm belief as a failure to act at all; Hoffer sees acting *according* to belief as a surrender of reason to passion. This is the "acting out" that the psychologist Robert Lindner diagnoses among the generation coming of age in the first decade of the Cold War. Observing "the tenacity of faith" with which so many cling to the "epic fiction" of communism, Lindner suggests that the problem with party loyalty is less a matter of belief than of taking literally what evidence reveals to be fictitious.[48] For Lindner, belief is problematic when it is literal rather than figurative, fundamental rather than provisional. To believe as an end in itself is to mistake the roles one plays in the scenarios prescribed by various "modern orthodoxies" for the real thing—an identity beyond pretense.[49]

It would thus be appropriate to describe the postwar university as enduring a seismic shift less from belief to disbelief than from belief to make-believe. Hence we find in the RAND Corporation nothing less than an "avant-garde research culture," as Sharon Ghamari-Tabrizi puts it, committed to "instilling tolerance for ambiguity and uncertainty" (170). RAND's origins illuminate not only the prestige of antifoundational thought at midcentury but also the perception of the university as its rightful custodian. Though born of the iconic public-private partnership in Cold War America—a defense contract between the US Air Force and the Douglas Aircraft Company—early on "RAND instituted a change in its nomenclature," according to Alex Abella, in order "to attract more academic researchers. . . . Divisions, originally named sections—which smacked of the military—became departments, which then grew exponentially to include a host of disciplines." But even more to the point, RAND's vigorous recruitment of a wide range of academics included "no test for ideological correctness."[50]

RAND sought to reproduce the university model both organizationally and pedagogically. "The terms with which they described gaming and simulation," Ghamari-Tabrizi argues of RAND "radicals" like Herman Kahn, privileged "a literary notion of realist description" over the "scientific idiom" (170). Ghamari-Tabrizi arguably overrates the "irrationalism" of RAND's discourse (169), but only because she underrates the objectivity and rigor that characterized Cold War literary criticism. For there is another sense in which Kahn's method was "literary": its precisionist attention to what in *On Thermonuclear War* Kahn called "*hypothetical experience.*"[51] What bound figures as unlike as the New Critics and the physicists at RAND was a novel empiricism. Positioning experience as central to the intellectual landscape of postwar America, these thinkers paid little mind to whether the experience in question was real or, as Ghamari-Tabrizi puts it, "synthetic" (161). The RAND radicals' theory was radical, as Richard Barringer and Barton Whaley explained in their 1965 article "The MIT Political-Military Gaming Experience," by virtue of its investment in a model of simulation underwritten by a powerful suspension of disbelief: "Gaming stretches the limits of one's imagination, of one's notions of the plausible and the possible."[52] "RAND's systems analysts," Abella observes, "refused to be constrained by existing reality."[53]

Yet it was less the case that systems analysts sought to exceed reality's limits than that reality in their view seemed to have acquired a kind of limitless unpredictability. The interest in improvisational strategies was driven by what RAND stalwart Norman Dalkey called the "stochastic variations" normative in Cold War culture.[54] Systems analysis was in Dalkey's estimation "a policy of flexible response to meet a wide variety of contingencies."[55] Dalkey was co-creator (with Olaf Helmer) of the "Delphi method," a forecasting technique that has been a standard tool in decision analysis for decades. "Its object is to obtain the most reliable consensus of opinion of a group of experts," Dalkey and Helmer explained in a 1963 paper, "by a series of intensive questionnaires with controlled opinion feedback."[56] Those questioned never see one another, though after each round of questions they have access to one another's answers. The goal is for experts to revise their beliefs toward a "convergence of answers" (465) in light of newly received information. What is worth pausing to consider is Dalkey and Helmer's presumption, widespread in postwar circles, that a self-revising method whose grounding is a salutary anonymity is obligatory for a stochastic world. If the rationale for the Delphi method was to give "best estimates in uncertain contexts" (463), its modus operandi was to take the Delphi participants' beliefs as the test subject. The crucial point here is that RAND perceived in Dalkey's "variety of contingencies" a reordering of the world according to what William Egginton calls the "potentially endless relativization of frames characteristic of theatrical space."[57] In confronting the recursive abyss of "uncertain contexts," RAND's thinkers evolved a skill set that found its optimum expression in assorted forms of playacting. Moreover, RAND's dramaturgical tools were honed to precision by their users' willingness to turn them on their colleagues and themselves.

From *Homo Academicus* to *Invisible Man*

The postwar university transformed the faculty's great liability, its supposed withdrawal from society at large, into one of the cardinal virtues disseminated to its client population. In the Cold War battle of ideas, university faculty purveyed a distanced engagement in which belief was held at bay, the better to observe the motives to which any ideology was beholden and the better to realize an equanimity that could withstand charismatic leaders and their cultic seductions. The term "seduction" is not incidental, for the style emanating from university culture was both gendered and eroticized. What the university offered was a competitive version of masculine agency distinguished by the ability to maintain a kind of equilibrium in the maelstrom of propaganda, institutional conflict, and mass hysteria that swept through Cold War America. Where the organization man was a pawn, the university man was a utilitarian who worked the system by keeping it at arm's length, all too aware of its artificiality.

"The revival of a genuinely tough-minded and principled liberalism may depend on a renewed sense of the vitality and significance of forms," the political scientist Cushing Strout argued in a 1955 essay that opposed utopianism to a "confidence in moral and legal procedures."[58] No less alert to "forms" than their counterparts in political theory, humanists were keen to advance the cause of an academic manhood whose signature was a "tough-minded" willingness to cope with ambiguity. According to one-time MLA president Henri Peyre,

> The study of languages and literatures is a difficult and very masculine subject indeed, and not at all one which should be left to girls along with music and sewing, while future "males" concentrate on engineering, accounting, marketing, compiling Kinseyan statistics. Young American men . . . label "feminine" what is both alluring but mysterious and difficult, for it requires more alertness of mind and more feeling for nuances than figures and quantitative statements and logically deduced but totally unconvincing assertions. The true courage, indeed, lies in facing those half-truths and imponderable but all-important values by which the world is in fact led and those shades of significance on which most problems hinge.[59]

Peyre's "very masculine" student of literature thrives in a social order that puts a premium on sensitivity to the workings of the system.

If the academic's nuanced manhood emerged as the corrective for a nation taken in by fanaticism and worst-case scenarios, its advocates were scrupulous in designating what social types were beyond irony's curative balm and likely to fall prey to the inauthentic by mistaking it for reality. Betty Friedan thus observes that her female subjects "are doomed to spend most of their lives in sexual fantasy," "acting out" erotic scripts learned from Tennessee Williams and other drama queens who prevent them from dealing with "complex modern reality."[60] This playacting can be remedied in the final analysis only by school culture. "Universities need," Friedan claims, "to become lifetime institutions for their students; offer them guidance, take care of their records, and keep track of their advanced work for refresher courses, no matter where they are taken" (372). Schooling functions here not only as a guarantor of civic competence but as a refuge from a deformed public sphere, a cordon sanitaire that protects its clientele from the unwitting passivity of what Herbert Marcuse called "one-dimensional society," with its true believers incapable of mustering consciousness of their own exploitation.[61] Yet even under the aegis of university culture, the quarantining of true believers was as risky as any efforts to keep contagion at bay. For while Friedan championed the university as a bulwark against an unreality embodied by queens like Tennessee Williams, school culture's defensive capabilities were continually being undermined in postwar America by the menace of a queer sensibility lurking within the ivory tower and ready to move, like a sleeper cell, against the salutary tough-mindedness prized by the era's fiercest critics.

To see how this threat unfolded, let us shift backward from *The Feminine Mystique* (1963) to Ralph Ellison's *Invisible Man* (1952), which entertains a critique of unreality comparable to Friedan's in its depiction of Harlemites whose "costumes" are "surreal variations of downtown styles" and whose surrender to "style" itself places them "outside the groove of history."[62] The novel's protagonist conceives of black consumers as "dodging the forces of history instead of making a dominating stand" (441). It is a forceful political critique, yet it is not at all clear whether we are meant to endorse it. Ellison's politics are notoriously ambiguous, and there is no clearer reminder of this than the fact that his novel begins in the pastoral environs of a black college whose chief administrator, the villainous Bledsoe, embodies the academic style that, in Friedan's estimation, thwarts the delusions of the culture industry. Ellison's own ironic powers were formed to a large extent within the precincts of the black college, which was both a variant of "mainstream" midcentury school culture and arguably that culture's model, insofar as the postwar university increasingly took upon itself the task of citizen making that had long been the purpose of black colleges like Tuskegee (from which Ellison departed one year shy of his degree).

To say that Ellison had an acute understanding of the school's fraught role in black life would be something of an understatement. The young Ellison delivered papers for Roscoe Dunjee's Oklahoma City newspaper, the *Black Dispatch*, to which he subscribed late in life, and later confessed to "being transformed," as he put it in a talk delivered in 1972, "by Roscoe Dunjee's editorials."[63] In that address, Ellison attributes to Dunjee "many of the gains which have transformed this country," not the least of which was that "through efforts he led as an official of the NAACP in Oklahoma, . . . the first real inroads for desegregation on the university level came out of Oklahoma City" (*CE*, 459). Ellison is referring to Dunjee's sponsorship of two lawsuits against the state of Oklahoma. In *Sipuel v. Board of Regents* (1948), Ada Lois Sipuel sued the University of Oklahoma Law School for sending black law students out of state in the absence of a "colored" law school in Oklahoma. In *McLaurin v. Oklahoma State Regents* (1950), George McLaurin sued the University of Oklahoma for segregating him from his white classmates in the doctoral program in education. Both plaintiffs made their way to the US Supreme Court, where their victory served as precedent for *Brown v. Board of Education* (1954).

The high praise Ellison heaps on Dunjee is worth remarking, for while there is no question that the latter deserves credit for the struggles in which he took a leading role, Ellison's encomium raises a number of questions over what those struggles meant. In his public lectures and occasional essays, we find a deliberate lack of specificity with respect to the subject at hand. To get a sense of this willful haziness, consider these sentences from the Dunjee address, where Ellison explains why black culture needs an independent press:

> If anyone thinks that a newspaper is an arbitrary enterprise, realize that our ancestors were responding to a very American situation in which we were exhorted to faith, to hope, to militancy. We had to be reminded that the way white Americans defined us was not what we were, and that the way we were described in the white press was not an adequate description. (*CE*, 461)

What, if anything, saves these sentences from being mere platitudes? Some version of this question must occur to many readers of Ellison's essays, which are rife with formulaic assumptions and high-flown diction ("to faith, to hope, to militancy"). "The way home we seek," Ellison writes in his acceptance speech for the 1953 National Book Award, "is that condition of man's being at home in the world, which is called love, and which we term democracy" (*CE*, 154). When faced with these and other sentiments in Ellison, we are forced to confront the relative emptiness of his democratic vision: "to project the possible, to inspirit the ideals of the Constitution, the Declaration of Independence, and the Bill of Rights into our own reality" (*CE*, 461). Yet we might respond to this perplexing feature in Ellison's discourse by coming at it aslant—by recognizing such sententious rhetoric, in other words, as a pretext for Ellison's equally recognizable habit of avoiding definitions. From this angle, the platitude stands as a kind of placeholder for an undisclosed and perhaps indefinable content. The negatives in this passage ("not what we were," "not an adequate description") might be seen as Ellison's real point, yet one so manifestly unsatisfactory in its refusal of definition that it obliges Ellison—who "despised concreteness in writing" (*CE*, 222)—to grant his listeners the commonplaces that will mitigate their frustration with his insistent negations.

What I have been describing will be fairly obvious to readers of *Invisible Man*, which elevates Ellison's refusal of specificity to a consummate artistry. It is, after all, a novel narrated by a character who declines to reveal his name, as well as a novel that—for all its historical interest—contains not a single calendar date. *Invisible Man* has routinely been taken as a critique of either black nationalism, popular front leftism, or the paternalistic liberalism of white supporters of the black race. By the same token, Ellison's own politics have been infamously hard to pin down. Separatist, integrationist, militant, accommodationist: at different times and from different views, Ellison reveals himself to hold any of these positions. Just as his own "cunning" (*CE*, 463) equivocation derives from what in the Dunjee address he calls his "easy rhetoric" (464), so the nimbleness with which *Invisible Man*'s narrator shifts in and out of the positions ascribed to him is accompanied by a fluency in the platitude. That Invisible Man (hereafter IM) is not quite capable of leaving the school that expels him is evidenced both by his mastery of the school's habits of pretending and by the persistence with which he measures his groundlessness in terms of a sardonic invocation of the hallowed figures in the American pageant (Franklin, Edison). Tracing his ancestry through this line of inventors, IM calls himself a "thinker-tinker." But as in postwar school culture at large, it is his very experience that becomes an experiment. Ellison recognized this linkage in his National Book Award speech, where he refers to his novel's "experimental attitude," which derived from his effort to "examine my experience through the discipline of the novel" because "so many of the works which impressed me were too restricted to contain the experience which I knew" (*CE*, 151).

In his curious 1970 bestseller *Future Shock*, Alvin Toffler heralds the arrival of a "novel, surprise-filled economy unlike any man has ever experienced," one in which "consumers" will "begin to collect experiences as consciously and passionately as they once collected things."[64] This economy, according to Toffler, will defy the binaries structuring the contemporary world. If "economists have great difficulty imagining alternatives to communism and capitalism," Toffler notes, in the future such "straight lines" (219) will give way to a system of "education" that "begins to employ experiential techniques to convey both knowledge and values" (234). Yet it is arguable that the future about which Toffler rhapsodized in 1970 had already come to pass, at least where the college as "experience industry" was concerned. For the university had long been purveying the "experiential benefits" (226) that Toffler saw as posterity's promise. Indeed, well before Toffler, its faculty had come to rely on "experiential production" (227) in order to demonstrate to students the folly of thinking in the "straight lines" of any particular ism. To anticipate the argument that unfolds in the next chapter, we might say that the greatest dividend of the academic commitment to ungrounded belief is that it accords a forceful primacy to open-ended experience. This privileging of experience, the core curriculum of the postwar university, evolves and is taken up so rapidly in midcentury American culture that by the 1960s the New Left can rally around experience as a viable political category both in and out of the university.

The school in *Invisible Man* is not typical, however, of the twentieth-century college. Ellison, let us recall, attended the all-black Tuskegee—a school that had for decades been the flagship of the policy position associated with its founder, Booker T. Washington, that black people did not want or need college in the traditional sense of that term. From its origin until well into the twentieth century, Tuskegee maintained a course of study in the "industrial and agricultural arts," staunchly flouting the liberal arts curriculum advocated by Washington's nemesis, W. E. B. Du Bois. Long before—and after—Du Bois published *The Souls of Black Folk* (1903), black colleges had a vexed position in the history of segregation.[65] They were institutions intensely desired by Reconstruction-era blacks *and* the products of Jim Crow, which authorized southern states to create separate colleges for black citizens after *Plessy v. Ferguson* (1896). The history of Tuskegee illustrates this ambiguity; in his infamous 1895 address to the Cotton States Convention, Washington promoted the school as the model for his accommodationist views.

All this is to say that *Invisible Man* brings a fairly conflicted account of the college to its pages. Even as it leans heavily on the syllabus of experience that was emerging from the midcentury college campus, it cannot but draw upon a knowledge of the difference that race makes to that account. Although the Reverend Barbee calls the Founder's vision a "great and noble experiment" (133), his "college for Negroes" (140) only imperfectly mimics the school as a laboratory for self-renewal or transformation. The lesson IM belatedly learns is that the experimentation with identity idealized by the postwar campus is one of the ruses that Bledsoe insists on seeing through even while he pays it lip service. When Bledsoe asks IM, "Did you forget how to lie?" (139), he calls attention to the fact that IM has come to believe in the mythology Barbee and others have concocted for white benefactors—that the school has given him "the only identity that [he] had ever known" (99) and other "vague notions of dignity" (144). Bledsoe sees such notions as "a lot of dead weight" (145) and insists that "to get where I am . . . I had to act the nigger" (143).

"Play the game," the vet tells IM on the bus ride North, "but don't believe in it" (153). This is an apt paraphrase of the advice Bledsoe gives IM earlier in the chapter, and it is fitting that the vet himself, a former brain surgeon who is now a mental patient on his way to St. Elizabeth's in Washington, D.C., should trace his own misfortunes back to his college days. Yet Bledsoe is a corrupt power broker who would "have every negro in the country hanging on tree limbs in the morning if it means staying where I am" (143), and the vet is quite likely insane. Thus, their cynicism about the school's ability to deliver a kind of Emersonian transformation is not necessarily reliable. Nor is it exactly true that for IM the college does not effect the forward momentum on which the midcentury college will set a premium for its student clientele. It is the catalyst of a hazardous perpetual motion, contained in Bledsoe's treacherous letters on IM's behalf: "Keep [this Robin] running" (193). Mobility in the book is equivalent to terror.

Of course, *Invisible Man* is not, strictly speaking, a campus novel. Its college scenes focus on IM the student (rather than the professoriat, the dramatis personae of the campus novel proper), and the novel rather quickly ejects IM from the college grounds. Yet two years before *Invisible Man* was published, there appeared a campus novel, Saunders Redding's *Stranger and Alone* (1950), featuring a black protagonist, Shelton Howden, who (like IM) starts off as a student at a "college for Negroes" and who (unlike IM) ends up at another such school, Arcadia State College, as a member of its faculty.[66] Ellison reviewed Redding's novel for the *New York Times*, where he faintly praised it for "reporting the little known role of those Negro 'leaders' who by collaborating with the despoilers of the South do insidious damage to us all."[67] Ellison thought of *Stranger and Alone* as little better than a documentary or, at best, a version of the "protest novel" that James Baldwin had disparaged the year before in *Partisan Review*. In a backhanded compliment that nodded to Baldwin's bête noire, Ellison referred to *Stranger and Alone* as "sociologically important."[68] In a small act of revenge, Redding in turn called *Invisible Man* "overblown" in a 1952 review.[69]

Redding endows his college president, Wimbush, with the bad faith and naked lust for power that Ellison's Bledsoe embodies. Indeed, precisely because Redding's book is not a very good novel, it tends to caricature its villain and thus make rather explicit many of the assumptions about school culture that the oversubtle *Invisible Man* leaves unspoken. If Ellison urges us toward an uneasy sympathy with Bledsoe's account of power, Redding lays out in much starker terms Wimbush's "cynical detachment," the opportunistic make-believe that he fosters in Howden, and the disdain we are intended to feel for a pragmatism that Redding sees as indistinct from "sportive malice": "There's nothing wrong with being the white man's nigger," Wimbush tells Howden. "It's only because of the concept that it seems contemptible . . . and the concept's not important" (136). Schooling Howden in the niceties of "disbelief" (134), Wimbush scorns what he calls "victims of a disease called racial absolutism, which blinds them to the fact that there are no absolutes: there are only continuing extremes which only fools try to reach" (135). Wimbush merges the midcentury academic's rejection of abstract ideals with a strategy of appeasement worthy of Booker T. Washington at his most objectionable: "It's only common sense," he tells Howden, "to accept the world as we find it" (135).

Redding's contempt for Wimbush's ironic instrumentalism is well attested. His 1942 autobiography *No Day of Triumph* records his perennial chagrin with school culture. Morehouse "disappointed me," he writes of a particularly unpleasant tenure at that historically black college. Its faculty "was effete, innocuous, and pretentious also, with a flabby softness of intellectual and spiritual fiber and even a lack of personal force."[70] This experience elicited a dismay from which Redding would never waver. Consider this broadside from *No Day of Triumph*:

> Negro schoolmen are terrific snobs, the true bourgeoisie. Grasping eagerly for straws of recognition, a great many of them proclaim loudly their race-faith. . . . In reality they look to the upper-middle-class whites for their social philosophy and in actual practice ape that class's indifference to social and political matters and reforms. They are a bulwark against positive action, liberal or even independent thought, and spiritual and economic freedom. (119)

We might note that Redding refused to share the conviction of other mid-century academics that "indifference to social and political matters" could itself count as "positive action" insofar as freedom to act meant freedom from "radicalism." He instead perceived the academy as both a restrictive space that compromised his intellectual freedom and a kind of forced march by virtue of the itinerant life it foisted on him. Redding was hardly unique in this respect. "Trained in prestigious white universities," Faith Berry notes, "black academicians were rarely invited to teach in those institutions . . . except as 'visiting professors.'"[71] The institutional detachment enjoyed by his white colleagues—fond of posing as invited guests in the colleges that housed them, with the added benefit of never being asked to leave—was hardly an option for Redding, who seemed incapable of remaining in the good graces of any one place for long.

His peculiar relation to the school, a place that until late in his career neither fully welcomed nor fully refused him, might account for Redding's Faustian view of the politics of make-believe that Wimbush instills in Howden.[72] What makes *Stranger and Alone* a campus novel, in fact, is what keeps *Invisible Man* from being one: its sense of the campus as forming a segment on a closed loop of power and politics from which there is no escape. For Howden, expulsion is not an option, and hence neither is the sort of existential drama to which IM lays claim. IM's solution to the problem of black performance is of course an embrace of invisibility that obliges him to disown the equation he has long maintained between public spectacle and conviction. If IM can convince himself that he is moving the masses at Madison Square Garden, for instance, the reason is that he has been moved by another's oratorical power. Thus, the Reverend Barbee, whose sermon rehearses the story of the college's founding, a story that every member of his audience knows, can make IM feel as though that story is an epiphany. IM makes for a good speaker because he has been a gullible audience. Given his opportunities to disabuse himself of the fallacious equation between performance and agency, from the battle royal to his discovery of Bledsoe's treachery to the Brotherhood's maneuvering to freeze him out, it is striking that it takes IM so long to extricate himself from the instrumental roles to which others subject him with his willing (if not exactly informed) consent.

One reason for this dilatoriness is that Ellison confounds the issue of performance by making the school into the backdrop of the bad-faith histrionics that true believers pursue and that the academic style seeks to counteract. As IM's response to Barbee's sermon confirms, the drama most likely to move him is that of the college as promised land. It is less the case that IM has been a bad student than that Ellison treats the college's pedagogy as fundamentally flawed, since it turns out to bear a startling resemblance to the very isms against which midcentury school culture seeks to inoculate its members. Far from bringing about the end of ideology, the academic style is just another *version* of ideology, replete with its own dogmatic content: "Play the game, but don't believe in it." IM is paradoxically too moved by this directive, too susceptible to its appeal as a life script, to heed its actual lesson. A kind of academic true believer, he is continually duped as a consequence of his zealous commitment to cynical reason.

Here we can observe one telling contrast between *Invisible Man* and *Stranger and Alone*. For Howden, there is no recourse to disowning one's role because there is no sense that the "gravy and play-acting" (129) he undertakes is ever other than a fraud so ever much of a problem to begin with. And it is his schooling that makes Howden a compelling instrument for use by others, as when he is summoned to "substitute" for Wimbush at a speech in front of a "Negro youth group" (127). It is thus slightly inaccurate to observe, with Lawrence Jackson, that Redding "had written a novel with a plot nearly the same as Ellison's: a poor black boy makes it to college only to be taken advantage of and become disillusioned."[73] Whereas *Invisible Man* records the gradual disillusionment of its true-believer protagonist, *Stranger and Alone* charts close to the opposite trajectory. It begins with its protagonist's education in "disbelief" and concludes with his having mastered others by strategically pretending to believe things he privately disavows—in other words, by absorbing the midcentury academic's commitment to make-believe as a way of life. It is as though *Invisible Man* were written with Bledsoe as its hero. In Redding's novel, the surrogacy of the professorial performer, allowing himself to be used by another in the service of a cause in which neither of them believes, is deplored with a moral certitude from which Ellison's book demurs.

But even if it withholds the harsh verdict that Redding renders on his characters, *Invisible Man* remains in crucial respects an idealistic narrative. Whereas the college teaches Howden that there is nothing beyond the act, it teaches IM that once the act is shed, there opens a world of indefinite possibility. Like his protagonist, Ellison found it somewhat difficult to extricate himself from school culture. A telling indication of what a powerful hold it maintained on Ellison is his reference, in "The World and the Jug," to "American Negro Life" as "not only a burden . . . but also a *discipline*—just as any human life which has endured is a discipline teaching its own insights into the human condition" (*CE*, 159). A basic feature of this particular discipline is the negative capability that shapes Ellison's "experimental attitude" (*CE*, 153) as surely as it lends its protean assets to the irony-rich humor pulsing through the body politic of the mid-century professoriat. Ellison's evasiveness and his flair for the truism, after all, feature prominently in the tool kit of the university intellectual, weaned on an appreciation for forms without content, for the ability to "project the possible" (Ellison's phrase) by leaving the "sanctum empty" (Daniel Boorstin's phrase).[74]

That expression appears in Boorstin's 1953 book *The Genius of American Politics*, a bracing corrective to the widespread lament over the absence of what Arthur Schlesinger called "a fighting faith" among a citizenry prone to disbelief.[75] "We should be inspired that in an era of idolatry," Boorstin claims, "when so many nations have filled their sanctuaries with ideological idols, we have had the courage to refuse to do so" (170). Boorstin's metaphor is a tribute to a pragmatism that pays respect to the same institutions it seeks to void of authorizing essence. The preceptors in Ellison's makeshift discipline possess a "coolness under pressure" (*CE*, 161) akin to the composure of the beneficiaries of the Cold War academic style. And just as Ellison exalts the "validity of experience" (*CE*, 161), so Boorstin's "pragmatic" (176) ideal rests on "the principle of the 'seamlessness' of experience" (175). Because Americans are de facto constructionists, perceiving "institutions" as "intimately related to the peculiar environment which nourishes them" (175), they cannot have beliefs in the pejorative sense: as doctrines always at risk of becoming orthodoxy. "Take our concept of equality," Boorstin writes,

> which many have called the central American value. No sooner does one describe a subject like this and try to separate it for study, than one finds it diffusing and evaporating into the general atmosphere. "Equality," what does it mean? In the United States it has been taken for a fact and an ideal, a moral imperative and a sociological datum, a legal principle and a social norm. It describes a continuum from physiology at one end to theology at the other. (177)

This is a remarkable statement to come across in a book published in 1953, within earshot of the *Brown* decision (1954), the Montgomery bus boycott (1956), and the descent of the National Guard on Little Rock Central High School (1957), and so in a context that might be thought to furnish some palpable connotations for the term "equality" or even to trouble the notion that it is the "central American value." And it is here that we must take note of a gap separating Ellison and Boorstin, the gap that "separate but equal" records. For even when he is most skeptical of normative definitions, it is hard to imagine Ellison conceding the dispersal of meaning that Boorstin takes "equality" to imply. The negations that cluster around the academic's "diffusing and evaporating" rationality would seem to stop short of an experience that, far from "seamless," literally cannot be shared across races: the benefits of white privilege in Jim Crow America.

It is thus striking to find Ellison not so much breaking faith with the antifaith of the Cold War academic as retaining that stance by enacting a distinctive vengeance on the academic's blithely ironic sensibility. This revenge, which ensures the preeminence of Ellison's own shrewd irony over the pallid versions to be found among his academic foils, consists in eliding the academic into his own worst nightmare: the queer man whose knowing embrace of make-believe travesties the social style of the professor class by twisting its penchant for "synthetic" experience in the wrong direction. In school culture, irony detaches the self from a society that covets relief from ambiguity. But in *Invisible Man*, the bearer of what Henri Peyre calls a "feeling for nuances" is its queer token, Emerson the Younger, who enlists ironic knowingness in the service of his *attachment* to IM as a fantasized object of desire. The scene of IM's encounter with Emerson is nothing other than a study in nuances. Emerson drops elusive hints about his interest in IM, clues that grow progressively less subtle as IM fails to pick up on his cruisy intimations. Among the various misunderstandings throughout their exchange, Ellison invokes a less noticeable but more pivotal confusion between queer subculture and the culture of the school. Prone to a "nostalgia for Harvard yard," Emerson begins his would-be seduction of IM by holding out the possibility that the latter might return to the college's warm embrace, even if it means transferring to "some school in New England" (183). Talk of the college thus functions like the phrase "Club Calamus" (185) a few pages on: a passport to illicit vice.

This is only to say that however else one parses what Daniel Kim calls the "homophobic symbolism that undergirds" Ellison's description of IM's visit with the "hip-swinging" Emerson (180), the latter cannot exactly be saddled with the *gullibility* that is as symptomatic of the Cold War queer as of the true believer.[76] Almost too oblique in his queries, Emerson pursues IM by forming and discarding his overtures with the skill of those well versed in the niceties of a noncommittal playacting. Whether posing as IM's prospective employer, as his secret sharer in "frustrated" potential (187), or as his co-conspirator in breaking the taboos ratified in the "mask of custom and manners that separate man from man" (186), Emerson maintains an "unmistakable irony in his voice" (185), an irony nowhere so evident as in his willingness to turn his corrosive wit on the school itself: "I guess one's college is really a kind of mother and father," he tells IM as he is about to reveal Bledsoe's betrayal, "a sacred matter" (183).

Emerson appears to use social scripts in the way that Cold War academics prefer: as conduits of enlightened self-interest, disowned or revised or selectively appropriated as the need arises. When the prospect of "naked honesty and frankness" proves a nonstarter with IM (186), he resorts to the constructionist's question of choice ("Who has any identity anymore?" [187]) before plying IM with an allusion to the period's most scandalous work of criticism, Leslie Fiedler's "Come Back to the Raft Ag'in, Huck Honey!" (1948): "With us it's still Jim and Huck Finn."[77] But it would be more accurate to say that Emerson approaches the scripts he borrows from postwar school culture's heterodox syllabus in the guise of the true believer so that Freud's *Totem and Taboo* and Fiedler's essay become the sort of how-to manuals in identity formation that true believers find in the writings of Lenin or Hitler. And it would perhaps be even more accurate to say that in Emerson's hands, the postwar academic style has itself become the kind of preformatted script that school culture disdains. When Emerson announces that "ambition . . . sometimes blinds one to realities" (184), that "some things are . . . too ambiguous for speech or ideas" (185), that "all our motives are impure" (186), or that "I must disillusion you" (187), he sounds as if he is parroting Niebuhr on the dangerous ruse of innocence or Daniel Bell praising "the claims of doubt" over "the claims of faith."[78] And he delivers these rote statements with the practiced ease of someone for whom they have become automatic responses, like a sequence of flash cards learned by heart.

That they are also as confining as the isms from which the school means to free the republic is made clear through an analogy so blatant, as the first-year composition student might say, that even Ellison's generally imperceptive protagonist could not miss it. Among the curios arrayed in Emerson's office is an "aviary of tropical birds" (181) that periodically jolt IM with their "beating and fluttering" (182). Emerson is also a creature given to "fluttering" (184); and even without the cigarette he always has in reach, he is as "flamboyant" as the birds whose "flashing" makes it seem as though they "had burst into spontaneous flame" (182). Despite his supreme facility in "evading [an] issue" in pursuit of a different or better possibility (186), Emerson remains trapped in what *Invisible Man* regards as the *cage aux folles* of the academic style, here shorn of the veneer of optionality that the professoriat imagines it enjoys with its campus employer. The take-it-or-leave-it attitude espoused by the faculty toward a university unable to inspire anything beyond a minimal sense of "belonging" becomes, in Emerson's case, a ploy for obscuring a cycle of dependence. Ellison describes a vicious circle in which Emerson's initial knowingness is made to curve around to the naïveté for which generations of critics have held him (or his romantic-racist paternalism) in contempt. I am suggesting that the content of his paternalism is less notable than its mode: the academic style centered on strategic make-believe.

Calling out the academic style in the figure of its abject double, the campy homosexual whose pragmatism lies adjacent to a shameless deviance, Ellison makes that style an erratic mannerist charade, the hallmark of the flaming sissy rather than the tough-minded ironist. In this move he would hardly be unique. It is worth noting here how often the campus novel caricatures the faculty by effeminizing it. Bill Sanders, a college administrator in Stringfellow Barr's *Purely Academic* (1958), "looked on professors as a special class of kept women."[79] Richard Waithe, a visiting writer at Cranton College in John Aldridge's *The Party at Cranton* (1960), realizes with the force of epiphany that the cynosure of the Cranton English department "radiated femininity."[80] When in *Night and Silence, Who Is Here?* (1963) Pamela Hansford Johnson describes the figures "burning up with brutal irony, original in their cruel sarcasms, verbally ingenious, arcane in inspiration," she is ostensibly attending to the professors whose "*furor academicus*" lights upon the "thousand pieces of suggestiveness" in a text.[81] But she might as well be alluding to the flaming creatures who gather in what Fiedler's "Come Back to the Raft" calls "the 'queer' café," what *Invisible Man* calls "Club Calamus."[82] Johnson's is one of dozens of campus novels in which the social style of the professoriat is stamped with a queer overlay.

Or specifically, a camp overlay. In "The Jig Is Up!" (1963), Fiedler defines "camping" as "an activity less than fully human: a slave's secret revolt that leaves him (even in his own deepest self-consciousness) a slave still."[83] In light of his more famous piece of writing, which reads the homoerotic off Huck Finn's bond with a man in bondage, Fiedler's equation of "camping" and slavery seems rather overdetermined. And as we have seen in Emerson's appropriation of Fiedler's "Come Back to the Raft" in *Invisible Man*, the effort to make school culture a sanctuary from camp's ineffectual "slave's revolt" is nullified by the ease with which the queer slips into the persona of the Cold War academic. Mustering a dubious sympathy for "the queer" who "must exaggerate flounce and flutter into the convention of his condition," as he puts it in "Come Back to the Raft," Fiedler treats the queer's forced exhibition as a performance he knows is false but cannot help reenacting.[84] Ellison in turn treats Emerson's "fluttering" hopscotch from one proposition to another as response conditioned by essays like Fiedler's.

Indeed, the identification of camp with the academic style had become so familiar in the decade between *Invisible Man* and essays like "The Jig Is Up!" and Sontag's "Notes on Camp" (1964) that by the time Louis Kampf published "The Scandal of Literary Scholarship" in 1967, his assault on the business as usual of the English department could almost read like a jeremiad directed at the camp fairy rather than the humanities faculty. Thus, when he claims that "our academics have released a flood of literary solvent . . . which promises to dissolve whatever standards we have managed to retain,"[85] he echoes Sontag's definition of camp as "a solvent of morality" that "neutralizes moral indignation."[86] And when he describes the "excrescences emitted by the corpse of literary scholarship," which "corrupt the language" and "sully our scholarly ideals" (86), he echoes Sontag's point that "camp discloses innocence, but also, when it can, corrupts it."[87] But Kampf reserves his harshest words for the fact that the discipline of English has devolved from a substantive research program to what he calls "an invitation to opportunism, . . . an opportunity for personal display" whose golden rule is for its novitiates "not to take their own role—the use of their intellects—too seriously" (87).

The problem with humanist study in the era of the New Social Movements, then, is that it has become *exclusively* a tutorial in style. It is thus strangely fitting that the same year Kampf's essay appeared, Students for a Democratic Society (SDS) member Mike Zweig sought to "suggest what a 'radical university professor' might do, what he might be like, in his effort to be part of a transformation of America," by granting primacy to the "question of personal style":

> The teacher himself ought to keep loose and avoid the trappings of constrained academic style that are imposed on him. . . . We should continue to be what we are in a natural way, in a personal way, because that is an important element of "radical style" which we should not allow to atrophy. We should be the way we ourselves

want, not the way others decide we should be, because that's one of the radical's threats to American liberalism.[88]

It is not clear what really distinguishes the "free and informal" or "nonprofessorial" style Zweig advocates from the style that Kampf condemns in his colleagues. Why should the former confirm something like a "natural" authenticity while the latter confirms Kampf's verdict on his colleagues as "hollow men" (86)? What makes this question hard to answer is that Cold War academics already took pride in a kind of loose style (although they declined to refer it to nature). The basic problem lies not in academic style as such but in the way that style is deployed. For style to serve what Kampf calls "freedom" (91) and "action" (90), it must stop wearing "a mask of irony" (88); for it to be "rigorous" (90), it must cease to be "pathological" (89) and "narcissistic" (90). For professorial style to be "effective" (90), it must stop being camp.

Invisible Man shows us the blueprint for Kampf's late-1960s critique of the professoriat as all style and no substance, able to "absorb all new cultural phenomena" (87) on the camp-inflected presumption that each is equally meaningless. Perhaps the most revealing confirmation of Emerson as an avatar of midcentury school culture is his fondness for analogizing, for deriving a claim about something on the basis of what that something is like. "I know many things about you," he tells IM, "not you personally, but fellows like you" (187). The trope of analogy drives the postwar humanities as firmly as irony steers the Cold War academic style at large. Indeed, the two gestures are symbiotic, but Ellison's strategy is to separate them, making Emerson's irony fail him at the moment when he shifts toward analogical thinking. Confidence in inferring what something is like is no less prevalent in Emerson's effort to forge continuities than in what Boorstin calls "'seamlessness' of experience." But the scare quotes around "seamlessness" signal Boorstin's awareness of the ad hoc nature of this unity, a condition in whose existence the reader is meant to entertain belief for the sake of argument but not necessarily beyond the latter's duration. Ellison by contrast withholds from Emerson camp's scare quotes. Making Emerson believe in the counterfeit likeness between a person and a category ("not you personally, but fellows like you"), Ellison diminishes the camp queen's irony in a bid to expose the credulous underbelly of the school's agnosticism. In turning Emerson into a joke, Ellison robs him of his sense of humor.

Humor is of course a central topic in *Invisible Man*. Rejecting forced analogies of the sort that Emerson presents because it sees them as perpetuating the coercion of blacks by whites through other means, the novel embraces the discordance of the blues sensibility, specifically as embodied in Louis Armstrong, a figure whose musical timing was paired with remarkable comic timing. Whereas Armstrong's rendition of "(What Did I Do to Be) So Black and Blue" inaugurates *Invisible Man*, the novel ends with IM reciting, "with Louis Armstrong, . . . Open the window and let the foul air out" (581), from Armstrong's cover of "I Thought I Heard Buddy Bolden Say," or as it is otherwise known, "Funky Butt Blues," a title that references the New Orleans club where Bolden held court.[89] IM glosses these lyrics as follows: "Of course Louie was kidding, *he* wouldn't have thrown the bad air out, because it would have broken up the music and the dance, when it was the good music that came from the bell of old Bad Air's horn that counted" (581). By this definition, jazz is a form made perfect by its studied imperfections, just as the blues are inconceivable without the pain and suffering that infuse blues lyrics.

As a consummate player in the jazz tradition, Armstrong was daily involved with the comedy at the edge of tragedy fundamental to the blues. The scatological humor Armstrong engaged in—that the blues always engage in—becomes crucial to *Invisible Man*'s sense of the black body, or rather to its reclamation of that body from the claims of white spectatorship. The distorted reflection that the novel repeatedly stages between a white-identified audience and a black performer finds a counterpoint, for example, in Armstrong's embrace of the minstrel tradition, a performance style synonymous with distortion. Ellison was intensely mindful of the implications of Armstrong's self-display, defending him against those who "fastened the epithet 'Uncle Tom' upon Armstrong's music" and thus "confused artistic quality with questions of personal conduct" (*CE*, 259). Crucial to the way Armstrong played with distorted racial images instead of simply embodying them was the instrument whose distortionary potential he exploited. I have in mind not just his iconic trumpet but also the innovative plug-in attached to the trumpet's bell, the plunger mute, an accessory pioneered by his mentor, King Oliver.

As Ellison suggests in his reference to "the bell of old Bad Air's horn," this plunger—a thing that was and remains the tool we use to unclog a toilet, the site of "bad air" and other bad matter—is associated with the wrong opening in the body, the anus and not the mouth, and is thus particularly relevant to "Funky Butt Blues," a tune long regarded as a composition on farting. The conflation of mouth and ass is even more pointed in light of the fact that in the wide catalog of frequently racist kitsch associated with Armstrong, no doubt the most familiar image is the effigy of "Satchmo" (short for Satchelmouth) with a clownishly enlarged maw on an equally clownish face, a mouth that seems optimized for the plunger mute precisely because it is forever plastered with a shit-eating grin. The inversion that Armstrong might be said to bring to "Funky Butt Blues" belongs to the larger play with dissonance central to the blues: transposing the "funky butt" to the trumpet-blowing mouth physicalizes the disjunctive poetics that the blues locate in such lyrics as "I'm white inside but that don't help my case / 'cause I can't hide what is in my face." These infamous lines come from "So Black and Blue," a song explicitly written for a female voice and first performed on Broadway in the 1929 musical *Hot Chocolates*, a musical in which Armstrong costarred. Armstrong appears to have been unruffled by the gender trouble that his cover of "So Black and Blue" implies. We might say that he brings to his rendition's implicit transvestitism the same comfort level he appears to enjoy with respect to the unease the song induces by way of its dysmorphic cross-racial fantasy.

If Ellison's novel adopts the absurdist consciousness of the blues tradition as a political posture designed to thwart the "false wisdom of slaves and pragmatists alike, that white is right" (95), that posture is supported by some rather selective borrowings from the blues repertoire. Toward the end of *Invisible Man*, Ellison makes several references to "plunging" (499): "Clifton had chosen to plunge out of history" (477); "I'd plunge in with both feet and they'd gag" (551); "someone, for some reason, had removed the manhole and I felt myself plunge down, down; a long drop that ended upon a load of coal that sent up a cloud of dust" (565). It is hard not to read these plunging moments in relation to the bodily inversion Armstrong makes apparent with the plumber's helper on the bell of his trumpet. IM's drop into a black mass that reads like cloaca encourages us to see in these references the symbolic immersion in the toilet that Armstrong's horn connotes. But if this is a connection Ellison recognizes, it is also one whose other inversions—of gender and sexuality—*Invisible Man* seems intent on denying.

Ellison takes plunging to mean a precipitous fall, an abject expulsion from the social order into an antisocial zone, whereas Armstrong takes plunging quite literally as an instrument of sociability. In addition, *Invisible Man* screens out the resonance between the anal semiotics of a song like "Funky Butt" and the casual sex change that Armstrong's "So Black and Blue" entertains, not to say the strong resemblance between the blues and the queer sensibility whose clownish spectacle Ellison uses to smear the academic style with the brush of deviance. We need not pore over the extensive and well-documented homo-erotic presence in the history of the blues, nor even press too hard on the fact that "So Black and Blue" began life as that queerest of numbers, a *show tune*, to take note of this resemblance. Just as the blues aesthetic is governed by an appreciation for counterfactual fantasy and jarring collisions, so the camp sensibility appears governed by its beholders' comfort with those familiar capsizals of gender and erotic normativity, the drag act and anal sex, so firmly cemented to the gay male body in the cultural imaginary that to call them signifiers is redundant.

Because it too revels in mixed messages and the gap between aspiration and experience (of the sort that the color line presents to the singer of "So Black and Blue"), because its followers share Armstrong's infamous willingness to preempt jokes at their expense by making a joke of themselves, camp might be thought to have as much in common with the blues habit of mind as with the academic style. In having his protagonist flee from the unwelcome advances of school culture's queer envoy, Ellison no less than the Cold War critic throws up a friable barrier between sensibilities whose likenesses would seem worth pursuing if not in fact admitting. Severing camp from professorial irony, Fiedler makes the former a tool of the slave in order to assert the latter as a tool of mastery. Ellison proceeds through a similar logic with regard to blues culture and school culture, with the latter now connoting a slavish gullibility that Ellison traces, counterintuitively though not uniquely, through a homophobic stencil. Making the academic style "like" the camp theatricals of Emerson, Ellison renders a shoddy version of camp, a camp that cannot laugh at itself.

2 Campus Novels and Experimental Persons

The School as Difference Engine

In a 1951 essay about a visit to her alma mater, Mary McCarthy admits her frustration with the Vassar student's "increasing dependency . . . on the college and its auxiliary agencies to furnish not only education but pleasure, emotional guidance, and social direction."[1] Yet where McCarthy regretted that "the extracurricular side of Vassar life has already expanded to the point where solitude and self-questioning seem regulated out of existence" (*OC*, 208), school culture's wardens took a different view. For them, the "intensification of the extracurricular life" (*OC*, 209) was beside the point. The self-questioning whose passing McCarthy lamented had been absorbed into the curriculum itself. Instead of vanishing from the midcentury campus, introspection had entered the course catalog.

McCarthy was a shrewd observer of the midcentury campus, and she gave freer rein to her misgivings about it a year later in *The Groves of Academe* (1952), her contribution to the era's strikingly prolific genre, the campus novel. Considering how much novelists' livelihood would come to depend on university stipends in the postwar era, either as freelance teachers or as recruits to the recently founded discipline of creative writing, it is perhaps no surprise that they turned en masse to a study of *Homo academicus*. "The proliferation of universities as settings for novels," Mark McGurl writes, "is what we might call a thematic symptom of a larger shift in the institutional arrangements of postwar literary production"—the rise of the MFA program—with the consequence that "all novels aspiring to the honorific status of literature must now be considered campus novels of a sort."[2]

The mutual distrust between the creative writer and the academic critic made newly intimate by a shared college campus is what Leslie Fiedler had in mind when he noted in a 1964 essay, "It is the revolt against school and in particular against the university which most clearly distinguishes the writers of the sixties from those who immediately preceded them." By the latter, Fiedler meant a group of novelists—including McCarthy, Bernard Malamud, Philip Roth, and Vladimir Nabokov—who had what he called a "primary commitment" to the university as either teachers or writers-in-residence or something in between.[3] Yet the establishment of MFA programs was but one stark manifestation of the massive enlargement of the university system in postwar society. It is this enlargement that interests me. Many writers, according to Fiedler, were well attuned to the gigantism of the school, which they imagined less as confining them in a disciplinary cage than as expanding so much that its borders threatened to become identical to the boundaries of the culture. Rather than depict the academy as "an adequate symbol of our total society," as Fiedler puts it, campus novels shared McCarthy's suspicion that the college had become a "total society" in its own right, not so much "reflecting the great world" (5) as aiming to supplant it.

Implausible though it may be, this dire view of campus life had the tactical advantage of reversing midcentury school culture's own self-promotion as a model for the open society. Campus novelists were keen to show how the university might be understood to camouflage its insidious kinship with the totalitarianism to which it was opposed. The most notable feature of the genre is thus its focus on protagonists who are indentured to school culture more or less permanently. Shifting attention to the professor and away from the student (the traditional subject of the college novel), campus novelists record a significant change in how one is meant to understand the academy. In campus novels, the college is not an interim social space, a way station on the road to bourgeois comfort, but a gulag that prevents its inmates from imagining any extramural setting in which their lives might unfold. The academic in thrall to the university is the genre's foil for the professor who understood himself as a resident alien in the institution, someone (as Niebuhr would say) both "within and above" whichever school happened to be paying his salary. If the professoriat understood all roles—even tenure—as fictive and contingent, campus novels exposed this posture of self-removal as itself fictive, a means for the professoriat to deny its dependency on an institution without which it could not survive.

Indeed, in the campus novel, the professoriat bereft of its customary detachment is instead driven toward one of two impulses that appear to run amok in every institution of higher learning: a single-minded quest for self-actualization and an equally quixotic pursuit of social revolution. Fixing on these traits, campus novels attempted to thwart the self-image of university intellectuals by equating their intellectual style with the utopianism that was roundly discredited in postwar thought. Yet in pursuing this likeness, the campus novel helped bequeath a potent new self-image that has since fused deftly, if paradoxically, with the ironizing *habitus* of the faculty, which could now find in the academy not only a congenial environment for self-discovery but also a training ground for successive generations of insurrectionists. Though the millennial effusion of academic memoirs suggests that the project of self-discovery has won out over the pedagogy of broad social change, the relation between these two impulses is actually quite knotty. Self-actualization and social revolution are less alternatives to each other than alternative versions—one turned inward; the other outward—of the commitment to "difference" with which the university has long since come to be identified.

For the postwar university, *making a difference* always begins at home. Across the spectrum of postwar higher education we find every sort of campus fashioning itself into a better version of itself. From the cow college on the land grant to the Ivy League citadel, midcentury school culture is distinguished above all by its striving, its pursuit of ever more students, faculty, departments, buildings, grants, and areas of expertise to augment its reputation, retool its mission, or surpass its competitors. While some of the most distinguished campus novels take place in avowedly "experimental" colleges (McCarthy's Jocelyn is based on Bard), it would be more accurate to say that every college as understood by campus novels is an experimental one.[4] And endlessly seeking to renovate its own identity, the college becomes the most auspicious venue for individuals to undertake their redevelopment. Even such a lackluster environment as Bernard Malamud's Cascadia College affords Seymour Levin, a recovering alcoholic, the glamorous fantasy of rebirth suggested by Malamud's title (*A New Life*). In the same spirit, John Barth's Jacob Horner takes a job at Wicomico Teachers College by order of "the Doctor," who prescribes this post as one among a "schedule of therapies" to overcome Jacob's mental "immobility" and to replenish what the doctor calls "the vacuum you have for a self."[5]

It is a hallmark of the campus novel that it portrays the college as much less interested in the older, genteel effort to buff up the manners of its charges than in the more exhaustive goal of remaking their identities and experiences from the inside out. We can trace this shift in emphasis by looking at a text that lies adjacent to the campus novel proper, B. F. Skinner's *Walden Two* (1948), whose central conceit is that school culture grants its beneficiaries privileged access to self-experimentation. Though Skinner's hero, Frazier, has "no current university affiliation" and appears to have "given up teaching," and though his would-be disciple, Rogers, insists that "you've got to . . . *experiment with your own life*" but that such "research" cannot be done "in an ivory tower," Walden Two bears more resemblance to a college campus than to the hermitage of its Thoreauvian namesake.[6] This is the case not just in its physical plant, an "architectural hodgepodge" of old and new (40), but also in its segmentation of work into various "departments" (30), each of which tends its own garden. Walden Two's residents understand themselves as both students and "teachers, at what I suppose you would call the 'college level'" (25). Frazier's scare quotes are intended to mock the analogy between utopia and university life, since in Walden Two they "dispense with half the teachers required" in the "system" of mainstream education, having mastered "techniques" by which their "children . . . learn things for themselves" (110). But Walden Two's "constantly experimental attitude toward everything" (25) mirrors rather than refutes the precepts of midcentury school culture, which is committed to an anti-institutionalism every bit as militant as Frazier's own.

Just as Walden Two furnishes its members with "a broad experience and many attractive alternatives" (47), so the postwar college sought to ensure that its clientele had at their disposal as many opportunities as possible to capitalize on their experience of inwardness. According to Harvard's landmark report *General Education in a Free Society* (1945), also known as the Redbook, "democracy imposes on all its citizens the task of responsible private judgment, and it is for the schools to fit them for this task by every possible means."[7] Despite its institutional provenance, the Redbook airs some serious misgivings about the school as intermediary. In tones echoing Frazier's reservations about the role of teachers in the learning process, the Redbook frequently disclaims the interposing of superfluous "information" (201) between the "private" mind and its proper objects. Thus, in the humanities curriculum, "knowledge through" is what matters and "comes only through immersion in the literature," while "knowledge about, though its origin and aim may be simply to aid the immersion, can in fact prevent and hinder its own purpose" (205). Whereas New Critics understood the training of students in the method of close reading as indispensable to both an aesthetic appreciation of literature and a technical understanding of its forms, the Redbook argues instead for the critic's sacrifice on the altar of a "direct access to the potentialities and norms of living as they are presented to the mental eye by the best authors" (107), a communion between the student and the text tradition undisturbed by the deforming lessons of the meddling preceptor. "Since the best commentary on an author is frequently some more of his own writing" (206), the report argues, "the instructor can only seek to be a means by which the authors teach the course" (207).

The Redbook's authors took as given "that rational explanation should accompany or follow habituation, . . . that, in short, mere habituation is not enough" (172). Just as it seeks to turn professors into "means" rather than ends, so the Redbook discounts education as inculcation (because it tends toward complacency) in favor of education as *process* (because by continual monitoring it delays the fossilization of knowledge into mere data). This perpetual method is epitomized in "composition, . . . a never-ending discipline which can be only begun in schools and must be continued in college" (198). Because a discipline is more or less infinite while college comes to an end, an enterprise like Walden Two seems necessary to its members in the first place. As opposed to "the educational process which comes to a dead stop somewhere around the middle of June in one's last year of college," Frazier points out, "in Walden Two education goes on forever" (112), and by the same token, "people in Walden Two never stop changing" (124). An insufficient guarantor of changing, no sooner producing those eager for alteration than it graduates them out of its ranks, the university creates a desire that, only partially satisfied under its auspices, can be adapted to a kind of "never-ending" experimentalism elsewhere. Hence Frazier's community does not replace so much as supplement the university, like an institute or think tank whose members can work unfettered "with an eye to possible improvement" of "every habit and custom" (25).

The objective of Walden Two, according to Frazier, is "to manipulate the environment in the required way" (70) in order to foster people who, instead of settling into predetermined roles, can keep on with the task of changing. This is why, in *Utopia and Its Enemies* (1963), George Kateb identifies Skinner's utopianism as more concerned with the "formation of character" than with the formation of a better society.[8] Nothing in Walden Two is fixed except the dictate that any element of it can be rearranged. The distress brought on by the radicalism of Skinner's thought would be mitigated, Kateb notes, were his "enemies" to realize that "behavioral engineering" is just an ungainly term for "a more effective kind of education" (143). Far from coercing people, Skinner merely aims to redirect their learning, Kateb claims, "so educating them as to make it easier for them to be good and to work well" (157).

Despite his sympathy for *Walden Two*'s educational utopia, Kateb finally rejects Skinner's model society on the grounds that, in seeking to make the attainment of virtue chief among the "aims of conditioning" (143), his vision does not go far enough. In presupposing *any* aims for education, according to Kateb, Skinner falls short of the radical implications of his own precepts. The heady idea of ongoing experiment given voice to in the early part of *Walden Two* turns out to be mere lip service; nothing short of a *moral* end point punctuates what had promised to be an investment in experiment for its own sake. Walden Two's precepts instill what Kateb calls an "indolence" (164) at odds with the community's stated objective to keep its members perpetually aiming for new "potentialities" (214). "Skinner," Kateb writes, "speaks as if his methods of education were such as to leave no room for either growth or effort" (160).

On the subject of education, Kateb favored the writings of Dewey, the founder of the progressive school movement and the advocate for what, in *Experience and Education* (1938), he called "a philosophy of education based upon a philosophy of experience."[9] "The office of the educator," Dewey claimed, is "to select those things within the range of existing experience that have the promise and potentiality of presenting new problems which by stimulating new ways of observation and judgment will expand the area of further experience."[10] "Potentiality" is Dewey's word—also the Redbook's and Kateb's—for describing the advantages of shifting persons from a view of themselves as "ends of *action*" toward a conception of themselves as "redirecting pivots *in* action."[11] Skinner's utopia reneges on its promise to keep its members changing when in Walden Two, Kateb notes, "The level of moral goodness is slightly raised; and it is made fairly easy for people to reach and keep that level" (216). Committed to a "static conception of man" (214), *Walden Two* fosters what the Redbook calls "mere habituation."

Toward an Education of Experience:
Hum 6 at Harvard, English 1 at Amherst

If Kateb reproaches Skinner for being "oblivious to the claims of any kind of *personalism*" (215), the reason is that during the time Kateb was writing *Utopia and Its Enemies* a preoccupation with what he calls "the 'inside' of human activity" (215) had accrued a certain urgency in the circles in which he moved. Trained as a political theorist, Kateb (like Skinner) maintained close ties with humanists throughout his career, first at Harvard and later at Amherst, where he taught for thirty years. The relation *Walden Two* advanced between educa-tion and "the formation of character" was crucial to pedagogical experiments at both these institutions, the most influential of which were Amherst's English 1 and Harvard's interpretation of literature course, or "Hum 6," introduced into the Harvard curriculum by Reuben Brower in the early 1950s after he moved there from Amherst. In answer to the crisis in "general education" that the Redbook exposed, Brower furnished a class, adapted from the introductory se-quence at Amherst, that put into practice the Redbook's reimagining of literary study as "knowledge through" and "immersion."

Hum 6 was an experimental undertaking based, we might say paradoxically, on the rejection of experimental methods. In their preface to a 1962 collection of essays authored by the course's past and present staff, Brower and Richard Poirier (one of Hum 6's instructors along with Paul de Man) note that Hum 6 aimed "less to create 'methods' than to resist them," since any "fixed" technique "may too easily become a substitute for the freer and more difficult activity of reading and of accurately describing what that activity was like."[12] While Hum 6 dispatched method, it retained the empirical scientist's commitment to "accu-rate" description. The crucible that mattered most to this inductive observation was the "literary experience" of the readers themselves (vii). In the volume's preparatory essay, Brower advocates "slowing down the process of reading to observe what is happening" (4) and "engaging in imaginative experience" (9). "Our aim," he argues, "is to get the student in a position where he can learn for himself" (8). Where Skinner sought to dispense with teachers in order to grant students a kind of unmediated entrée to learning, Brower envisioned a pedagogy in which "mere teachers of literature . . . might in time quietly disap-pear from the academic scene" (21), allowing students to "carry on internally . . . an independent performance for an attentive critical audience of one" (17). The essay's imaginary course (based on classes "given at Amherst College and Harvard" [3]) thus concludes with a period "when the students are given two or more weeks without classes in which to read new material—poems, plays, or novels—with no teacher to guide them" (10).

In addition to freeing up the professor's own schedule, Brower's proposed hiatus sought the far nobler benefit of securing what Frazier calls "a broad experience" for the student granted an unencumbered few weeks at semester's end. Yet Hum 6's goal of "accurately describing what the activity [of reading] was like" was somewhat at variance with the premium the course placed on holding the observer's experience open to what Poirier called "a beautifully liberating instability."[13] In *The Resistance to Theory*, de Man admits to having "never known a course by which students were so transformed."[14] The absence of referents for this transformation reveals as much about de Man's elliptic style of argument as about Hum 6's cultic reverence for the inaccessible substantive. De Man's highest praise for the course thus concerns its ability to expose by way of "mere reading" the "deeply subversive . . . power of literary instruction" (2). Poirier fills in something of what de Man means by "subversive" by noting that Hum 6's "exercises made reading an acutely meditative process without ever inviting anything so mechanical as the mere tracking of images."[15] Hum 6 bred the "feeling . . . that the human presence in any gathering of words was always elusive" (183).

Implicit in these claims about subversion, transformation, and elusive presence is a view of literary study as the occasion for analyses that, as Poirier puts it, "should never end" (193). Hum 6 aimed "to practice the art of not arriving" (182), the better to carry on the "acutely meditative process" of an indefinite if not indefinable reading. This technique had a clear forerunner in the work of Kenneth Burke, who identifies his "pragmatic" approach in these terms: "By inspection of the work, you propose your description" of a text's "equational structure," by which he means forming "relevant observations" of "what goes with what."[16] Befitting its pragmatist roots, such criticism refuses certitude; the best it can hope for is "closer approximations," plausible estimations of what a text is like.[17] Postwar humanists drew not only on Burke's sense that the "equational" structure of texts licenses reading for *analogy* but also on his suspicion that reading is no more than informed guesswork.

"Experience" does a good deal of rhetorical labor in both *Walden Two* and Hum 6. But where Frazier lectures on the advantages of "broad experience," Hum 6 and its parent class, Amherst's English 1, were eager to advance the virtues of *new* experience. Hence the definition of experience in these courses was a purist version of Dewey's claim that "experience in its vital form is experimental, an effort to change the given."[18] Hum 6's sense of its curriculum as a journey without "arriving" evolved out of the intimacy that many of its instructors had with English 1—a course Walker Gibson, who taught it in the 1950s, describes as "dynamic" rather than "static, . . . not a body of knowledge to be readily laid out on paper" but "an ongoing activity."[19] Like Hum 6, English 1 was designed around the autodidactic fantasy that, as its founder Theodore Baird put it in a 1954 memo to his students, "whatever answers you reach in this course . . . will be your own."[20] But even more than Hum 6, which was bound to the subject matter of the literary canon and so to some version of tradition, English 1 (which used only writing prompts) emphasized the class's "ongoing" innovativeness to the exclusion of everything else. "Every year, this teaching staff makes a new sequence of assignments," Baird wrote in his 1954 memo, "so that for all concerned, teacher and student, this is a new course" (*FW*, 250).

Such newness served as the basis for what English 1 saw as a productive disorientation of the undergraduate's experience. "We frequently had assignments that asked," Armour Craig recounts in an interview about English 1, "'You are in a situation where you're at a loss. What does it feel like? How do you know you're at a loss?'" (*FW*, 121). English 1 required its students not only to fix on but to distance themselves from their experience. "In the last few assignments you have been asked to characterize a writer's 'voice,' to construct a personality for the character you 'hear talking' in a piece of writing," Baird reminded his students in a lesson reproduced in Varnum's book. "Suppose you now try doing this with your own work" (*FW*, 48). The assignment predicates its completion on the student's ability to entertain the thought of being in two places at once: inside and outside his own head, performing a "personality" on the written page that he must then "characterize" through the equally fabricated role of listener.

We might reasonably infer from the dislocated self implied by English 1's assignments that the class sought to remake its students' identity in the image-ideal of the ironic professoriat whose intellectual style I examined in the previous chapter. "Among other things," notes William Pritchard, who took English 1 as a freshman in 1949 and taught it as a professor beginning in 1959, "the course was an elementary education in irony."[21] That irony finds its way into Baird's last assignment for his fall 1963 English 1 class, where he cautions his students that the course's "Real Subject exists only as you think of it."[22] Where the Cold War academic's consensus of make-believe paved the way for a politics of the noncommittal, Baird's similarly counterpoised dynamic of owning and disowning authenticity went hand in hand with renewal. The teachers of Hum 6 and English 1 understood individuals in terms of their opportunistic promise—the promise, that is, to be perpetual means. The ideal person in this account would, like English 1, begin afresh each autumn.

English 1's fetish for "potentiality" is subjected to withering scrutiny in a late-period campus novel that both entertains and debunks the idea that the self can be educated into a state of ceaseless innovation. In Alison Lurie's *Love and Friendship* (1962), Emmy Turner's husband, Holman, teaches a barely fictive replica of English 1, called Hum C, at Convers College, an equally transparent facsimile of Amherst. The novel is intent on dispelling the mystifications that cluster around Hum C and its tyrannical director, Oswald McBane, modeled on Baird. Holman, "sophisticated enough to have grasped" the basics of Hum C's "Socratic method," is "really concerned . . . to discover the inner power politics of both Hum C and the Languages and Literature Division," although "in this area he had accomplished nothing."[23] Meanwhile, Emmy, "pretending that she was taking Hum C along with her husband's classes" (19), makes Holman bring home the class assignments for her to puzzle through. Emmy and Holman's Hum C ritual always ends with her frustration at "this stupid word game" and her husband's realization "that his wife had little aptitude for abstract ideas" (20). But the problem put this way misses Emmy's real anxiety: "She felt that there must be some more important secret, if only from the gnomic behavior of her husband and the other Hum C instructors" (20).

Refusing to believe that Hum C is based on a resolute positivism rather than a metaphysics of depth, Emmy thinks the class is "like Emerson" in that the assignments "keep asking questions simply to clear away all the rubbish that everyone takes for granted and what's left is what you really believe." Holman, on the other hand, "despaired of trying to explain to her why the course was not a program of self-analysis, but completely the opposite." Yet Emmy is closer to the mark than her husband, who sees Hum C as a set of "principles . . . which could be applied to the criticism of literature." Holman commits the sin of reifying Hum C into "a technical matter" (62); "the use of words like 'positivist' and 'principles,'" as Holman knows, "was absolutely taboo" (17). In an Emersonian mood, Emmy sees the course less "from an emotional point of view" (62) than from the vantage of the ever-changing self that appears to be "what's left" after stripping away "the rubbish that everyone takes for granted." Though Hum C has virtually no commitment to "what you believe," as we might expect of a course in the postwar college, it is intensely committed to deposing any established conventions—preconceived "rubbish"—that stand in the way of the student's acts of self-questioning.

Another way to put their difference of opinion is to say that both Emmy and Holman find in Hum C a model for self-renovation. But whereas Holman's transformation entails his breaching Hum C's "inner power politics" in the hope of getting tenure, Emmy's takes her in a much more unsettling direction. Emmy's desire for "some more important secret," after all, leads to her affair with another instructor at Convers, Will Thomas. Failing to get the gist of Hum C, she imbibes enough of its lessons to master the "levels of experience" that Baird described as the chief skill imparted by English 1.[24] By "levels," Baird did not exactly mean duplicity, but this is how the course's lessons unfolded in the classroom, given that they enjoined students both to use and to distrust their experience in pursuit of "answers."

As one of her early Hum C assignments, Emmy is given "a photograph, an airview of Convers College," on the basis of which she is meant to "a. assume you are now somewhere in the middle of the area contained in the photograph and you recognize this as a photograph of the spot you are now on" and "b. define in the context of a. 'the spot you are now on'" (19). This is an example of what Craig would call a "situation where you're at a loss," and indeed Emmy casts about in despair for some purchase on the lesson, first wondering whether there is "some trick" and then confirming that the "airplane photograph really is of Convers" because she descries "Baird Hall, with those funny Gothic windows" (19). Though "Baird Hall" is an obvious swipe at Theodore Baird, the nature of the insult needs explanation. The "funny Gothic windows" no doubt refer to Baird's habit on the Amherst campus of climbing through a window into his classroom and then asking his students the Humean question, Why they shouldn't thus call the window a door? Yet Lurie's windows also suggest that rather than the insignia of a fashion-forward epistemology, Baird's query dresses medieval scholasticism in modernist attire—just as, when not clad in Jeffersonian brick, the built environment of higher learning typically gestures toward the twelfth-century cathedral or its Oxbridge simulacrum.

In addition to the compromising reunion of its estranged married couple, *Love and Friendship* ends with a student uprising whose logic becomes clear in the context of Baird Hall's ersatz traditionalism. The Convers students riot against a "new Religion Building" whose design, rather than "given to a good modern architect, . . . was a brick cake iced with white shutters and columns and gables in the best Traditional Colonial Split-Level Ranch-Style" (296). Hum C's staff is enlisted to break up the protest at the excavation site, which catches fire when Holman pushes a torch-bearing student, Dicky Smith (whom he wrongly takes to be Emmy's partner in adultery), into the debris from the dig. This scene presents a complex convergence of the novel's concerns even as it introduces some unexpected ones at the eleventh hour. There is, for instance, the translation of Hum C's rhetoric of the new into the demand on the part of Hum C's conscripts for a built environment that reflects newness as such. Yet this revolutionary spirit is limited by circumstance to the school itself, which becomes the battleground over the question of "life style" (153). *Love and Friendship* accompanies its diminution of campus politics with an equally dismissive discourse on sexual politics, insofar as Lurie conflates heterosexual adultery and homosexual identity in order to render both these illicit categories strangely docile. Emmy's would-be lover, Dicky, is thus simultaneously and paradoxically someone Holman accuses of being "a homosexual," or someone who at any rate "runs with queers" (318).

We learn of the protest over the architecturally retrograde building through Allen Ingram, a writer-in-residence and an actual rather than hypothetical homosexual, whose letters to his New York lover provide the novel with a parallel story line in which Ingram comments quite archly on the minutest happenings of the Convers community. *Love and Friendship* does not deny so much as ghettoize the cattiness endemic to the campus novel, delegating its bitchiest voice to Convers College's queer onlooker. No one in Convers is safe from Ingram's "screwdriver-like eyes" (180). Emmy is thus an "enthusiastic, Bryn Mawr type of deb" who happens to be "hopelessly suburban" (206). Then too, as "a real-life demonstration of the love that dare not speak its name" (26), Ingram is not just an observer but a spectacle himself, whose experience of erotic difference substantiates the oscillation between observer and observed that Hum C's curriculum demands of its freshman recruits. It is in his capacity as an observer that Ingram's own formative experiences have in fact transpired. "So many of these Convers boys are like Mr. Smith," Ingram writes to his lover, "absolutely untouched. When I think what *I* went through . . . at thirteen, with that episode at Newport the day of the boat race which, although (or because) I was in the main a spectator, certainly marked me for life" (254). Just as Baird liked to claim that part of English 1's objective was to get the student to recognize that "a large area of experience" remains "quite beyond his powers of expression," so Ingram both concedes this point and turns it around by alluding to experiences—sexual in nature, maybe pedophilic to boot—that are not so much incommunicable as denied expression by polite consensus.[25]

Compared to what presumably occurred at the Newport boat race during Ingram's thirteenth summer, the experiences of Hum C's students—"sent out," for example, "with a tape measure to measure the length of their feet" (17)—seem rather tame. And from this perspective, Ingram emerges as the evil twin of Hum C's idealized student-experimenter. He has surely learned from his experience, as well as how to step outside it and judge it as a "spectator," but—like the adulterous Emmy Turner after her bout with Hum C's rigors—he has just as surely learned the wrong thing. The "more important secret" that Emmy seeks behind Hum C's experiments in "semantics" (17) turns out in more than one case to be the experience of erotic trespasses that, because they cannot be "broken down" and described in quite the same way as measuring one's feet, can never be submitted to interpretation as such. There are no precise words to describe the ever ambiguous homosexual; hence, Holman finds himself going back and forth in his estimation of Dicky Smith. If the latter "runs with queers," it is because the queer is always on the run.

The point here is not exactly to suggest that through her gay writer-in-residence Lurie means to claim that underlying a curriculum like English 1 is the epistemology of the closet. It is rather to suggest that in the effort to demonstrate how Hum C and its real-life equivalents both overrate and trivialize experience, Lurie reaches unhesitatingly for the counterexample of illicit sexualities under the assumption that they are possessed of a truth index that academic courses cannot accommodate except through the expedient of hypocrisy and subterfuge. Yet it cannot escape our notice that the pedagogic insistence on a certain vigilance and deniability with regard to experience suggests an uncanny likeness between teachers like Brower, Baird, and Poirier and inhabitants of the pre-Stonewall gay underground, ever mindful of their self-presentation and adept at course correcting in any given environment. This parallel is strengthened by the view, increasingly common among proponents of the New Left, that having a "real" identity, homosexual or otherwise, would oblige one to reject the lessons of Hum C along with the institution that teaches them—an opinion rooted in a long-standing equation between homosexual artifice and academic style.

Ingram provides *Love and Friendship* with an ironist whose knowing urbanity competes with Hum C's "abstract" and "metaphysical" lessons (180). Putting the camp in campus novel, Ingram offers a counterpoint to Hum C largely through maxims that appear straight out of Oscar Wilde ("What is success, after all, but the proof that one has come to terms with society?" [108]). But we should not let the alternative to Hum C that Ingram represents lead us to conclude that real social change for Lurie takes place outside—and in hostility to—the school. The novel understands Ingram's eccentricity as compatible with the commitment to privilege the school legitimizes. It is a mistake, Lurie insists, to equate personal style with political change even if it takes the form of the overtly gay Ingram and his Wildean aesthetic (founded on an equally Wildean appanage). And if Ingram seems ideally positioned to ferret out the unreal pretenses of the school, it is less that he has an allegiance to objectivity than that he embodies, like the rest of his kind, a casual relation to the real. He is thus less a foil to the extravagant abstractions of the self favored by midcentury humanists than the latter's unmentionable star pupil.

Totalitarian Humanism: *The Groves of Academe*

I have been arguing that midcentury school culture came to champion experiment and difference as the keystones of higher education. Heeding Dewey's lessons, literary critics in particular supplemented the traditional course of undergraduate study with what we might call the "syllabus of experience," which advanced the text tradition as the sole authority the student need reckon with (since the canon was understood to teach itself). "It is essential to hold firmly to the totality of the reader's experience," Louise Rosenblatt writes in *Literature as Exploration* (1938), a textbook for teachers commissioned by the Progressive Education Association (and so informally under Dewey's auspices) and a book that was as influential in its own way as *Understanding Poetry*, the primer of New Critical pedagogy.[26] By the time the 1952 edition of *English Language Arts* acknowledged that the "primary objective" of English was the teaching of "literature as focused experience," the interchangeability of literature and experience in the postwar university was more or less complete.[27]

Alongside the veneration of experience, the commitment to viewing students as the object of their own ongoing experiment was the feature of postwar pedagogy that campus novels like *Love and Friendship* spent the most energy deriding. Lurie does so by equating self-exploration with solipsism. "If you don't express" something, Emmy Turner asks herself while lying in the woods with her lover, "does it exist?" (201). The something in question is her affair; and to the extent that it is exposed against her will, the answer to her Hum C–

inspired question must be "yes." The signature move of the campus novel is the "reality check," the gesture of disillusionment that finds the protagonists of campus novels disabused of the fluid relay between introspection and the world at large. In Malamud's *A New Life*, Sy Levin's "purpose as self-improved man," as he thinks to himself in the English department bathroom, "is to help the human lot, notwithstanding universal peril, anxiety, continued betrayal of freedom and oppression of man." Self-fashioning of this sort is an unproblematic conduit to larger social change. It is also, as Levin knows, unrealistic—hence his self-deprecating "bow at the toilet" in response to the "prolonged applause" he imagines greeting his equation of personal and political betterment.[28] At the heart of Malamud's view of academic life as theater lies the assumption that school culture's unreality renders academics indistinguishable from the utopians that the postwar campus understood itself fending off. Levin's redemption from this stage requires him to embark upon a more securely heterosexual course of study. The end of *A New Life* finds him driving away from Cascadia College with his department chair's wife and children in tow.

The juxtaposition that Malamud poses between theatricality and realism is pursued with bracing vigor in the work of Mary McCarthy, whose brief career as a theater critic allowed her to hone her own commitments to a literary authenticity that the midcentury stage failed to deliver. In "The Fact in Fiction" (1960), she writes: "We not only make believe we believe a novel, but we do *substantially* believe it, as being continuous with real life, made of the same stuff, and the presence of fact in fiction . . . is a kind of reassurance—a guarantee of credibility."[29] Like numerous other observers in midcentury culture, McCarthy refers the rejection of the real to the spurious promises of a managerial culture to which her contemporaries have succumbed: "Today the writer has become specialized, like the worker on an assembly line whose task is to perform a single action several hundred times a day" (*BB*, 201). Conflating the aesthetic problem of verisimilitude—"the fact in fiction"—with the philosophical problem of realism ("We know that the real world exists, but we can no longer imagine it" [*BB*, 203]), McCarthy traces both of these crises to the rise of an instrumentalism that makes a fetish of performance and so misconstrues to its detriment "the reality, the factuality, of the world" (203).

What gives special point to McCarthy's investment in realism, and why it bears special notice in a discussion of campus novels, is that McCarthy consistently understood the antithesis between reality and unreality in sexual terms.

Whereas Lurie uses her queer writer to debunk the delusions of the school, McCarthy was far more inclined to treat queerness as synonymous with delusion. Consider her biting appraisal of one of midcentury American theater's most celebrated figures, Tennessee Williams. *A Streetcar Named Desire* was a play, or so McCarthy claimed in a 1948 review, about a man driven to rage because his sister-in-law has locked herself in his bathroom. McCarthy's review opens as follows:

> You are an ordinary guy and your wife's sister comes to stay with you. Whenever you want to go to the toilet, there she is primping and having a bath or giving herself a shampoo and taking her time about it. . . . My God, you yell, loud enough so that Blanche can hear you, can't a man pee in his own house, when is she getting out of here? (*BB*, 40)

In this review McCarthy's sympathies clearly lie with Stanley, the "realist of the bladder and the genitals," over his creator's "painful falsity," which uncannily mirrors Blanche's "arty decorations" (*BB*, 42). For McCarthy, Williams's "literary ambition" takes on not only Blanche's "attempts at decoration" but also her bathroom odor. "The smell of careerism" in *Streetcar* McCarthy likens to the "reek of cheap perfume" women like Blanche sometimes employ to camouflage a particularly noisome emission (*BB*, 42).

The gendering here is not incidental. McCarthy took aim repeatedly at Williams's lapses in realist decorum in such feminizing terms. "The less a playwright can write prose," she argued in "The American Realist Playwrights" (1961), "the more he wishes to write poetry and to raise his plays by their bootstraps to a higher realm. You find these applications of beauty . . . in Tennessee Williams; they stand out like rouge on a pitted complexion; it is as though the author first wrote the play naturalistically and then gave it a beauty-treatment or face-lift" (*BB*, 69). What McCarthy understands as a vainglorious toilette whose impressions trick no one but their maker entails an elaborate staging of the self that routinely gives way to a threat of overextension, whereby persons engaged in perpetual self-display risk not only exposure or embarrassment but *supplication* to an audience on which they become unwittingly dependent. In McCarthy's account of realism, then, the problem with Williams is that he doesn't know where his own performance ends and where the audience begins. This is the inverse of the solipsism to which Emmy Holman is given; whereas her life is a study in interiority, Williams—like innumerable gay men before and after him—cannot keep his feelings to himself. As a result, he turns himself into a spectacle of instrumentality, a figure whose ridiculousness is measured precisely by his willingness to pander for and live by the approval of others. What she disdains about *Streetcar* is its very "box-office draw," which she attributes to a shameless appeal to an audience of "peepshow enthusiasts" (*BB*, 42). Far from ignoring its audience as McCarthy thinks a good play should (here Ibsen is Williams's foil), *Streetcar* relies, like its doomed heroine, overmuch on the kindness of strangers.

McCarthy's phobic response to Williams takes the interesting form of laughing at his camp melodrama while imagining that the playwright himself constructs his plays in deadly earnest. As with Ellison's derision of Emerson the Younger, McCarthy refuses to see the queer as in on the joke. We might even say that Williams provides McCarthy with an easy target in a battle for realism whose most vulnerable theater of operations is not the midcentury stage but the midcentury campus. And what makes the latter struggle dire is that the subversions of the reality principle in school culture are not, like Williams's, on the surface. The protagonist of McCarthy's *The Groves of Academe*, Henry Mulcahy, possessed of an "imagination that is capable of seeing and feeling on many levels at once," combines the pandering McCarthy locates in Williams with an unassailable narcissism irreducible to the reality checks found in *Love and Friendship* or McCarthy's theater writing.[30] Mulcahy's mental stylings epitomize what McCarthy's friend Hannah Arendt identified as "the capability to press on to conclusions with a total disregard for all reality," a "pure logic" that was, she claims, "Hitler's greatest gift."[31]

Mulcahy not only dominates the novel's action with his intrigues but dominates its narrator with his own rather elaborate thoughts, a turbulent stream of consciousness on whose rapids the narrator is frequently swept away. Whereas Mulcahy sees that "in order to win" reappointment at Jocelyn College, "it would be necessary to shut his mind to its own settled purpose" and to assume for himself "that obstinate feigned *madness* of Hamlet's" (10), McCarthy confessed to having a much harder time mastering point of view in regard to distinguishing her own thoughts from her character's during the novel's composition. In the 1961 essay "Characters in Fiction," she writes:

> I wanted to know how it felt to be raging inside the skin of a Henry Mulcahy and to learn how . . . he arrived at a sense of self-justification and triumphant injury that allowed him, as though he had been issued a license, to use any means to promote

his personal cause. . . . Certain characters, in their impudence or awfulness, have the power of making us feel *bornés*, and in a sense I wanted to tiptoe into the interior of Mulcahy like a peasant coming into a palace. (*OC*, 286)

Like Arendt, McCarthy is interested in the workings of the totalitarian mind: "If I could make myself *be* Mulcahy," she writes, "it would get me closer to the mystery, say, of Hitler and of all the baleful demagogic figures of modern society whom I could not imagine being" (*OC*, 286).

Despite the loathing she appears to have for her creation, McCarthy nonetheless stands in awe of him, feeling limited (*bornée*) in the face of his Machiavellian "license." But in her equation of Mulcahy and Hitler, McCarthy mistakenly attributes her character's "impudence" to "demagogic" speech, rather than to mentation, in the effort to delimit as much as possible the identification between author and character. The truly odd notion this description encourages us to concede is that her character apparently influences McCarthy as much as she influences him. "There are moments when one would like to drop the pretense of being Mulcahy," she writes, "and go on with the business of the novel" (*OC* 287). McCarthy thus appears at a massive disadvantage: Lacking Mulcahy's ability to "shut his mind," she seems unable to "drop the pretense" and restore the proper relation of mastery over her subject. In writing a character possessed of an imagination unconcerned with moral stays, McCarthy would have us believe that she has in turn been victimized by that imagination herself. Whereas Tennessee Williams's problem in McCarthy's view is that he cannot distinguish himself from his admirers, and becomes more or less a character in his own work, the novelist betrays a similar failing with regard to her creation, albeit through no fault of her own. In the hands of the overreaching Mulcahy, the experimental personhood favored in midcentury humanism turns out to mean the disintegration of personhood, of the line between self and role.

Yet McCarthy's judgment is more than a little disingenuous, for Mulcahy's imagination *just is* McCarthy's, the same way that the "business" of writing a novel *just is* the exercise of a dictatorial imagination over characters and scenarios that exist wholly at the whim of the novelist. "My characters," as Nabokov puts it in a statement that applies to the characters of all novelists, "are galley slaves."[32] Accusing Mulcahy of the worst crime an author can imagine—usurping her own omnipotence—she casts her fictional academic as a villainous rival with whom she must battle for the right to determine the direction her narrative will take. If this claim appears strained, we need only remind ourselves that Mulcahy's stratagem for holding on to his job entails inventing a past as a member of the Communist Party, a past for which he then accuses Jocelyn's liberal president, Maynard Hoar, of blacklisting him. In other words, McCarthy's framing of Mulcahy for a crime against her authorial mastery replicates the sort of fabrication on which the character himself bases his alleged persecution and consequent vindication. "He was the first," Mulcahy imagines, "in all history to expose the existence of a frame-up by framing himself first" (98).

Just as McCarthy wanted to "know how it felt" to be someone like Mulcahy, so *The Groves of Academe* continually ponders what things are like and how things are like other things. In particular, it is concerned with the analogy between the world imagined in art and the lived experience of Jocelyn's small but dedicated literature faculty. For some faculty—Domna Rejnev, for instance— even to pose such an analogy is a corruption of art's spirit, since it makes literature utilitarian and turns readers into instrumentalists. Domna is an absolutist and a "libertarian" in both aesthetics and morals (275), but even she accedes to analogy as an unwelcome but unavoidable moral yardstick, hence her "obsession" with addressing "moral imperatives" by asking herself, "What would Tolstoy think?" (252).

Domna is committed to an ethics that assigns an intrinsic worth to persons irrespective of how they compare with other persons. "There is," she declares, "in each individual the faculty of transcendence" (213). Mulcahy's own "habit of universalization" (210) by contrast assumes that persons are defined by their being eminently translatable into other types of persons. Domna's principles are decried by her colleagues as "feudal, . . . a certain *noblesse oblige*" deriving from her "privilege" (131); and Mulcahy calls Domna (as McCarthy calls herself in regard to Mulcahy) "*bornée* in your thinking" (54). Whereas Domna's Kantian morals require a static world, Mulcahy's pragmatic ones respond nimbly to the "freakish conditions" at Jocelyn, whose "tides of opinion" (100) ebb and flow according to no discernible chart. For this reason, despite his colleagues' reservations about his "fit" at Jocelyn (165), Mulcahy is more comfortable in its progressive environs than the aristocratic Domna is. Jocelyn's students are "a strange new race" (68) whose "rawness and formlessness" (64) made them "*more* dependent" on the sort of "authoritarian leader-pattern" Mulcahy supplies (63). Thus, a female student tells Domna that "the boys in her circle were 'slaves,' . . . revolving around Mulcahy in charmed servitude" (244).

Whereas Domna sees persons or poems as ends in themselves, Mulcahy takes "the purely utilitarian view" that persons have a higher potential "value" based on their aggregation in a social assembly (131). While this attitude prompts Domna to claim that Mulcahy himself, like his students, "has the soul of a slave" (213), it is the peculiar gift of his analogical mind that he is capable of recognizing that Domna's absolutist gestures betray a rather mundane psychology: "At bottom she was conventional, believing in a conventional moral order and shocked by deviations from it into a sense of helpless guilt toward the deviator" (52). By "conventional," Mulcahy means conformist in both the pejorative sense (obedient to type) and what we might call the formal sense, as one might refer to "the standards of a poem" (123). In this double meaning, poems are like persons in that both have the capacity—however unique or original a poem or person may seem—to be categorized as like something else. Because he is able to analogize with respect to Domna, despite her "illusion . . . that her own life was free" (252), the novel prefers Mulcahy's imaginative powers to hers. Domna's transcendental ideal might have virtue on its side, but Mulcahy's "purely utilitarian" take on persons has the ability to propel narrative interest, since Mulcahy is capable of transforming any "deviations" in his own story into plausible links in the causal chains he adeptly forges.

Mulcahy's greatest talent, after all, is his ability to shape unlikely associations or assertions into believable ones. Whereas Domna is preoccupied with "the criteria of truth and falsity," Mulcahy "looks at truth with the eyes of a literary critic and measures a statement by its persuasiveness" (206). And even if John Bentkoop calls this habit "real alienation" and likens Mulcahy's "inner life" to "a busy rehearsal" (206), Mulcahy's powers of persuasion incite in Bentkoop and his colleagues a kind of wonder. "One begins by persuading *oneself*," Bentkoop notes, "and the germ of persuasion is infectious." In his view, Mulcahy starts with an advantage in this epidemic of persuasion because of his "gift for being his own sympathizer."

> He's loyal to himself, objectively, as if he were another person, with that feeling of sacrifice and blind obedience that we give to a leader or a cause. In the world today, there's a great deal of free-floating, circumambient loyalty that fixes itself on such people. . . . It's Hen's fortune or his fate to have achieved this union with his own personality; he's foregone [*sic*] his subjectivity and hypostasized himself as an object. (205)

Such a description is no doubt meant to confirm McCarthy's contempt for Mulcahy as one of those "baleful demagogic figures of modern society whom I could not imagine being." But in this account Mulcahy seems to have less in common with Hitler and Stalin than with the preceptors of English 1 and Hum 6, for whom the education of experience is founded on the presumption that students should think of themselves as their own analogies or examples. We have good cause to be wary of McCarthy's disdain, moreover, not least because the outrageous analogy McCarthy forges between Mulcahy and Hitler does not itself contain a particularly virulent "germ of persuasion." The *reductio ad Hitlerum* by which McCarthy renounces a character that she has invented mimics Mulcahy's own rather elaborate and unwieldy inventions; like her character, McCarthy could be justly accused of taking "refuge in my irony" (57).

That phrase occurs to Mulcahy in a conversation with Domna during which he confesses his communist past. If Mulcahy's problem is to convince others to see him as he sees himself, his success in this endeavor depends on his being able to convince people that he belongs to a very distinctive type about which they themselves have only the most anecdotal knowledge: the lapsed party member who is now that group's covert enemy. The most striking proof that *The Groves of Academe* is committed rather than opposed to Mulcahy's version of things is its narrator's tendency to follow Mulcahy's example in establishing the novel's characters through analogies that appear not only strained but coercive. The pages of *The Groves of Academe* bristle with generalizations so audacious that, like Mulcahy's communism, they must be taken on a faith that feels like a connivance between the author and her reader to suspend disbelief. This connivance in turn appears suspiciously like McCarthy's roguish exploitation of readerly weakness. Here are some examples:

> Like many teachers of English, he was not able to think very clearly and responded, like a conditioned watch-dog, to certain sets of words which he found vaguely inimical. (118)

> Like many sentimental people he really felt things more deeply than those who characterized him as sentimental. (122)

> Like most Russian women of her class, she had a horror of the bizarre that could only be tamed by mirth. (170)

> Like all such official types, he specialized in being his own antithesis. (172)

Like most administrators, he was a man who felt himself to be misunderstood. (180)

Dr. Muller, like many historians, had certain regressive tendencies arising from the nature of his subject, which called forth a tolerance for the past. (266)

This narratorial tic might be said to *thematize* analogical thought, to make it so central a cognitive habit that characters cannot have coherent identity apart from their resemblance to some larger category, however narrowly or broadly construed. In some of these examples, the category being generalized about ("Russian women") is so particularized that we can never have satisfactory proof of its cogency. In others, the example appears to undo the very purpose of analogy ("types" who are their "own antithesis"). In yet other cases, the analogy is little other than tautology (the "sentimental people" who are "sentimental"). Thus, even as the novel introduces analogies for the sake of generating coherent descriptions, it also undermines them. Or rather, like Mulcahy faced with his colleagues' skepticism about his former party membership, the novel dares us to remain unconvinced by its analogies at the cost of our trust in the narrator's mastery and at the arguably higher cost of our own sophistication. The suspect commitment to analogizing as a limitless practice, for which *The Groves of Academe* ostentatiously holds Mulcahy in contempt, turns out to be its most consistent narrative device.

Academic Anomie: *Bend Sinister* and *Pale Fire*

While her equation of Hitler and Mulcahy may be just as implausible as her character's own analogies, McCarthy was hardly alone in looking to the academic humanist for evidence of what Arendt calls totalitarian "logic" in action. We might see her novel's elaboration of the unfettered analogy as making visible the liabilities of a reading practice that appeared to originate in the postwar college classroom even as it threatened everywhere to leap that enclosure. I have already described how some of that classroom's stewards sought to reframe literature as a matter of experience, further aiming to dispatch any "methods" that might come between reader and text by imposing content or context from outside. Only by separating the reader from technique may "poems," as Brower writes in the introduction to a 1966 anthology, "come to stand in a student's mind as platonic forms of true and complete literary experience."[33]

It is not difficult to see how loosening the constraints of shareable or external claims on reading might lead to the implication that any reading practice (or any reader for that matter) can be justified solely on the basis of personal experience. Nor is it difficult to see how the affirmative turn toward individual experience, which looks at first like a liberating practice in its resistance to the dictates of imposed techniques, finally reveals itself in the work of liberals like McCarthy and Arendt as even more despotic than its avowed pedagogical nemeses. For the twin dividends of academic humanism's instrumentalist poetics, inwardness and potentiality, result in a reading practice limited in its freedom to generate resemblances only by the reader's own imagination. And the consequence of such a reading practice is not merely a turn toward authoritarian coercion, the despotic will of the unchecked reader, but an equally disastrous turn toward the asocial, toward a solipsistic dissolution of collective life. If this view of the humanist classroom appears improbably sinister, we need only look to another novel, a favorite of McCarthy's, to witness how readily the postwar academic's preference for exegesis by resemblance could be equated with a dictatorial power play. In Nabokov's *Pale Fire*, as McCarthy pointed out in her review of the novel, "semblance becomes resemblance" (*BB*, 87). As Zembla's deposed head, moreover, Charles Xavier, a.k.a. Kinbote, practices all manner of Mulcahy-like *dissemblance* alongside his willful analogies (as between the Zemblan revolution and John Shade's poem) in the effort to conceal while yet retaining his claim to Zembla's throne.

When he began to write in English, Nabokov developed a penchant for academic characters: *Bend Sinister*'s Adam Krug, *Pnin*'s Timofey Pnin, *Lolita*'s Humbert Humbert, the unnamed protagonist of "The Vane Sisters." All of these characters habitually overrate the power of their acumen to guide them through the world beyond the page. *Bend Sinister*'s Krug may be his country's most distinguished intellectual, but he tragically misreads the lay of the political land when he assumes that his public stature makes him invulnerable to the dictatorship of Paduk, an old schoolmate who has risen to power as the head of the Ekwilists, the "party of the Average Man."[34] Krug has built his career on a policy of "creative destruction" (173), routing the pieties of other philosophers and making a habit of "not join[ing] any group whatsoever" (73). Yet Krug's nonconformist stance is really another name for an insularity that makes him "chary of squandering in idle conversation such experiences as might undergo unpredictable metamorphoses later on (if left to pupate quietly in the alluvium of the mind)" (30). Kinbote is scarcely unique in the Nabokov canon in taking private experience—the Rosetta stone of midcentury humanism—as the basis on which to interpret the texts around him.

"Paronomasia is a kind of verbal plague," Nabokov writes in the preface to *Bend Sinister*, "a contagious sickness in the world of words; no wonder they are monstrously and ineptly distorted in Padukgrad, where everybody is merely an anagram of everybody else" (xv). This is an odd statement from a writer who seems incapable of resisting any chance to treat language as child's play. Singling "paronomasia" out for contempt may be Nabokov's way of glossing over the fact that while the villainous Paduk "had an irritating trick of calling his classmates by anagrams of their names—Adam Krug for instance was Gumakrad" (68), the latter deals in equally treacherous wordplay. By reverting to Paduk's schoolboy nickname, "Toad," even though "there was nothing in his face suggestive of that animal" (67), Krug imagines that he can reduce Paduk to the role he occupied when Krug, a vicious teenage bully, "used to trip him up and sit upon his face" (50). But the analogy that had worked only by virtue of Krug's domineering school-yard physique is untenable in the new order.

Krug remains "something of a bully" late in life (50). His arguments entail "not an admirable expansion of positive matter but a kind of inaudible frozen explosion . . . with some debris gracefully poised in mid-air" (173). Yet this far-reaching academic nihilism discloses an old-fashioned idealism in keeping with the campus novel's rewriting of the professor as a true believer. "We speak of one thing as being like some other thing," Krug laments, "when what we are really craving to do is to describe something that is like nothing on earth" (174). Nabokov sees the commitment to invented likenesses as indistinct from the will to power. When his son David is mistaken for another boy whose father is also a professor with the same last name ("Arvid Krug, son of Professor Martin Krug" [215]), Krug thus faces an apparatchik's obstinate refusal to concede that Arvid is not David: "Are you *quite* sure . . . this little fellow is not your son? Philosophers are absent-minded, you know" (216). As a result of this logic, David takes Arvid's place as a "release-instrument" in a sadistic experiment for the "interesting inmates" in "the Institute for Abnormal Children" (218), at whose brutal hands David dies.

Michael Wood finds the torture and death of David a virtuosic flight that measures the profundity of Nabokov's ethical vision. "The pain of a child," he writes, "is Nabokov's dominant image of moral horror."[35] Here Wood follows Richard Rorty's lead: "The death of a child is Nabokov's standard example of ultimate pain."[36] Yet reduced to a statement like "torturing children is wrong," such an axiom might be said to have the same moral force as a bumper sticker that advertises a motorist's opposition to drunk driving. What would it mean to be *for* such a thing as the death of a child? The defense of Nabokov as a moralist on these grounds obscures the extent to which his description of David's murder by psychotic teenagers fits with unsettling neatness into a pattern that *Bend Sinister* forces us to ponder. For the adolescent Krug's torture of Paduk finds a suitable narrative revenge in those hubristic sins of which Krug is guilty: forcing resemblances and doing violence to one's inferiors.[37]

It would be perverse to read the text of *Bend Sinister* with Krug as the villain and Paduk as the hero. This is the type of misreading the novel mocks in the conversation between Krug and his friend Ember, a translator who regales Krug with the "sheer stupidity" (111) of a German scholar who has argued that "the real hero of *Hamlet* is Fortinbras" (108). Yet we need not root for Paduk, any more than we need condemn Krug, to wonder at both the symmetry with which Nabokov lays out his narrative and the brutality he bestows on it. Even to call the dead or abused child a "standard example," as Rorty does, is to invite more questions than answers. If examples are meant to be "standard," the lesson that doing malice to children is wrong surely doesn't need much repeating. Nabokov's resort to this "standard example" is at least slightly gratuitous, and to reduce the surplus of tortured or dead children in his work to some repeatable standard is to ignore its virulent antisocial charge through a premature domestication of the unbalanced equations (as between torturing and misreading) on which his prose insists.

In *Bend Sinister*, for example, the case of mistaken identity occasioned by poor reading—Arvid for David—is inseparable from the violent abolition of David's person. These different orders of violence (to the text, to the body) are made to seem structurally equivalent. Can misreading really be as momentous as murder? According to those who have aimed to take Nabokov's morality seriously on the basis of his recurrent depictions of the death or abuse of a child, the answer to this question seems to be yes. "Both Kinbote and Humbert," Rorty writes, "dramatize, as it has never before been dramatized, the particular form of cruelty about which Nabokov worried most—incuriosity." What Rorty means by claiming incuriosity as Nabokov's most worrisome form of cruelty is that Humbert and Kinbote are selective readers, cherry-picking the information at their disposal for what "provides expression for their own obsession."[38] Rorty does not really describe a morality so much as moralize the act of reading. Yet it is not at all obvious that Nabokov shares Rorty's conclusions.

If incuriosity is unforgivable to Nabokov, after all, curiosity is scarcely a lesser sin, since the curious reader who follows the details through Nabokov's book will inevitably discover that Krug has brought his—and his child's—suffering upon himself. Nabokov's readers manage to resist the sin of incuriosity in *Bend Sinister* only to discover that the pattern the author has hidden for them to hunt down is one in which Krug appears to merit his fate, because Krug must be understood as guilty of the incuriosity Rorty finds in Kinbote and Humbert. When Krug is arrested "on the night of the twenty-first," it is to him wholly "unexpected," Nabokov writes, "since he had not thought they would find the handle. In fact, he had hardly known there was any handle at all" (203). The handle is David, the attachment to the child that Krug, alone among the characters in *Bend Sinister*, finds it almost impossible to acknowledge. When Krug tells his friend Maximov that he wants "to be left alone," Maximov retorts that "'alone is the wrong word. . . . You have a child'" (90). But Krug turns out to be no more capable of understanding this lesson than of conceding that there are *right* words. "When Krug mentioned once that the word 'loyalty' phonetically and visually reminded him of a golden fork lying in the sun on a smooth spread of pale yellow silk," Nabokov writes, "Maximov replied that to *him* loyalty was limited to its dictionary denotation" (87).

Nabokov by contrast insists that language may be subjected to any number of trespasses, but it cannot be the private, self-referential invention of a single individual. If in *Bend Sinister* we are dazzled by the narrator's frequent lapses into Krug's native language, the reason is that the immediate provision of a translation into our own forestalls our suspicion that Nabokov is merely indulging a verbal whim. Nabokov's parenthetical translations show him to be both a renegade and a law-abiding citizen of the symbolic order. They register both his inventiveness and his awareness that such inventiveness must be circumscribed by an indexical relation between imagined and real-world referents. "Loyalty" for Nabokov retains its "dictionary denotation." Yet despite his fondness for his "traveling companion, Webster's Collegiate," it would be premature to elide Nabokov's position into the "stolid" Maximov's, given that, so far as loyalty itself goes, Nabokov took a certain pride in having none.[39] Nabokov's life was strewn with the corpses of abandoned languages, relinquished nations, and disowned friendships. "My aloofness is an illusion resulting from my never having belonged to any literary, political, or social coterie," he told an interviewer in 1969. "I am a lone lamb" (*SO*, 156).

In *Lectures on Literature*, Nabokov elevates this dissociative habit to an aesthetic tenet: "The artist . . . disconnects what he chooses."[40] If loyalty was not high on Nabokov's list of values, what did matter to him, as he took every opportunity to insist, was a preference for the particular over the general, for "the sway accorded to a seemingly incongruous detail over a seemingly dominant generalization" (*LL*, 374). Nabokov's interest in the incongruous over the systematic resonates with the position advanced by Niebuhr in *The Irony of American History*. As I argued earlier, Niebuhr and his associates in "the school of irony" situated midcentury academics as the bearers of a secret weapon for use against the institution that employed them: a disloyalty informed by an awareness of the university's internal contradictions. Nabokov's version of this attitude combines a mastery of any game's (linguistic, institutional) rules with a blithe, if feigned, indifference to remaining its player.

With Kinbote, Nabokov revives the portrait of the academic as solipsist that he brought to bear on Krug. Holed up for the length of *Pale Fire* in a "desolate cabin," Kinbote is no less antisocial than his Padukgradian predecessor.[41] But whereas Krug's narcissism prevents him from taking note of the patterns all around him, Kinbote is wholly preoccupied with affinities, nearly all of which become highly personalized. The only thing stronger than Kinbote's nostalgia may be the tenacity with which he holds a grudge. Though he "can forgive anything save treason" (26), the latter is a roomy category in Kinbote's world. Hence, Sybil Shade's failure to invite him to her husband's birthday party resurfaces in the latter's "treacherous" (272) failure to transcribe the saga of Zembla with which Kinbote has entertained him over the months leading up to the composition of "Pale Fire." For each instance of perceived disloyalty, Kinbote seeks revenge: he gives Sybil a copy of *Swann's Way* with a bookmarked passage about backstabbing socialites and resituates Shade's poem in the mists of the Zemblan revolution.

While Kinbote's dubious loyalty to originals is the target of Nabokov's satire, it is also the source of some of the novel's darker musings. His inability to be faithful to Disa causes him to dream repeatedly about a fealty that in waking life he cannot muster. Loyalty for Kinbote is something that, like predestination, cannot be practiced so much as taken on faith. The religious analogy is apt because Kinbote is, by his own admission, a "true Christian Zemblan" (219), prone to "the burning desire for merging in God" (222). The joining of these two qualities in his narrator—a loyalty that shades into vengeance and a theism that verges on fundamentalism—reveals much about Nabokov's attitude toward reading habits on the college campus. For the very traits that Nabokov spurned among his colleagues in literature departments from Wellesley to Cornell find themselves distilled to a toxic draft in the alembic of his Zemblan impostor.

"My approach and principles irritated or puzzled such students of literature," Nabokov recalled of his teaching days, "as were accustomed to 'serious' courses replete with 'trends,' and 'schools,' and 'myths,' and 'symbols,' and 'social comment,' and something unspeakably spooky called 'climate of thought'" (*SO*, 128). Though the riot of scare quotes points to Nabokov's cynical verdict on the professionalization of reading, it is not easy to say precisely what would count as a proper approach in his view. In the introduction to *Lectures on Literature,* he disdains the attitude that "the reader should identify" with a book's hero; yet he also praises the reader with "memory" and "imagination" (*LL*, 3) and concludes with the maddeningly vague statement that "fiction appeals first of all to the mind," which "is, or should be, the only instrument used upon a book" (4). Given that his interpretation of Shade's poem is mediated exclusively through his memory and imagination, it is far from clear that Kinbote makes for a poor reader on Nabokov's terms.

Yet *Pale Fire*'s favorite joke is that Kinbote assumes he is being faithful to the text by continually referring to his own irrelevant experience of it. The laughter occasioned by the content of Kinbote's referents has eclipsed any real focus on the form his analysis takes. Critics take it for granted that the ludicrousness of Kinbote's Zemblan examples carries over to the interpretive protocol by which he arrives at them. "He does not bother to trace sources in the original language, fails to identify natural objects, and misconstrues the mores and milieu of his poet," Brian Boyd writes, "because he is too preoccupied with his own Zembla."[42] Their sense that Kinbote is a lazy reader has prevented scholars from considering any possible overlap between the fictional critic's reading habits and those of his maker. It thus seems worth looking at whatever "principles" lie behind Kinbote's commentary.

First among these is a rather un-Eliotic prizing of originality. Although a tireless seeker of correspondences, Kinbote cannot abide intertextual ones, "condemn[ing] . . . the talent that substitutes the easy allusiveness of literacy for original fancy" (240). His preference for originals over allusions positions Kinbote as the experiential reader par excellence. This appears to reverse Nabokov's view of literary interpretation. In addition to deploring the "lowly kind" of "imagination" that Kinbote evinces, "which turns for support to the simple emotions and is of definitely personal nature" (*LL*, 2), Nabokov was a legendary pedant. But Kinbote is not precisely Nabokov's opposite. He may prefer subjective impression ("original fancy") to objective reference ("easy allusiveness"), but he shares his creator's disgust with symbolism. Consider the image in *Pale Fire* of Shade "shaking and howling with laughter" as Kinbote regales him with the "symbolic" methods found in "a book [he] had filched from a classroom: a learned work on psychoanalysis, used in American colleges, repeat, used in American colleges" (271). And just as Kinbote derides symbol, so Nabokov was actually a devotee of experiential reading. "In reading the great artists," he writes, "the main thing is to experience" what he calls "the pleasure of pure art" (*LL*, 382). Nabokov's claims about the function of reading—that it avoid symbolic systems, that it be physically pleasurable—make it hard to pinpoint his attitude toward his creation. Is Kinbote a bad reader or a good one, a foil for Nabokov or his surrogate?

Lectures on Literature ends with Nabokov condemning the reading habits bred in college classrooms "for the academic purpose of indulging in generalizations" (*LL*, 381). If Nabokov holds generalization in contempt because it is liable to tyrannize the "incongruous detail," he condemns "the symbolism racket in schools" because it functions solely "to keep schoolmen busy" (*SO*, 305). The latter are "resolved to follow a system . . . invented for the express purpose of following it" (*LL*, 374). While this is hardly the first time the academic reader is understood to betray the text on behalf of a system, Nabokov's innovation is to configure such treason in the stark terms of the ideological struggle at the heart of *Bend Sinister*: through the literary critic, the lowest common denominator subsumes the unique specimen, the Ekwilist triumphs over both the intellectual giant (Krug) and the little guy (Krug's son).

This critique of the critic may seem a little tired because we have heard it many times before—in fact, from within the confines of the discipline of literary study itself. It has long been obligatory for academic critics to deplore the twin evils of method and generalization, especially in scholarship other than their own. Just as it was incumbent on the teachers of Hum 6 and English 1 to accuse New Critics of an overbearing technique, so Cleanth Brooks had felt compelled to oppose "the mechanical attempt to pile up as much symbolism as possible" among New Criticism's own detractors.[43] Criticism is peculiar among the disciplines in evolving its protocols by disowning not just previous methods but the very idea of method. When Nabokov observes of his teaching that "none of my questions ever presupposed the advocacy of a fashionable interpretation or critical view" (*SO*, 129), he adopts the stance that has prevailed in humanism from at least the mid-twentieth century to the present. "Surely, we of all people should know something of the history and the principles of new historicism," Stephen Greenblatt and Catherine Gallagher write in the introduction to *Practicing New Historicism* (2001), "but what we knew above all was that it (or perhaps we) resisted systematization."[44]

In addition to echoing the postwar critic's refutation of method, *Lectures on Literature* reveals what looks like a debt to the interpretive habits of Hum 6 or English 1. Just as Reuben Brower's practice consists of "slowing down the process of reading . . . in order to attend very closely to the words,"[45] so Nabokov's "plan" is "to deal . . . in loving and lingering detail with several European masterpieces" (*LL*, 1). Yet even Brower's antisystemic criticism appears to overreach for Nabokov, who insists that anything beyond informed summary or the barest paraphrase of a text invites the threat of faulty analogies. *Lectures on Literature* treats reading as so self-evident that there is no point—there is nothing but presumption—in the redundant task of proposing, along with Poirier, what reading is "like." Abetted by lavish helpings of citation, Nabokov's synoptic appraisals of Jane Austen, Gustave Flaubert, and other novelists imply that the only direct road to authorial intent entails summarizing the author's own words.

In every discussion of the "European masterpieces" under review in *Lectures on Literature*, Nabokov's critical lexicon rotates around the familiar touchstones of "theme" and "structure," but these terms mean something more basic in his hands than in those of the "schoolmen." Thus, in discussing *Bleak House*, he speaks of "the Chancery theme" (*LL*, 70), the "bird theme" (73), the "Skimpole theme" (88), "the doctor theme" (89), "the child theme" (91), "the mystery theme" (91), "the resemblance theme" (103), "the Tulkinghorn theme" (112), "the fog theme" (114), and a throng of other themes. In every instance the theme referenced functions as a redundant placeholder locked on to a transparent dimension of Dickens's novel. This multitude of themes has the effect of preventing Nabokov from zooming out to any broader analysis of them, not even one so uncontroversial as their "formal unity." Their paratactic enumeration means that none is allowed to overtake the others, as though singling one theme out would risk committing Nabokov to something as gauche as a thesis, a claim on what the novel is about. Whereas *Pale Fire*'s Zembla theme entails a reading as remote from Shade's poem as Kinbote's "distant northern land" (315), Nabokov's close readings refuse any heuristic move further afield than the page in front of him.

"All we have to do when reading *Bleak House*," Nabokov tells his students, "is to relax and let our spines take over" (*LL*, 64). If critics in the mainstream of humanist practice treat reading as what Poirier calls "an acutely meditative activity," reading for Nabokov demands a passive receptivity. I have argued that the construction of reading in the postwar classroom followed the experiential model that Dewey set forth in the interwar years. "There is no limit to the amount of meaning," he wrote, "which reflective and meditative habit is capable of importing into even simple acts."[46] What Dewey saw as lively intellection Nabokov sees as unseemly grasping. At the heart of symbolic reading, Nabokov finds a spurious analogizing justified only by a Krug-like insistence on equivalence. To borrow his own parody of symbolic interpretation, "'Wickedly folded moth' suggests 'wick' . . . and 'wick' . . . is the Male Organ" (*SO*, 305).

Yet this complaint about the "abhorrent" (*SO*, 305) system of symbolic criticism depends on a strange pair of assumptions. The first is that the world of fiction is less contingent and indeed more truthful than we customarily understand it to be, and the second is that critics who pursue the symbolic route do a disservice to fiction's "reality" by reading back into the fictive world references from an outside understood as less real. This is not merely a case of Nabokov's preferring the verisimilitude of a well-made story over the often strained readings brought to bear on it. Rather, it involves an ideal of purity that analogical reading violates. "Literature is not about something," Nabokov claims; "it is the thing itself" (*LL*, 116). William Wimsatt calls this a "curious" statement about literature's ontology. "For if anything about poetry is clear," he argues in *The Verbal Icon*, "it is that a poem is not really a thing, like a horse or a house, but only *analogically* so."[47] Insisting on literature as a real thing, Nabokov denies the claim that literature is apprehensible only through analogy. "In the case of a certain type of writer," he observes, "a whole paragraph or sinuous sentence exists as a discrete organism, with its own imagery, its own invocations, its own bloom" (*SO*, 305).

Precisely because of the force with which he commits himself to the opposition between arbitrary symbolism and language as an "organism," Nabokov proves crucial to understanding the broader antagonism between the school and its constituencies that shadowed the decade in which *Pale Fire* appeared. That antagonism was mediated through the ideal of authenticity that the student movement conceived as a rebuke to the technocracy and its professorial enforcers, "those who are," Nabokov writes in his *Bleak House* lecture, "immune to . . . authentic literature" (*LL*, 64). It is in this context that we must consider Kinbote's line at the end of the foreword of *Pale Fire*: "Without my notes Shade's poem simply has no human reality" (28). Kinbote's grandiose gestures of authentication, executed by reading into the poem a reality it might not already possess, are of a piece with his hallucinations of deposed kingship. The problem *Pale Fire* seeks to redress in its toppling of his fantasy structure is Kinbote's cavalier admission that poems and other fictions do not in fact command the same authenticity as the real world. The assignment of different values to different types of reality is keyed to an erotic caste system; in the novel's hierarchy of experience, Shade's happily married heterosexuality takes unambiguous precedence over Kinbote's boy love. Kinbote's penchant for correspondence never appears more preposterous than in his translation of the conjugal idyll extolled in Shade's poem into the homo-utopia of his pedophilic fancy. In this view Kinbote is a daft queen rather than a tragic king, and his Zembla but a camp fantasia.

If the forced correspondence of discordant things is the critic's prerogative, in other words, then the novelist goes out of his way to play that move for laughs. Thus, when Brian Boyd claims that "amid all the mayhem Kinbote causes," Nabokov "allows us the pleasures of form, the satisfaction of sensing the author's order everywhere behind the commentator's chaos" (21), he gets it exactly backward. Nabokov indicates that the chaos attributed to Kinbote is instead the prerogative of the novelist, the poet, or other world-making creative types. It is the critic who takes perverse "pleasure" in "order." When Shade discovers that there is no "affinity" or "sacramental bond / uniting mystically" (30) his life with that of a woman who has also had a near-death experience, he settles for "making ornaments of accidents" (31). Contrary to Kinbote's insistence, any perception that experiences correspond across different people is only coincidental. Shade's discovery returns us to Nabokov's pronouncement that the artist "disconnects what he chooses." The ability to dissociate from institutions was emblematic of the attitude toward academic life enjoyed by the professoriat, whose preferred self-image took the form of a loosely affiliated cadre of voluntary agents. When Nabokov shifts the powers of detachment from critics to creatives, it is unsurprising that he begins by exposing his fictive professors as fetishists of connection.[48]

Believing that coincidences are more than "accidents," after all, Kinbote seeks to turn random "possibilities" (31) into plausible chains of correspondence. And while no one would deny that formal and thematic intricacies abound in *Pale Fire*, it is only the critic who delights in following the links in a correlative chain or, more precisely, who equates the task of finding correlations with gratification. Boyd's extreme contempt for Kinbote ("a pathetic, lonely paranoid, utterly deluded about himself" [61]) might be said to emerge from the biographer's need to disavow an uncomfortable likeness, given that paranoids no less than critics are adepts in forging associations undetectable by the naked eye. Compare Kinbote's reserves of memory and imagination in parsing the subtext of Shade's poem, and the hopscotching strategy he recommends in essaying his nestled commentary, to Boyd's advice on how to read *Pale Fire*: "If Nabokov wants us to understand something essential, he plants it firmly within the covers of his book, or indicates—if we exercise just a little curiosity, memory, and imagination—exactly where we should look for it elsewhere" (82). In fact Nabokov had a rather ambivalent view of patterning. The mental patient in "Signs and Symbols" (1947) who suffers from "referential mania," for example, "must be always on his guard and devote every minute and module of life to the decoding of the undulation of things."[49] Interpretation is here indistinct from pathology.

Eric Naiman has observed that the pleasure "good readers" of Nabokov take in their interpretive mettle is never far from the specter of humiliation encoded in the pleasure-seeking queers who populate his novels. From this perspective, Kinbote—who insists on reading associations in Shade's poem in the service of the most arbitrary system imaginable, a self-authored erotic utopia—appears less as foil than gothic double to the professional Nabokovian, the Hyde to Boyd's critical Jekyll. For both the fictitious critic and the real one commit to a pleasure of the text derived specifically from the practice of interpretive association. Whereas critics of late have referred Kinbote's queerness to the Cold War panic over the homosexual menace, the salient referent in *Pale Fire* is the institutional reading practice in which such critics are most intimately engaged. Rejecting all systems and methods, the perpetually self-fashioning Kinbote stakes out a hermeneutics in which the claims of experience move in tandem with the inventive self-reflection that disciples of Brower or Baird equated with literary reading.

This is not to say that the mileage Nabokov gets out of casting his narrator as a lover of boys is not tightly braided with Cold War culture's demonizing of homosexuality, communism, or other un-American activities. It is rather to suggest that whatever contempt Nabokov expects his reader to hold for Kinbote is just as closely linked with the dubious pedagogy of the humanist classroom. It is safe to say that by the early 1960s the style of interpretation preferred in that venue had come to feel patently unsatisfactory to a rising generation of students, who strenuously rejected the instrumentalist thinking found in the school—with its commitment to the pragmatist view that analogical resemblance is a passable enough version of reality. For Fifties Cold Warriors as much as Sixties radicals, the disparate categories of professors, closet queens, and bureaucrats were enmeshed in a dense weave of impersonality, artifice, and instrumental logic. All these types were indifferent to experience as an end in itself in favor of a referentially indefinite system.

Kinbote's readerly pathos is again instructive. Hasn't his experience of "inenubilable Zembla" (288) been forever compromised on his own admission by Shade's failure to render it clearly, as though its being mirrored in the poem "Pale Fire" were crucial to the experience's having any meaning at all? It was such vicarious engagement, spurred on by an overactive textual play, that the New Social Movements abhorred. Like Nabokov, the student radicals of the 1960s would discriminate intensely between levels of experience and seek authentic experience in a language uncontaminated by "spurious symbols." And in asserting their contempt for a bankrupt liberalism, radicals in the 1960s adopted Nabokov's tactic of eliding school culture's devious reading practices into deviant sexuality.

3. Liberal Perversion and Countercultural Commitment

Political Statements

In *Revolutionary Suicide* (1973), Huey P. Newton recalls that in the early days of the Black Panther Party, he was "vehemently attacked by black students" for advocating "strong and meaningful alliances with white youth."[1] Newton likens these students, in their refusal of any compromise with white America, to the "prisoners in Plato's cave" (183), an analogy to which he often refers as "a symbol of the Black man's predicament" (249). "Far from preparing them to deal with reality," he concludes, "college kept their intellects in chains." Newton thus vows "to implement . . . a true education for our people" (183) by pursuing more vigorously "Point 5" of the Black Panther platform: "We believe in an educational system that will give to our people a knowledge of self" (123). The need for such knowledge is confirmed by Newton's own example. His "years in the Oakland public schools" did not afford him "one teacher who taught me anything relevant to my own life or experience" (20). It was only by sharing his older brother's college course work that he acquired a taste for "literature and philosophy" and, from there, for radical consciousness. "When my brother and I analyzed and interpreted poetry," Newton writes, "I was becoming familiar with conceptual abstractions and beginning to develop the questioning attitude that later allowed me to analyze my experiences" (34).

Newton's mixed feelings toward a college that kept the intellects of black Americans in chains when it neglected to teach them a knowledge of self make clear that, in repudiating school culture, the New Left rejected not the syllabus of experience but the perpetually revisionary project to which that syllabus was beholden. In Newton's view, school culture's fetish for deferral and disorientation afforded a pedagogy unsuited to the "awareness of reality" (4) that the Panthers, like those white students with whom Newton sought to affiliate, saw as key to radicalization. This chapter surveys the predominance of the reality principle in Sixties culture, specifically in the terms that Newton understands it: as the basis for the commitment to what he calls "essential meaning" (3). It was in pursuit of such essence that the New Left came to understand the school as the enemy of change. In New Left thinking, school culture's focus on estranging and refracting experience did not add up to a meaningful program so much as confirmed the college in its role as apologist for an incoherent society. While the attitude that led Newton to analyze his experiences bore resemblance to the close reading of Hum 6 or English 1, the "shared sense of purpose" he found in the party could not be more remote from the atomizing and anomic experiments of the midcentury classroom.

The New Left was fiercely critical of the interpretive vertigo to which school culture was prone. Though Sixties radicals appeared to share the antisystemic views of the literary critics discussed in the last chapter, their notion of system—unlike that of the critic, who conceived of system as "formula"—was an amorphous network of hidden operators that included the faculty itself.[2] Like campus novelists, Sixties radicals treated the postwar humanists' prizing of ambivalence as a denial of real-world certitudes. Yet unlike campus novelists, who condemned analogy as a form of coercion, radicals were committed to drawing examples. "Black men and women who refuse to live under oppression," Newton writes, "become symbols of hope to their brothers and sisters, inspiring them to follow their example" (172). If *Revolutionary Suicide* devotes much attention to defending the principle that setting good examples makes for good radicals, it is equally forthcoming on another tactic that appeared fundamental to New Left ideology: "the significance of words in the struggle for liberation," especially "in the important area of raising consciousness" (173). The desire to free not only persons but discourse itself from the state's rhetorical sleights galvanized the New Social Movements.

The emphasis on authentic language committed many radicals to advocating the spoken over the written word. To explain why the sheer act of speaking held such a robust charge for the New Social Movements, we can begin by noting that the explosion of speech during the 1960s marked a kind of linguistic watershed different from the proliferation of documents, files, and memoranda that appeared to be the chief dividend of bureaucracy. The speaking subject came to stand in redemptive opposition to the subject-less writing of the institution. The bid for an authentic language was carried out under the assumption that, like the most "relevant" education, such language ought to be directly personal. Hence, Newton's aim in shaping party rhetoric was to clarify an ethical imperative: "As far as I am concerned, if men are responsible beings, they ought to be responsible to each other" (180). During the 1968 Columbia strike, SDS-organizer-turned-Weatherman Mark Rudd defended the release of documents in President Grayson Kirk's office on the grounds that "they were proof of our thesis that decisions are made behind the scenes." Like Newton's "responsible" speech, Rudd's exposure accrued force and value against the rambling paper trail that the "power-broking" Kirk contrived in order to "manufacture propaganda" in support of the American overclass.[3]

Even though it formed a centerpiece of New Left thought, the equation between bureaucratic language and an overreaching power structure did not originate with the New Left itself. From C. Wright Mills's *The Power Elite* to Dwight Eisenhower's invocation of the "military-industrial complex" during his farewell address, it had become a standard assumption in the postwar era that bureaucracies rather than electorates controlled governance. In his 1963 book *The Paper Economy*, the social critic David Bazelon indicted what he called "private government," a "second non-democratic government" that—shadowing "its weak sister, the official government"—"governs mostly by denying its own existence" and "by domination and perversion of the entire national culture."[4] Bazelon poses several themes that I will take up in detail, the most salient of which is his use of terms like "perversion" and "weak sister," words that speak to an alignment of government with the limp-wristed physique and vicarious passions of the Cold War homosexual. Bazelon's effeminizing rhetoric underwrote a critique embraced by New Left radicals, who availed themselves of a well-established hermeneutics for deciphering the secret government when they turned to the techniques for wedging open the closet in order to expose its elusive yet all too recognizable occupants.

The embrace of both authenticity and speech in the 1960s depended not only on eliding discourse with bureaucracy but on conflating bureaucracy with closeted homosexuality. Equipped with this metaleptic conceit, radicals tied the defeat of the national security state to the eviction of the closet queens presumed to throng its warrens. A notable irony of this radical stance is that such housecleaning had periodically served the state's own system of checks and balances. The countercultural offensive against establishment liberalism had a precedent in the Eisenhower-era purge that David Johnson calls "the lavender scare," the panic fomented by Cold Warriors to combat the plague of career deviants staffing the federal government.[5] While "homophobia united the left," as Van Gosse notes, the homophobic critique of bureaucracy also united radicals with their avowed enemy: a hypertrophied state whose postwar legitimacy had been secured in part by making an example of the queer civil servants in its ranks.[6]

"The language of the establishment is mutilated by hypocrisy," Tom Hayden noted in the aftermath of the Chicago Seven trial, during which one of the many charges leveled at the defendants was "obscenity." "Perhaps our language would be acceptable if it were divorced from practice."[7] Hayden's commitment to the reciprocity between statement and action—his insistence that each refer back to the other—resonated into much of the countercultural Sixties. Compare Rudd's comment on how "obscenity" helped the Columbia student strikers "define [their] struggle": "We could use our own language, much more expressive than the repressed language of Grayson Kirk."[8] In fact, despite what its founders (including Rudd) understood as a repudiation of Hayden's New Left, the Weather Underground Organization (WUO) carried Hayden's vision of linguistic integrity into its practice. WUO statements were hardly cryptic. They were models of highly self-conscious explicitness. WUO envisioned a communicative ideal in which there were no mistaken meanings. *Prairie Fire*, its 1974 statement of purpose, opens with a litany driven by the conviction that it is politically irresponsible to let one's intentions remain unspoken: "Our intention is to disrupt the empire. . . . Our intention is to engage the enemy. . . . Our intention is to encourage the people. . . . Our intention is to forge an underground."[9] In WUO's account of language and power, only the most resolute overemphasis might negate the mystifications of the state. Whatever misgivings they had about the SDS precepts they had abandoned, WUO members remained committed to the Port Huron Statement's goal of "making values explicit."[10]

What is striking about the varied manifestoes of the New Social Movements is their reliance on overstatement, a kind of redundancy at every turn in the speech act. "This is Bernardine Dohrn," opens WUO's first communiqué. "I'm going to read a declaration of a state of war."[11] In 1969, some 250 college student-body presidents signed a letter to President Nixon that not only declared their refusal to register with Selective Service but also declared this open declaration as such: "We publicly and collectively express our intention to refuse induction" (*TS*, 245). In March of that year, the group D.C. 9, following its decision to "spill human blood and destroy the files and office equipment" in the Washington headquarters of Dow Chemical, composed "An Open Letter to the Corporations of America" that declared, "By this action, we condemn you, the Dow Chemical Company, and all similar American Corporations." In New Left discourse, only the most hyperbolic exposition of one's meaning can counter the impassiveness of the "faceless and inhuman corporation" (*TS*, 251).

The epicenter of this rhetorical strategy was the Berkeley campus in the fall of 1964. It was there, under the auspices of what would quickly come to be known as the Free Speech Movement (FSM), that what SDS president Greg Calvert called the "authentically revolutionary movements" (*TS*, 126) found their basis in a model of freedom grounded in linguistic integrity. In "An End to History" (1964), FSM leader Mario Savio drew a startling parallel between the civil rights struggle against racial injustice and the Berkeley students' struggle against the University of California Board of Regents, who had sought to shut down antiwar tables in Berkeley's Sproul Plaza. Claiming that southern blacks and UC students have "the same enemy," Savio observes that both groups have "come up against what may emerge as the greatest problem of our nation—depersonalized, unresponsive bureaucracy" (*TS*, 112). The analogy between "the problem of automation and the problem of racial injustice" weaves through Savio's essay to ballast the assumption that bureaucracy's interest in severing speech from its consequences is identical to the exploitation of human beings (*TS*, 113).

That "speech with consequences" (*TS*, 115) should become a whetstone for the insurgent Left in the next decade still posed something of a puzzle, however, if only because it was hard to imagine why "effective speech," as Jerry Rubin called it, "speech which moves people" (*TS*, 192), was any more likely to move them toward insurrection than toward complacency. The New Left coped with this technicality in various ways, not the least of which was the prestige it conferred on "automation" and "unresponsive bureaucracy" as the "greatest problems" that the student radicals had to overcome. "The FSM was an excuse for many to vent their wrath and pent-up hostility at a university which seems at times to be made by, for, and of electronic computers," observed Robert Kaufman and Michael Folsom. "The IBM machine" thus "comes to stand for the sense of administration and education without people."[12] The Port Huron Statement saw its task as "countering perhaps the dominant conception of man in the twentieth century: that he is a thing to be manipulated."[13] And crucial to this regime of manipulation was what Theodore Roszak called the "lieutenancy

of counterfeiters, . . . men who have risen above ideology," whose "clever falsifi-
cations" obscure the fact that words like "education," "democracy," and "pluralism" no longer represent the things they are intended to mean.[14]

That representative government was no longer representative had become
movement gospel by the middle of the 1960s, when Casey Hayden, in the SDS
article "The Question of Who Decides" (1966), heaped contempt on "the now
sterile and nearly meaningless patterns of representative democracy" (*TS*, 82).
In politics and language, representation had given way to manipulation. Such
was the conclusion David Wise and Thomas Ross reached in their exposé of
the "invisible government" in a 1964 book of that title.[15] This shadowy cabal
at the heart of the American power structure ("How many Americans have
ever heard of the 'Special Group?'" [6]) thrived on "whispered" (5) exchanges
suited to the domain of gossip and innuendo. Its preferred speech act was the
rumor. The invisible government used language opportunistically, favoring a
"lack of signs" (219) over the indexical transparency central to New Left politics. Nothing incensed the FSM quite so much as the tendency of its bureaucratic opponents to engage in what Wise and Ross call "secrecy for the mere
sake of secrecy" (264), which FSM consistently aligned with a pejorative notion
of impersonality. "There are many impersonal Universities in America," Mario
Savio writes in his introduction to Hal Draper's *Berkeley: The New Student Revolt* (1965), but "there is probably none more impersonal in its treatment of
students than the University of California."[16]

If it often appears that for Savio free speech reduces to the problem of
simply giving students more face time with their absentee faculty, the reason
is that the exemplary instance of the university's "impersonal" structure is "the
teacher" who "will be very seldom available for discussion with his students."[17]
"Even after all of the suffering which has occurred in our community," the
Berkeley psychiatrist Neal Blumenfeld notes ruefully in "Human Dignity and
the Multiversity," "the overwhelming majority of faculty members . . . have
not really listened to our voices."[18] On the basis of these examples, we might
conclude that the FSM crisis entailed two competing claims, tied together by
the common term "speech" but actually involving rather different assumptions. On the one hand, FSM was dedicated to upholding the constitutional
guarantee of freedom of speech and assembly, a commitment to a formal right
irrespective of content. This indifference to content explains why the FSM coalition could include such otherwise opposed groups as Students for Gold-

water and the Congress on Racial Equality. On the other hand, FSM seemed less interested in free speech in the abstract than in what we might call *meaningful* speech. Here the goal was not to defend the ability of people to have their say but to create the circumstances in which people would be able to say something interesting or valuable to others.

FSM turned the difference between free speech in the abstract and meaningful speech, "speech with consequences," into a choice between two types of social order: on the one hand, a world of committees pledged to clandestine activity, in which "free speech" means the free-floating and disembodied circulation of discourse; on the other, a community of persons organized around intimate contact and utterances that serve as vows or bonds. "The Regents meet in secret," according to FSM activist Michael Nelken, "because factional dispute and maneuver need to be masked in judicial calm and unanimity."[19] "Unanimity" here shades into anonymity, into an erasure of individuation that mirrors the denial of accountability to which secret meetings are conducive. Thus, when the authors of *We Want a University* (1964) claim that "we must insist upon meaning" in spelling out their objectives in the aftermath of the free speech crisis, they also insist that such meaning can come only from the dialogue found in "a community of furiously talking, feeling, and thinking human beings."[20] Or as Nelken puts it, "We must speak man-to-man without waiting for committees to meet."[21]

The student Left was powerfully drawn to an account of language as primarily and directly *testimonial*, on the assumption that the sort of "man-to-man" declarations Nelken endorsed afforded the means of restoring integrity to words that the establishment had abstracted of meaning. Describing what it felt like to be a part of the events in Sproul Plaza, Michael Rossman writes in *The Wedding within the War* (1971), "Words like 'democracy' and 'moral commitment' . . . had become alive and real."[22] Yet this claim speaks to an uncomfortable truth that FSM activists finessed. As we saw in Chapter 1, and as UC president Clark Kerr infamously observed, the university has long prided itself on requiring virtually *no* "commitment" even from its permanent members. If this is true of its tenured faculty, it is much more true of its students, who cannot be committed to the campus except temporarily. Rossman touches on a dim awareness of this fact when he notes that "the only chance for responsible continuous leadership in student affairs lies with the graduate students, who stay here for years" (97). That the undergraduate is always an impermanent member of her class makes for some oxymoronic pronouncements across a student movement that Rossman describes as the "evolution" in "every college" of "its captive transient population" (13). Captive maybe; transient definitely. In placing "moral commitment" at the center of the FSM ethos, Rossman suggests that the school has betrayed its clientele by not keeping it "captive" enough.

"For millions," John Searle observes in *The Campus War* (1972), "the university has ceased to be a voluntary institution. From being voluntary members of a limited-purpose community of scholars, they have become compulsory members of what they regard as a campus city-state."[23] Viewing its linguistic determination as a species of coercion, Searle had little patience for the New Left ideal of message discipline. "One never sees tenses or particles," the speech-act theorist writes regarding the utterances of the student radicals, "only the imperative" (83). If the student movement embraces "a politics of feeling and not a politics of reason" (57), according to Searle, it is because the students, "who are often quite unsuited to the peculiar demands of the university" (177), are not quite bright enough to think their way to revolution. We need not share his contempt for the students in order to take note of Searle's insight that, as an institution that everywhere trumpets its dedication to change and transformation, the school is at odds with what Rossman calls the "primitive moral ideology, . . . the simple, naïve, and stubborn cry that distinguishes the new radicals: 'This is *wrong*, it must stop!'" (80).

Resonating through much of the student Left and beyond, the force of this statement derives from its literally conservative verdict on the nihilistic dynamism understood to characterize the central institutions of the national security state. This verdict coexists uneasily alongside the commitment to transformation that Rossman also claims as a "trademark of the new radicals" (80): "We were *turning*: not so much to the left or right, and not only against, but *into* . . . something else" (76). In the effort to separate itself from the processing of the multiversity (committed after all to nothing *but* the transformation of its students into "something else"), the FSM alighted with surprising frequency on variants of Rossman's interjection. It would not be a misreading to take the antecedent of the "it" that "must stop" as the willful metamorphism of the university, the strategies of deferral and regrouping backed up by what Rossman calls the school's "successive reinterpretations" of its own "Directives" (101).

This explains why free speech finally seems beside the point. Since free speech could not be aligned with consequences any more readily than technocratic speech, FSM radicals reframed their commitment to free speech as a commitment to authentic speech, the purest version of which was straight description, the statement that directly pointed to unequivocal claims ("this is *wrong*"). Yet it would be more accurate to say that authentic speech, language not prone to misinterpretation, came to inhere for the student Left in action itself. "Action," in Theodore Roszak's definition, "gives voice to our total vision of life" once "we think of conduct as a vocabulary."[24] Hence Savio's rejoinder to the "problem of automation" was not just the articulation of "speech with consequences" but the body that spoke for itself: "You've got to put your bodies upon the gears and upon the wheels, upon the levers, upon all the apparatus," he famously announced, "and you've got to make it stop. No more talking" (*TS*, 111).

The Counterculture's Poetics of the Closet

The "media" of "mass communication," Allen Ginsberg wrote in his "Independence Day Manifesto" (1959), "are exactly the place where the deepest and most personal sensitivities and confessions of reality are most prohibited, mocked, suppressed."[25] Ginsberg saw in this "suppression . . . a vast conspiracy to impose one level of mechanical consciousness on mankind." While his animosity toward the culture industry was hardly novel, Ginsberg's assault on the "systems" of mass media arrayed against "unconditioned individuality" was uniquely capacious, inclusive of "journalists, commercial publishers, book-review fellows, multitudes of professors of literature . . . [and] post-office employees."[26] The inclusion of the post office is especially notable since, as the first federal bureaucracy, it had been the object of conspiratorial scorn for centuries (as Thomas Pynchon's *Crying of Lot 49* soon attested). Given his commitment to a personhood and a reality principle besieged by a system that works toward their elimination, it is little wonder that Ginsberg should often be understood as producing an account of language that conforms to the New Left ideal of authenticity.

Yet while Ginsberg's vatic pronouncements share in the general New Left ambition to perform the change their makers want to see, they do not do what the signatories to open letters to Dow Chemical or WUO members aspire to effect in their own performative statements: the establishment of first-person identity as a bulwark against anonymity. "It's an important human experience to relate to yourself and others as a hunk of meat sometimes," Ginsberg told Allen Young in a 1973 interview. In this exchange, Ginsberg expresses strong

misgivings about the gay liberation movement, precisely because his preference for "losing ego" conflicts with the liberationist's demand for asserting
self-identity. Few things are more remote from the agenda of the New Social
Movements than Ginsberg's encomium to "being reduced to an anonymous
piece of meat, coming, and recognizing your own orgiastic anonymity."[27] Nor
can we fail to observe that in contrast to the New Left commitment to expressive authenticity, Ginsberg's statements demur from the work of any straight-
forwardly *meaningful* communication. They fail to deliver on the linguistic
determinations for which FSM and other groups pleaded. The "glossolalia"
that Amy Hungerford cites as Ginsberg's signature speech act may well be a
form of authenticity, but it does not conduce to referential transparency.[28] It
is as though Ginsberg, pledged to solidarity with the New Left, cannot carry
through on its program of explicitness. His commitment to authenticity takes
him only so far along the trail blazed by FSM radicals. His path diverges from
theirs when, instead of a hallowed personhood, he opts for "impersonal meat
orgies, with no question of personality or character or relating to people as
people."[29] Ginsberg's hesitancy toward expressive authenticity has everything
to do with his queerness, which took shape in a period when the demand for
truthful expression looked far less appealing, erotically speaking, than it would
in the heyday of the New Social Movements.

Thus far I have looked at the privileging of authentic language across the
New Left. Here I describe a specific route by which the New Left arrives at
this investment, one that Ginsberg helps us complicate. The commitment to
linguistic integrity relied on an account of statism as fundamentally corrupt-
ing of language because the state was, first and foremost, guilty of the corruption of morals. Repeatedly in movement literature, this corruption took
the shape of an occlusive homosexual menace. And the defense against this
corruption in turn took the shape of a policy of acting out. Despite their enthusiasm for imposture and masquerade, for example, the Yippies understood
their activist stagecraft as a rebuff to what Guy Strait called "the straight game
of camouflage" (*TS*, 311) rather than its apotheosis. Shedding the public world's
coercive impression management, the Yippies' corrosive exhibitionism targeted
a conformist culture that presumably could not withstand the indecorous exposure of things that ought to remain unsaid.

In repudiating "the latent drama of repression and discontent," Jerry Rubin
writes in *Do It!*, "our tactic was exaggeration."[30] Far from rejecting the expres-

sive authenticity found throughout the more idealistic precincts of the New Left, the Yippies, bearing witness to the separation of meaning and action, demanded their restoration by any means necessary. Their object was to stabilize an action's meaning against any potential misconstruction. "Dyeing all the outdoor fountains red," Abbie Hoffman explains, "and then sending a message to the newspaper explaining why you did it, dramatizes the idea that blood is being shed needlessly in imperialist wars."[31] Yet like Mario Savio willing to throw his body on the "gears" of the "apparatus," the Yippies aspired to actions possessed of a self-evidence that rendered speech superfluous. This is what Rubin means when he says that "the revolution is nonverbal" (105) and why he calls the Yippie's "basic informational statement . . . a blank piece of paper" (80). Freedom of speech comes to be defined as freedom *from* speech, on the view that the latter is always prone to distortion.

The idea that language is corrupt did not originate with the Yippies, of course, or even with the New Left. When Rubin notes that "words have lost their emotional impact" (108), he might be parroting Allen Tate or any advocate of the view that language has fallen victim to that Eliotic malaise, the dissociation of sensibility. Whereas the New Critic tends to take this dissociation in stride, arguing for the sanctity of poetry that flaunts the gap between usage and meaning, the Yippies are strict intentionalists. "The ideological left is made up of part-time people whose lifestyle mocks their rhetoric," Rubin complains. "There's a thousand miles between their actions and their ideology" (114). It is thus fitting that the Yippies aim their most withering invective at a university culture that encourages appreciation rather than repudiation of the ironic distance between words and their objects. "Take no action, take no stands, commit yourself to nothing," Rubin writes. "Abstract thinking is the way professors avoid facing their own impotence" (213). The capacity to act one thing while saying another marks the professors not as dissidents but as what Rubin calls "house niggers" (215).

Gone is the antisocial threat, the slippery nihilistic slope, that the campus novel located in the academic's privileged relation to irony and imposture. Taking its place is the abject specter of a deviant longing. Singling out "the 'nice' Deans of Men who put one hand around our shoulder while the other hand gropes for our pants" (215), Rubin sums up liberalism in the figure of the academic as a suppliant queen. The vilification of the queer professor is a recurrent motif for the student Left. In "The Student and Society" (1970), Jerry Farber blames the "totally useless" busywork of freshman English on "who teaches the course, . . . some well-meaning instructor or TA whose own writing achievements" are composed "in pretentious faggot-academic."[32] The elision of "academic" with "faggot" was already implicit in Farber's earlier essay, "The Student as Nigger" (1967), where he puts his colleagues' "timidity" down to their being "short on balls," before likening their hypocritical stance to the passive role in anal intercourse: "They lie flat on their stomachs with their pants down, mumbling catch phrases like 'professional dignity' and 'meaningful dialogue'" (94). Farber traces the absence of a "free unashamed sexuality" to the fact that "academic training itself forces a split between thought and action." "Sexuality has no place in the classroom," he observes, except "in certain perverted and vitiated forms" (96). The unity of thought and action became a rallying point for Sixties radicals facing down the minced words and mincing bodies of the professoriat.

The homophobic language in Farber was not incidental to the ethical position he and other radicals advanced. Privileging speech over print, community over bureaucracy, the student Left simultaneously fostered an indicatively gendered and eroticized version of this choice. The "man-to-man" honesty that Michael Nelken promoted during the FSM crisis emerged in its full potency against the degraded spectacle of what Robert Kaufman and Michael Folsom called the "bevy of academic 'white glove girls' who are at the beck and call of industry and government."[33] Likewise, Mario Savio described the university professor as a "whore" unlawfully joined" to "industry and government."[34] Whereas Savio imagined the professoriat in an illegitimate union with the state, Kaufman and Folsom's professors were *noncommittal* in their mercenary dalliances with the power elite ("white glove girls" were the trademarked temps of Manpower, Inc.).

This view of the professoriat as erotically compromised and implicitly feminized by its entanglements with technocracy drew on a long-established association that would have been as familiar to Alger Hiss or Adlai Stevenson (both of whose lives were grist for the homophobic rumor mill) as to FSM or the Yippies: the mingling of politics in the national security state with the epistemology of the closet. As the locus of the alibi, the discreet and disowned encounter, the closet became synonymous with the deniability that the New Left deplored in politics as usual, yet this idea was hardly novel to the student movement. It was received wisdom that the federal government had since the New Deal been colonized by "fairies" who, according to CIA director Roscoe Hillenkoeter in 1950, formed "a government within a government."[35] The closet had functioned for decades as a privileged mode of cognition and contact among Washington elites. Tallying more than three hundred thousand pages, Hoover's "Sex Deviates" file contained information that the FBI had accrued since 1937 on the lives of gays and lesbians regardless of office or rank. The file remained classified until Hoover's death and was destroyed in 1977 in the massive purge that followed the passage of the Privacy Act. In keeping this material in check, Hoover's concern was not privacy but leverage. As Robert Dean argues, Hoover "used the mandated employee investigations to honeycomb the federal government with FBI informers."[36]

It is no small irony that Sixties radicals would turn against the invisible government by mobilizing the same demonizing rhetoric that early Cold War Republicans mustered against the Truman administration in their effort to combat the threat of a federal bureaucracy presumably staffed by subversives and perverts alike. As Hoover's deployment of the closet to recruit informants across government agencies suggests, there was a certain truth to the claim that the administration of the national security state was indeed a rather queer enterprise. "I think orgies should be institutionalized," Ginsberg told Allen Young in 1973, apparently unaware that for many a Cold Warrior, such institutionalization had long ago passed from theory to practice in the various branches of the Eisenhower State Department.[37] The rationale for rooting "perverts" out of government, of course, was their liability to extortion. Yet while those tasked with handling security risks insisted that homosexuals posed a threat to state secrets because they were incapable of keeping their mouths shut, it is hard not to observe that the policing agencies of the civil service promoted a vision of the chattering queen distinctly at odds with the fact that, in Cold War America, one was unlikely to find a group more discreet than the men who traveled in queer circles. Such figures were understood to be masters in the arts of anonymity, which they had perfected in cruising for sexual contacts and in other necessarily clandestine activities. The penchant for anonymity and episodic relations also made them perilously unaccountable. On this account, the queen was prone to spill state secrets less because he could not help himself than because he had no loyalties whatsoever: the indifference to commitment in his personal life augured a fatal lack of commitment to the national trust.

From this perspective, the queen was dangerous less because he departed from the Cold War social style than because he took it to an intolerable—or un-American—extreme. As we have seen, the proponents of that style took a rather sanguine view of "the art of commitment."[38] That phrase comes from the economist Thomas Schelling, the most forceful defender of the view that commitment was a strategy akin to moves in a game rather than another name for holding beliefs. In *Arms and Influence* (1966), Schelling maintained that "credible" commitments, of the sort that would carry weight with America's enemies, required a "public ritual of getting ourselves genuinely committed" (50); that is, the "process" (49) of commitment was a performance. For Schelling, the crucial point was not whether you held a commitment in earnest (whether it was meaningful to you) but whether you managed to impress your enemies that you held it in earnest (whether it was meaningful to them). The doxastic value of the commitment thus ceded pride of place to "fidelity of perception" (274).

Whereas Cold Warriors like Schelling fostered what I have called the consensus of make-believe to safeguard the national security state, their critics in the 1960s worked to rescind that accord by highlighting the link between the establishment's embrace of ironic performance and the stigmatized role-playing of the erotic outcast. This stigmatization rode in tandem with the condemnation of the school as the locus of a closeted erotics. Through the bad example of the closet, what Farber calls the "impersonal and coercive" nature of school culture inches toward the more sinister implications of the "automated" social order condemned by Mario Savio. Through the "heavy irony" with which its instructors aimed to "crush objectors," Farber argues, the school turns out not only "clever robots" (23) but also a generation of deviants: "With us the perversion is intellectual, but it's no less perverse." The deception crucial to the closet is built into the college classroom: "You walk in and everyone's face is a mask" (26).

Couched in a less demagogic idiom, Farber's views on the academic style and its tendency toward hollowness and perversion were the cutting edge of Sixties highbrow critique. In the title essay of *Against Interpretation* (1966), Susan Sontag takes aim at the systematic meaning making that appeared to dominate midcentury academic thought. Whereas Sontag's contemporaries tended to locate interpretive opaqueness in the complexity of the social and natural world (Parsons and Wiener are the relevant examples), Sontag faulted what she saw as a compulsion toward hermeneutics among intellectuals who made the world more complicated than it needed to be. Worst still in Sontag's view, in its fetish for complexity, interpreters hollowed out the authenticity in any object they chose to encipher. Hence, "to interpret is to impoverish, to deplete the world—

in order to set up a shadow world of 'meanings.'" Sontag's experts treated the object world as process rather than substance, which "amounts to the philistine refusal to leave the work of art alone."[39]

The imperative of meaning making thus paradoxically results in a world of meaningless gestures, the "shadow world" here coming awfully close to the dicey milieu that John Rechy illuminates in his 1963 chronicle of male prostitution, *City of Night*. Like the Professor in that novel, an academic who cannot keep his hands off the hustler protagonist, Sontag's academic expert, in his "refusal to leave the work of art alone," looks more like a pervert than a specialist, his interpretive overreaching made to seem indistinguishable from the bad touch of the molester. "I am a P-H-D," Rechy's Professor tells the narrator, "a Doctor of Learning: I don't cut up people; I dig into their minds to find, perhaps, a latent jewel!"[40] One way to construe the oblique sentence with which "Against Interpretation" ends—"In place of a hermeneutics, we need an erotics of art"—is to see Sontag's juxtaposition as both an aesthetic and an ethical claim, the choice of a committed and meaningful sexual practice over the intellectual dilettantism that takes its cues from the transient and fetishistic "shadow world" of cruising and hustling.[41]

Thomas Pynchon's *The Crying of Lot 49* (1966) likewise exploits the resemblance between the academic's shadow world of meanings and the shadow world of erotic dalliances favored by the sexually noncommittal. The specter of male homosexuality at its most clandestine (not to say villainous) looms large in Pynchon's synopsis of Richard Wharfinger's *The Courier's Tragedy*, the play-within-the-novel, during which "three figures, long-limbed, effeminate, dressed in black tights, leotards and gloves, and black silk hose pulled over their faces, come capering on stage and stop, gazing at [Niccolo]," the "rightful heir and good guy of the play."[42] Pynchon follows through the implications of Sontag's suggestion that hermeneutics is equal not just to the perversion of meaning but to perversion in general. Oedipa is drawn into the mystery of "Tristero's shadow-state" (163), after all, partly through her encounter with a Wharfinger scholar, Emory Bortz, who has "smuggled out" of the Vatican library "illicit microfilms" (154) of its "pornographic *Courier's Tragedy*" (151). It is as though Pynchon goes out of his way to highlight the complicity of the academic's interpretive prowess with both a suspect erotics and the stealth maneuvers of the shadow state.

The Crying of Lot 49 is equally intent on stressing the proximity of perverts and organization men. Consider Oedipa's encounter with the "aging boys in

Roos Atkins suits" in the vicinity of a "fag joint" called "The Greek Way" (110). These men in corporate attire attest to the link Pynchon forges between white-collar labor and gay life on the basis of their shared penchant for nondisclosure. Inside the bar Oedipa finds herself talking to a member of Inamorati Anonymous (IA), a group whose mission is to break people of "the worst addiction of all"—being "in love" (112). And though the IA rep professes asexuality, the fact that his group's founder "could not make a decision without first hearing the ideas of a committee" (113) suggests that his presence in the bar is not merely in the cause of equal opportunity. For if the IA does not discriminate between straight and queer "addiction" with respect to being in love, it favors the path of noncommitment broken by the "aging boys" of the queer "underworld" (116), entry to which has been decided, so to speak, by committee. The atomistic collectivity for which the IA strives, where "nobody knows anybody else's name" (113), is modeled on the "society of isolates" alleged to constitute gay life (116). That pattern in turn derives from Pynchon's belief that the queer world and the bureaucratic world shadow each other. The Greek way weaves like Ariadne's thread through the labyrinth of "the corporate root-system" (113).

Coming Out Straight

Whereas in *Crying of Lot 49* homosexuality is illicit and spectral, in *Gravity's Rainbow* (1973) it has become the open if not exactly proud servant of state power, which now targets a heterosexual vitality that has itself become illicit if not outlawed. Hence, it is their craving for what Pynchon calls "the penis of official commendation" that leads "federal cowards" to take down John Dillinger "with their faggots' precision," as though the Chicago gangster were a menace less because he robbed banks than because of his lusty heterosexuality.[43] "Anything but a 'common criminal'" in Pig Bodine's estimation, Dillinger had to be eliminated because he "socked Them right in the toilet privacy of Their banks" (756)—a view that equates Dillinger's assault on law and order with a quest to disinfect officialdom's preferred stronghold: the closet that postwar culture identifies categorically with the tearoom.

Recasting the queer from a sleeper agent within the corridors of power to the flunky of an establishment that actively rewards obedience with homo-erotic favors, *Gravity's Rainbow* sees queerness not as the underbelly of the national security state but as something like its frankly acknowledged rationale: "Homosexuality in high places is just a carnal afterthought now" (627). The reduction of queerness from anomic threat to the perfunctory business as usual of the social order has a specific historical explanation. The difference between *The Crying of Lot 49*'s oblique homosexuality and *Gravity's Rainbow*'s ostentatious homosexuality is the difference that Stonewall makes. Pynchon joins a formidable array of countercultural writers who treat the coming to visibility of gay and lesbian liberation as the normalization of deviance, a pattern that such writers take as clear evidence that the forces of normativity themselves are fundamentally corrupt. This judgment leads to what is perhaps the most unusual development in the counterculture's struggle against the "system": the embrace of gay liberation's coming-out narrative on behalf of a straight identity understood as the vanguard of revolutionary politics.

Taken together, *The Crying of Lot 49* and *Gravity's Rainbow* exemplify the range of opinions on the lavender menace throughout the radical Sixties, which tended to see the enemy as combining two queer stereotypes: the soulless authoritarian thug and the flamboyant queens who are unable to resist him. The "antiwar broadsheets" that, as Terence Kissack notes, "portrayed the U.S. military as a conclave of macho homosexuals" circulated in a counterculture that used "faggot" as an "all-purpose insult" for "weak men . . . who had sold out to the system."[44] "Homosexuals are docile and subservient," Newton writes in *Revolutionary Suicide*. "They tend to obey . . . regulations" (271). Newton might have been taking dictation from Theodor Adorno, whose 1963 essay "Sexual Laws and Taboo Today" deprecates "that type of homosexual whose admiration of virility is coupled with an enthusiasm for order and discipline."[45] Such assumptions about queer compliance overlapped, somewhat paradoxically, with the perceived licentiousness of gay experience, a sexual freedom that some activists saw as no different from anarchism. It was on the basis of his "libertarian" queerness, according to Greg Calvert, that he was frozen out of the SDS leadership in 1967.[46] But this only appears to be a contradiction; for the soft spot the queer had for the fascist was of a piece, in the New Left mind, with his being simply soft on order in general. Anarchism and fascism manifested the same disdain for the right kind of order, the discipline of authentic community, in favor of the wrong kind of desire. What Eldridge Cleaver calls "the root, the fountainhead, of the homosexuality that is perennially associated with the Omnipotent Administrator" is the latter's irresistible attraction to "Supermasculine Menials" whom he "cannot but . . . envy" and "worship."[47]

Given gay male culture's eroticizing of anonymity no less than interchangeability when it comes to objects of desire, it is thus surprising to find that the counterculture's effort to discredit the establishment by linking it with a calculating and servile queerness could scarcely outpace the use of this shaming tactic among some gay liberationists. In the aftermath of the Stonewall riots, Yippie-turned-gay-radical Jim Fouratt thus denounced those gay men interested in "dialogue" rather than protest for their readiness to "sit and accept" the "soft, weak, sensitive . . . homo stereotype," a "role society has been forcing these queens to play."[48] Preferring action over words, Fouratt accuses gay men of a girlish passivity that would have been obvious to Jerry Rubin, his erstwhile compatriot, or to the Weathermen, who viewed "anything on the moral level," according to a reporter, as "sissy talk."[49] In "The Fairy Princess Exposed," which appeared in the landmark anthology *Out of the Closets* (1972), Craig Hanson urged gay activists "not to fall into the lavender cesspool" of preliberationist gay men, the casualties of a "princess syndrome" that Hanson deemed a form of "cultural conservatism."[50] As the "beautifiers and decorators" (*VG*, 266) of the "establishment," these "perverted half-men" also connived in the sub-rosa workings of Amerika: "victims of the princess syndrome probably account for a large proportion of the male membership in the manipulative sects and cults" (267).

Even when they declined to lay the counterrevolution at the feet of the princess, gay radicals shared Hanson's equation of the closet queen's "conscious make-believe" and the "authoritarian" abuses of bureaucracy (*VG*, 269). "One of the ways bureaucracies find us useful," Mike Silverstein writes in "Gay Bureaucrats," is to turn gay men into "eunuchs . . . totally loyal to the administration" (*VG*, 166). "Invisible and depersonalized" within the managerial gulag, such men "do all kinds of embarrassing little nasty hatchet jobs for the boss," in return for which they "can swish around the office and camp it up" (*VG*, 166). The bureaucratic hive becomes a roomy and well-appointed closet. Coming out and rejecting bureaucratic "despotism" (*VG*, 165) go hand in hand for Silverstein on the assumption that by exiting the closet, one came out into "personhood"—or, as the Radicalesbians put it, "our own selves as absolutes" (175). For this reason the Gay Activists Alliance listed among the aims in its 1971 constitution not only "the right to be persons" but also "the right to express our feelings in action."[51] Such invocations of the person demonstrate the degree to which the post-Stonewall gay movement structured the coming-out narrative with an eye toward the New Left's modeling of the closet as a stronghold of bureaucratic impersonality.

The elaboration of this narrative was under way even before the seismic events of summer 1969. The reformist gay activists of the early 1960s also framed their coming out as a refusal of unaccountability. "I intend to take an active role in the determination of my own fate," the gay rights pioneer Franklin Kameny asserted in a 1965 essay.[52] Kameny, a target of the lavender scare who had unsuccessfully sued the federal government for wrongful termination in 1959, was instrumental in turning gay rights into a national issue. And while he patterned his politics on the civil rights movement, Kameny's rhetoric reveals an equal if implicit debt to the student movement's reverence for "determination" and transparency. He thus urges "a clear, definite, unambiguous stand" and, as though embracing FSM's notion that the most authentic language is nonverbal, also urges a "move from endless talk . . . to firm, vigorous action" (*WA*, 335). The penchant for ambiguity associated with establishment liberalism and its tweedy enforcers in the "ivory-tower" (*WA*, 336) can only obstruct what he calls "a unified, coherent, self-consistent philosophy" of homosexual identity (337).

Kameny's assimilationist politics sidelined the camp follower because his flamboyance was at odds with the homophile movement's tactic of respectability. His advocacy of homosexuality as "nothing other than a non-pathological preference" (*WA*, 368) thus obliged Kameny, in "Gay Is Good" (1969), to assert that "very few homosexuals are effeminate" (373), on the presumption that "the average, ordinary, guilt-free, unanguished, reasonably untroubled, basically happy homosexual" disallowed the sissy as a category (367). Although the gay liberationists who came after him had more sympathy for fairies than Kameny (or Hanson) did, they were equally keen to fasten on identity as what gave *purpose* to gay life. In "A Gay Manifesto" (1970), Carl Wittman thus refuses to "indict . . . the queen" (*VG*, 334) whom Kameny finds a bad example of gay identity, even if he shares Kameny's demand that "closet queenery must end" (334).

We can measure the difference between liberal and radical gay politics by reference to the rationale each brings to this imperative. In the view of a reformer like Kameny, coming out of the closet allows individual self-expression, the prerogative of any citizen in a pluralist democracy. In the view of radicals like Wittman, coming out of the closet means that broad social change will ensue. Yet for Wittman no less than Kameny, "nellies" are not a good model for liberation. However much he "suffers from being open," the nellie is not living what Wittman calls a "role-free" existence (*VG*, 334). More to the point, the role he continues to play offers no toehold for a larger social purpose. His being out makes no difference. "Adopting a gay identity in 1969 meant more than simply affirming one's same-sex orientation by declaring oneself 'a homosexual,'" as Justin Suran notes. "It meant positioning oneself in relation to a clearly articulated set of commitments and ideals associated at the time with radical politics."[53] This statement aims to register the separation between the homophile and the liberationist. But gay liberation's articulation of its "commitments and ideals" depended on the movement's differentiation from an even more pressing foil: the inconsequence that both homophiles and liberationists, like Cold War liberals and Sixties radicals, located in postwar queer life.

A former SDS leader, Wittman drifted away from that group in 1967 (after Tom Hayden made plain his hostility to gays). Wittman's bid for a "role-free social structure" was strongly colored by his early formation in the New Left's "politics of authenticity," to use Douglas Rossinow's phrase. By the terms of that politics, radicalization meant an insistence on "self-liberation," which in turn demanded a perpetual autocritique aimed at reckoning with "radicals' persistent fears of their own inauthenticity."[54] The continual self-examination advocated by midcentury humanists like Theodore Baird resurfaced in radical discourse, albeit with a crucial revision: the goal was not to ferret out a naïve unity of self, as it was for English 1's "education in irony," but to bring such a unity into being. In this regard, Huey Newton's widely bruited entente with gay liberation in 1970 is most revealing for what it tells us about the framework in which any aspiring radicalism was constrained to announce itself. "We must relate to the homosexual movement because it is a real thing," Newton writes in "An Open Letter from Huey to the Revolutionary Brothers and Sisters about the Women's Liberation and Gay Liberation Movements." "We should try to judge, somehow, whether they are operating in a sincere revolutionary fashion and from a really oppressed situation" (*WA*, 405). Newton's modifiers ("real," "sincere," "really") indicate the degree to which gay liberation would stand or fall on its commitment to the reality principle basic to revolutionary politics, a principle that entailed endlessly monitoring any and all claims to authenticity.

That commitment would prove continually challenging for gay liberation, given the high bar for authenticity set by radical discourse. "Real human life and real human flesh," according to Bobby Seale (ventriloquizing Eldridge Cleaver), are the casualties of the "homosexuality . . . rampant" among "the omnipotent administrators," who "taboo these things" on behalf of a "brainwashing" campaign designed to cut the people off from the facts of life: "The *fact* is that a man and a woman relate to each other, that through sexual relations they produce another real human being."[55] We might call this fact the definitive overstatement of Sixties radicalism, in the sense outlined earlier: the gesture of conferring political meaning on acts by highlighting their obviousness. It is a tribute to the primacy of this tactic among Sixties radicals that gay liberation embraced the New Left discourse of overstatement even while gay liberationists themselves could rarely attain its generative (procreative) ideal. "As liberated gays," Wittman writes, echoing the appeal to referential certitude that characterizes both Black Panther and FSM politics, "we must take a clear stand" (*VG*, 334). If gays could not meet Seale's standard of realness, they could nonetheless seek to join the revolution by asserting the clarity of what Suran calls their "commitments." Yet this assertion required liberationists to undo the long association of homosexuality with noncommitment.

The most recognizable watermark of New Left discourse in the documents of gay liberation is the latter's recourse to a Marxist idiom of social class in the analysis of nonclass categories. The queen is thus understood to be "acting out of false consciousness" (*VG*, 295), and his favorite pastime, "the cruelest of human games known as cruising" (264), is a version of capitalism's divide-and-conquer strategy. At the upper reaches of the class system, Hanson's "princess" is an establishment eunuch, a courtier to the power elite; at its lower end, the "nellie" is a sort of lumpen insensible to organization. Both are lost causes. Hence, gay liberation's consciousness raising is bent not on changing the princess and the nellie but on preventing the liberationists themselves from lapsing into their "inflexible" (*VG*, 334) and "programmed" (252) roles. "I don't think that anything is negative about gayness except for the roles" (*VG*, 109), Ron Vernon observes in "Sissy in Prison." An ex-convict whose "consciousness" has been made "entirely different" by liberation, Vernon claims that the prison uses roles as both a form of coercion and a sure path to recidivism for its gay population: "having to play those roles . . . was why so many of us kept returning to the institution" (*VG*, 107).

That there was something inflexible about gay liberation's fixation on the perils of role-playing is a subject I take up in the next two chapters, which elaborate on the alternatives to understanding role as synonymous with a "prison-like, straight-jacketed existence" (*VG*, 351). At this point we need only note that vilifying "role" allowed radicals to confer on gay identity a specificity that role-playing apparently undermined. "Homosexuality is *not* a lot of things," Wittman insists. It is "not a *makeshift*" but "*the capacity to love another person of the same sex*" (*VG*, 331). Such exactitude belies the fact that this capacity would turn out to be rather commodious in liberationist rhetoric. But this is to say that gay liberation's interest in exactitude in no way limited its pursuit of the most varied kinds of political possibility. Gay liberation's adherents often argued that coming out was capable of effecting a vast array of political changes far removed from the self-expression it nominally denotes. "Gay is good if we declare it so," a Gay Liberation Front–Chicago pamphlet reads. What follows from this declaration is a host of other "goods," which I quote at length to give a sense of the global consequences that coming out might entail:

> A higher level of gay is good is as a tool to break down enforced heterosexuality, sex roles, the impoverished categories of straight, gay, and bisexual, male supremacy, programing of children, ownership of children, the nuclear family, monogamy, possessiveness, exclusiveness of "love," insecurity, jealousy, competition, privilege, individual isolation, ego-tripping, power-tripping, money-tripping, people as property, people as machines, rejection of the body, repression of emotions, anal-eroticism, authoritarian anti-human religion, conformity, regimentation, polarization of "masculine" and "feminine," categorization of male and female emotions, abilities, interests, clothing, etc., fragmentation of the self by these outlines, isolation and elitism of the arts, uniform standards of beauty, dependency on leaders, unquestioning submission to authority, power hierarchies, caste, racism, militarism, imperialism, national chauvinism, cultural chauvinism, class chauvinism . . . maybe even up to private property and the state. (*VG*, 258)

Given that the conditions into which coming out is imagined to ramify presuppose a macrolevel upheaval, the pamphlet's late demurral over "the state" sounds slightly off-key. Although this is the sort of document that leads Kissack to call gay liberation's "theoretical analysis . . . not, in general, very sophisticated," it would be hard to imagine that charge carrying much weight with the liberationists.[56] A lack of sophistication, after all, often counted as a virtue in New Left circles. "The simple, naïve, and stubborn cry that distinguishes the new radicals," as Michael Rossman put it, resurfaces in gay liberation's subsumption of categories like "the nuclear family" and "elitism of the arts." The point of such drastic simplification is precisely its refusal of the forensic spirals of the establishment. It is against interpretation with a vengeance.

Yet even as it embraced a militant naïveté in keeping with the student Left's rejection of school culture, gay liberation nonetheless retained a telling affinity with the midcentury university's interpretive protocols. What the campus novel condemned as the academic's grossest vice turned out to be gay liberation's virtue: the habit of analogizing from personal experience to social transformation. But where the university venerated experimental personhood, gay liberation privileged authentic personhood. Excluded from the social contract and its invidious prejudices, according to the drafters of the Gay Revolutionary Party Manifesto, gay people "have had no investment in dogmatism, sexism, racism, and nationalism," so "have been able to see the essential nature of human personhood" (*VG*, 343). The antisystemic proviso of midcentury academic humanism, which led its practitioners to an account of persons as continually in flux, here gives way to the opposite conclusion: detachment from isms shows gay liberationists not that persons are always fabricated but that they are always authentic. The close attention to freedom from role reveals that the account of authenticity favored by Sixties gay activists shared in the larger New Left equation between authenticity and autonomy. And while both homophiles like Kameny and gay liberationists like Wittman owed an undeniable debt to the FSM-inspired project of establishing personhood and (to cite SDS) of "making values explicit," it is less frequently noted that the counterculture took up with gusto the enduring contribution of gay liberation to identity politics: the coming-out narrative. The counterculture adapted that narrative to a story line in which one broke from a shamefully unreal life into a politically satisfying heterosexuality that embraced the risk taking and self-determination, the radical individualism, of expressive authenticity.

How else to explain Norman Mailer's assertion, in *The Prisoner of Sex* (1971), that "all men are homosexual but for the choice not to be," as though homosexuality were the dominant structure of feeling in a social order that disallowed expressions of heterosexual desire?[57] Three years earlier in *The Armies of the Night*, Mailer had already specified a version of this conceit when he wrote that "you earned manhood provided you were good enough" to withstand a culture "designed precisely to drive men deep into onanism and homosexuality."[58] It is hard not to read the "transgressing" (137) that takes place in that novel—Mailer's arrest after rushing a police blockade during the March on the

Pentagon in 1967—in terms of the counterintuitive scenario Mailer elaborates: a world of *homosexual presumption,* given to us not only in the presence of the "sexologue" Paul Goodman and his "damnable tolerance for all the varieties of sex" but also in the guise of the Pentagon itself, a "foe" whose "every inch they could explore," including his "symbolic loins," and "still know nothing about him" (289). "Every aspect of the building was anonymous," Mailer writes, "monotonous, massive, interchangeable" (228).

No less inclined than J. Edgar Hoover to see behind every government agency a queer specter, Mailer pitches the Pentagon on the cruising grounds of gay male desire for which Goodman, who "looked like an old con who had first gotten into trouble in the YMCA" (29), might be the ambassador.[59] *The Armies of the Night* draws out the resonance not merely between Goodman and the guardians of American military overreach but also between the latter and the "liberal academics" whose opposition to the Pentagon provides superficial cover for a much deeper continuity between the Defense Department and the ivory tower: the commitment to the noncommitment afforded by the closet. Whereas the Pentagon's apologists embrace instrumental reason under the pretext of national security, the liberal academics embrace "oversecurity" under the pretext of instrumental reason (24). Like the gay male erotic style it resembles, the academic style that refuses commitment (because any "concept" is "always to be relinquished for a better concept" [15]) is for Mailer less an open buffet than a moral dead end. Since their "private loves . . . were attached to no gold standard of the psyche" (15), Mailer thus sees liberal academics as "the natural managers of that future air-conditioned vault where the last of human life would still exist" (24).

This is not to say that *The Armies of the Night* simply condemns the American war machine or its unlikely accomplices (Paul Goodman, liberal academics) on the basis of their perceived queerness. Indeed, the novel's most compelling feature is Mailer's deep ambivalence regarding the perversions of the statist institution it contests. Following his arrest, Mailer describes the "collective journey through the dark when strangers are brought close" on the bus that takes him to his detention center and recalls "that restful silence of men traveling, that sense of security in their muscle and in their number" that makes him feel "almost glad he had not yet been released" (174). We might be excused for remarking in Mailer's bus ride an affinity with the dalliances of another class of male "strangers" who meet under cover of darkness and conduct their affairs likewise in silence, given how closely it follows on the tussle that precipitates Mailer's stint in jail. "Some unfamiliar current," Mailer writes of his confrontation with an MP at the blockade line,

> was evolving from that quiver of the club, and the MP seemed to turn slowly away from his position confronting the rope, and the novelist turned with him, each still facing the other until the axis of their shoulders was now perpendicular to the rope, and they still kept turning in this psychic field, not touching, the club quivering, and then Mailer was behind the MP, he was free of him, and he wheeled around and kept going in a half run to the next line of MPs. (130)

Mailer plays this scrimmage as a fantasy of homoerotic encounter organized around the "raised" (130) and "quivering" phallus of the MP's formidable "club." (In *Gravity's Rainbow*, "coppers" [579] also "show up" with "black dildos in nervous hands" to quell a civilian gathering [580].) As befits their role as the shock troops of the Pentagon, the MPs are distinguished by a macho-fascist sex appeal that would have been as obvious to Theodor Adorno as to Tom of Finland.

Read in the context of the prison bus ride, this dalliance with the MPs signals Mailer's commitment to the view that any "psychic field" surcharged with a homoerotic "current" is bound to end badly for its participants, however dynamic and thus freeing it might at first appear. Despite the pleasure he feels among his fellow passengers "in their muscle and in their number," that experience of "security" remains one of bondage. Yet this is only to say that the experience of detainment exists in *The Armies of the Night* as the means for its author to provide his hero with an incentive for being "released." Mailer of course never intends jail as a one-way trip. It is only a rung on the "moral ladder" at the top of which he descries a chastened liberty (212). The object of going to jail consists in acceding to and then escaping from the security of muscle and number in order to disavow the pleasures of a life in which one's actions are severed from one's instincts. While *The Armies of the Night* provides momentary glimpses of the warm glow to be had in the embrace of a benevolent totalitarianism, or in the security of the anonymous collective, its conclusion restores the terms of approbation and disapproval to their rightful places. As counterpoint to the liberal academic in his "air-conditioned vault," Mailer's book ends with a view of the "last pacifists" of the Pentagon protest, "naked Quakers" who, by virtue of their hunger strike, find "the cells of the brain contracting to the crystals of their thought, essence of one thought so close to the essence of another" (287).

If the detachment of the liberal ironist fosters a promiscuous intellection, a serial choosing among equally desirable and vacant concepts, the example of the fasting Quaker body, reduced to its essence by deprivation, makes commitment to one's thought look like monogamy. Recasting the Quakers' pledge of non-cooperation with their jailers as a version of companionate marriage ("essence of one thought so close to the essence of another"), Mailer thus restores to his ambivalent narrative the body whose obdurate matter served Mario Savio as a means to disrupt "the apparatus," a way to "make it stop." The Quakers' bodies are antecedent to the novel's final body, "America . . . heavy with child, . . . a beauty" who "languishes in a dungeon whose walls are never seen." This over-wrought figure of parturition occasions an equally baroque series of questions and injunctions: "Can she, poor giant, tormented lovely girl, deliver a babe of a new world brave and tender, artful and wild? Rush to the locks. God writhes in his bonds. Rush to the locks. Deliver us from our curse" (288). The image of America as a pregnant body consummates the logic Mailer introduces with the protesters "born again" at the end of the previous chapter (281). That would be the logic of consummation itself.

Like Bobby Seale, Mailer sees not only heterosexual intercourse and conception as unassailable signs of realness but also that realness in turn as having radical political meaning. *The Prisoner of Sex* picks up and elaborates on the figure of childbirth with which *Armies of the Night* concludes. Mailer writes that women who "choose to have no children" face "the possibility of some unnameable harm to that inner space of creation their bodies would enclose" (*PS*, 59), and thus makes giving birth appear as an analogy for escaping from prison. Men must voluntarily risk imprisonment so that they will recognize the necessity of escape from a homosexuality always pressing down on them, since "buggery is as fundamental to prison as money to social life" (*PS*, 165). "In full possession of a mysterious space within" (*PS*, 59), women by contrast are blessed with the ability to play out the drama of liberation through an act that until recently, Mailer observes, entailed "the dramatic possibility of a fatal end" (126). Thus, Mailer insists on treating the capacity for childbearing as a rebuff to "every attempt at uniform behavior" (61). Far from making women captives to biology, the "womb" (*PS*, 61) instead furnishes the means for nonconformity, for thwarting the reduction of "separate institutions" to "one institution" and of heterosexual diversity to a homosexual default. The literal embodiment of expressive authenticity, the womb expresses personhood by giving rise to persons. But its capacity to deliver such realness has been undermined by what Mailer calls "that single permissive sexual standard where a man's asshole is the democratic taxpaying equivalent of any vagina" (*PS*, 113).

Resurrecting the twin culprits of *The Armies of the Night*, *The Prisoner of Sex* contrasts them with the pregnant body to make the point that the radical moral choice is not to pretend that one is not imprisoned (like academics in their "vault"), or that there are no taboos holding one back (like Goodman with his "varieties of sex"), but rather to act as if one is continually threatened with a captivity from which one continually strives to escape. Childbearing thus does not so much liberate women as provide a meaning for liberation by virtue of its perpetual reminder of their own struggle against the tyranny of biology. Borrowing Marcuse's argument from *One-Dimensional Man*, which also condemns permissiveness as a ruse of domination, Mailer suggests that a world distilled to one institution, by disallowing distinctions, likewise threatens the self with the prospect of not being able to locate the outside, the line that marks the difference between freedom and nonfreedom. The way to defeat the flattening of institutions from the many to the one is to defend such institutions as marriage and family by making them appear like the radical entrée to the promise of a committed life.

It says much about his allegiance to the sex-gender system that Mailer figures risk taking as parenthood, arguably the path of least resistance in a heteronormative world.[60] Yet whatever bad faith this figuration implies is secondary to the more interesting development that it allows us to witness in the context of gay liberation's insistence on coming out as a politically valuable act. Mailer's example suggests that the logic of political expressivity that underwrites coming out makes itself available to positions quite remote from—and, indeed, antagonistic to—same-sex desire. Identifying the military-industrial complex with the "oversecurity" of establishment liberalism, both of which in turn epitomize the prison-house of an implausibly hegemonic homosexuality, *The Armies of the Night* sets the stage for the coming-out narrative that *The Prisoner of Sex* exploits: the embrace of a daring and provocative heterosexuality. In *The Prisoner of Sex* Mailer announces his fidelity to straightness not merely as a sober reconciliation to adult sexuality, a putting away of childish things, but as though it were the outcome of a gratifying bout of *consciousness raising*. "The sexual force of a man," Mailer insists against the view that it is merely the "luck of his birth," is "his finest moral product" (*PS*, 45). The "passion to be masculine" (*PS*, 69) acquires an epic stature "in that ubiquitous bisexual world where men and women were as interchangeable as coin and cash" (71), which is to say that the assertion of a manly heterosexuality is less a prerogative for Mailer than a revolutionary act, a strike against "the free market," the "technologizing of sex" (71), and other sins of the liberal state.

It is from this vantage that we can see why, in *The Prisoner of Sex*, the prison functions less as a foil to the technocracy and its "single permissive sexual standard" than as its test laboratory, the leading edge of liberalism's effort to neuter its subjects into a state of uniformity. In prison the "choice not to be" homosexual thus "loses all social support" (*PS*, 170). As evidence of this logic in action, Mailer presents "two affidavits," sworn by prisoners at "the Long Island City Men's House of Detention," detailing a scene in which inmates are required to stand nude, "*pricks to asses*" (*PS*, 163), with the further stipulation that anyone in "this naked line of convicts" who gets "a hard-on" would also get "dispensation" (164). Like Pynchon in *Gravity's Rainbow*, Mailer concludes from this line-up that the custodians of power actively foster and reward homosexual expression, embodied in the "phallus erect" (*PS*, 164), since "the man to get a hard-on would be made on the spot an official favorite, would be incorporated temporarily by the law" (167). "Why else would prison reform never succeed in allowing convicts to be alone with their wives or mistresses" (*PS*, 170), Mailer asks rhetorically, were not "Establishment" (170) committed to equating punishment with forbidding "human life to rise above what is easiest and most routine for it" (178)? "The real journey," he writes, "would be through homosexuality itself" (*PS*, 162).

As with "the journey through the dark" on the prison bus in *Armies of the Night*, the "safety" (*PS*, 163) to be had from the prisoners' public surrender to arousal is no less false than the "single permissive standard." What thus makes a journey through homosexuality real, a path whose terminus is authentic heterosexual self-knowledge, is the confrontation it forces with the prison's effort to make all inmates into "artificial queers" (*PS*, 170) and thus oblivious to "the first knowledge, that the physical love of men and women, insofar as it was untainted by civilization, was the salvation of us all" (141). It is worth recalling that gay liberationists also drew an analogy between coming out and escaping from prison. "Now we are becoming free enough," Wittman argues, "to shed the roles which we've picked up from the institutions which have imprisoned us" (*VG*, 333). Political change, Gay Liberation Front cofounder Martha Shelley writes in terms that Mailer would have appreciated, concerned the effort "to reach the homosexuals entombed in you . . . locked in the prisons of your skulls" (*VG*, 34). Yet while the presumption that "men and women can survive only if they reach the depth of their own sex down within themselves" informs both Mailer's and Shelley's views (*PS*, 147), it is hard to imagine Shelley ceding Mailer's point that the enemy is an "Establishment" that subdues men by compelling them to turn "from the vagina to the anus" (*PS*, 162).

This is only to say that in figuring the coming-out narrative through the conceit of the prison, liberationists vied for rhetorical leverage with radicals who were often opposed to gay and lesbian expression—or who treated such expression not as a means of fighting power but as hegemony's most glaring symptom. The pride Mailer takes in a defiant heterosexuality resurfaces in the work of more than a few of his contemporaries, along with his attitude toward the prison as the training ground for "artificial queers." In *The Book of Daniel* (1971), E. L. Doctorow's novel of a fictive Julius and Ethel Rosenberg told from the perspective of their orphaned son, the salient feature of imprisonment is the severing of the heterosexual union. For Daniel Isaacson, a doctoral student who spends his days in Columbia's Butler library ostensibly working on his thesis but in reality chronicling the fallout from his parents' trial and execution, the chief consequence of the Isaacsons' sacrifice on the altar of the national security state is his own inability to arrive at a sense of legitimate commitment, a concept to which he lacks the most basic access: "How do you spell comit [*sic*]?" he asks.[61] Daniel's fumbling toward commitment, reflected in his troubled marriage to a "child bride" whom he treats to humiliating sexual abuse (6), is given point by the even worse definition of commitment to which his student-radical sister is condemned: institutionalized at the novel's start, she ends it by dying in a sanitarium.

Daniel views this terminus as of a piece with the institutional world of postwar America as he has come to know it: a succession of interlocking disciplinary spaces, from the grade school to the university to the mental hospital, each constructed on the model of the prison. Given over to arbitrary "rules" (168), such institutions are invested in depleting commitment in the positive sense in favor of what Daniel calls "sequence," a sham version of progress that occludes a process close to amnesia, an inability to treat "feelings" as other than "indiscriminate" (160): "Is there nothing good enough to transfix us?" (245). Treating sex with his wife as a series of one-night stands, Daniel links marriage with the impermanence of promiscuity: "If she is truly worth fucking why do I have to fuck her again? . . . The monstrous reader who goes on from one word to the next. The monstrous writer who places one word after another. The monstrous magician" (246). Evoking the "trick," that shibboleth of gay male subculture, the "monstrous" sleight of hand that confers meretricious meaning on transient encounters recalls *Armies of the Night's* academics and their "unassailable logic of the next step" (86). If academics blithely relinquish one commitment for another, Daniel despairs of a world in which seriality affords no more than the *illusion* of choice. In *The Book of Daniel*, where officialdom insists that "everything is elusive" (42), the fetish for "sequence" is a ruse of power: "The world wanted you to forget who you had been and what had happened to you" (125).

Doctorow treats Daniel's capacity for commitment as fatally compromised by his early exposure to the welfare state. Interned at the East Bronx Children's Welfare Shelter during his parents' trial, Daniel encounters a homoerotic dystopia: "There was a lot of homo wrestling. One kid liked to jerk off in the middle of the room where everyone could see him. Once there was an attempted sodomizing" (164). This ambient queerness accompanies an injunction to "perform" in order to get ahead (171): a "challenge," of course, since any skilled performance "without the right attitude, without the right tone, is disastrous in that situation—you end up as some kind of over-articulate fag intellect and you're out in the cold" (170). Captivity by institutions for Doctorow means forcible homosexuality and an equally compulsory familiarity with the closet and its delicate balancing act of self-monitoring masquerade. Daniel has been "perverted by institutions" because those institutions are thoroughly perverted (184). His sense that "all our environments are wrong" (26) derives from the conviction that the same-sex environs of the "city barracks for children" (231), like those of the prison, are contrived to block the formation of durable bonds, specifically the ties that conjugal desire binds.

Hence Daniel's attraction to the "digger" Artie Sternlicht, who exposes the collusion between "corporate liberalism, and George Washington and the fag peace movement" (137). Artie is "probably a champion fucker," a "revolutionary stud" Daniel pictures having sex with his wife and giving her "the right choice, all her rhythm liberated," instead of keeping her "in bondage" (152). The novel dwells at length on such heterosexual liberation. Whereas the Isaacsons "used to make the whole house rock" with their unashamed sex life—"they balled all the time" (42)—prison interdicts their red-blooded lust. Thus, Daniel envisions his parents' final night in jail as "a reconciliation in heat and love and terror, while the jailers fled the corridor and the stones groaned and the bars rattled; and they rippled and spasmed and shook and trembled as if electrocution was something people did together" (282). By way of this erotically charged last meal, Daniel imagines his parents' revenge on the penal state that would forbid the expression of heterosexual desire in the effort to queer its inmates into submission.

One of the key subplots in *The Book of Daniel* turns on using the Isaacson children's trust fund to establish a foundation that, aiding progressive causes, would help retrieve the family name from disgrace. An idea that his sister has originated and that he has resisted ("I'm not ashamed of the name," she rebukes him; "I'm proud of who I am" [80]), Daniel comes finally to embrace the Isaacson Foundation for Revolution. "A foundation," he concludes, is the only thing "worth desiring" (171). In the context of the foundation, which affords Daniel the grounding he has long sought by obliging him to own a name he has long denied, his final act in the novel—leaving the library, now under siege, and "walking out to the Sundial" in the midst of the 1968 Columbia student strike—might be seen as a coming out of the sort that Mailer enacts in *The Prisoner of Sex*. Although the student who urges him out of the library asks in an exasperated tone, "What's the matter with you, don't you know you're liberated?," the question at this point can only be rhetorical. For immediately before this moment, Daniel lets us know what form his liberation takes; at his sister's funeral, he tells us, "I hold my wife's hand. And I think I'm going to be able to cry" (302). The gesture embodies a connection that Daniel has been unable to feel with his wife, attachment to whom now becomes the source of emotional authenticity.

It is helpful to recall Michael Rossman's claim, in *The Wedding within the War*, that during the student movement "'moral commitment' became real" for people like Daniel as never before. The title of Rossman's book suggests why this should be, given its reference to the vows exchanged by a couple in an occupied building during the Columbia strike. Like Mailer, Doctorow structures what we might call the *commitment to commitment* along the lines of the coming-out narrative, but with heterosexual courtship now standing in for gay expression as the means to access authenticity. Like those who came out during gay liberation, Mailer's prisoner and Doctorow's Daniel appear to go through the motions of straight existence. Yet unlike gay liberationists, who move from pretending straightness to embracing homosexuality, Mailer and Doctorow register the shift from ritualistic heterosexuality to a full-bodied experience of it. What is striking about this shift and the political promise it heralds is that it depended on picturing statist anonymity and opacity on the model of queer life at its most purposeless and misdirected. The closet from which the would-be straight radical escaped into a meaningful commitment was a world, as Mailer describes it, "designed precisely to drive men deep into onanism and homosexuality."

While Mailer's and Doctorow's deliberations on the jail are largely vicarious, the logic that informs their account of the queer penitentiary assumes a documentary salience in the writings of Huey Newton, who actually did time and whose favorite parable, we may recall, is Plato's allegory of the cave, which he renames "the story of the cave prisoners" (77). Given the fluidity of real and metaphorical prisons in *Revolutionary Suicide*—"prison is a microcosm of the outside world" (5), Newton maintains—it is revealing that he characterizes the California Penal Colony, where he spent nearly two years, as a "model prison" whose "calm reputation" (270) is owing to the fact that "80 per cent of the prisoners were homosexual, and homosexuals are docile and subservient." This proclivity made it "hard to politicize men who lived largely for the next sexual encounter," according to Newton. "To them, sex was all." But even more to the point, the guards—many of whom "were themselves homosexuals"— used the prisoners' already submissive orientation against them to "undermine their normal yearnings for dignity and freedom." Like the "sequence" that Doctorow's Daniel cannot abide or the "logic of the next step" that Mailer scorns in liberal academics, chance encounters replace the chance for liberation among the prison's queer inmates. If prison ushers in "the reign of homosexual life," it does so because the queen serves as the figurehead for a "system" (271), within and without the prison, imagined to thrive on an opposition between sexual gratification and the risk of commitment, between the immediacy of the flesh and the sustainability necessary for revolution.

That Newton should specify such gratification and immediacy as homoerotic is slightly peculiar, since by his own admission he both enjoyed promiscuity and rejected "bourgeois marriage" as "one more imprisoning experience within the general prison of society" (93). But any common ground between Newton and the gay liberationists, whose similar efforts to overturn the sanctity of the marriage contract were also pursued in the name of freedom, erodes under Newton's acknowledgment that a refusal of marriage by no means equals a refusal of commitment. Indeed, his "inability to make a total commitment" (97) to a single person turns out to be the challenge whose defeat results in the birth of the Black Panther Party, that is, in the "total commitment" to a plurality of people: "We have the closeness and love of family life" (98), Newton writes, "a fighting family that is a vital unit in itself" (100). Such vitality is rooted not only in necessity—"We need a family, because every man and woman deserves the kind of spiritual support and unity a family provides" (100)—but also, and far more strikingly, in a principle of transgression: "Our unity has transformed us to the point where we have not compromised with the system" (98). Newton makes the embrace of family values over into the most defiant stance one can take against oppression, a means of "staying outside the system" by committing oneself to the institution the system values most (100).

Like Mailer's equation of childrearing and emancipation, Newton's encomium to the family shows us why gay liberation's adoption of the rhetoric of authenticity could actually backfire on that movement, or at least reveal an impasse between gay liberation and the New Left at large. For however deep the commitment to commitment may have been among gay liberationists themselves, such an investment never encompassed monogamy or family planning as sufficient or even welcome avenues of personhood. It was perhaps inevitable that the insistence on a reciprocity between institutions and their commitments, an insistence often coupled in the 1960s with an esteem for face-to-face oaths, would draw radicals to the marriage vow, the definitive interpersonal pledge. If, as Rossman insists, "we must take care that the Wedding go on within the War" (25), the reason is that the emblematic struggle of Sixties radicals was to restore substance to merely ceremonial forms. It is fitting that *The Wedding within the War* itself ends with Rossman greeting the arrival of his newborn. As Seale and Mailer confirm, the birth announcement serves as the objective correlative for a realness founded on resistance rather than concession to an uncommitted life nowhere so sterile as in the specter of a childless existence. But the "I do" of the marriage ceremony was simply not in the vocabulary of the Sixties gay radicals, however strenuously they sought to break free of the inconsequence that gay life connoted. Despite the efforts of gay liberationists to reconcile their aims with the broader New Left, they would always find themselves uninvited to the latter's weddings.

From Impression Management to Expressive Authenticity

Fragile Institutions and Processed Goods

Though Berkeley's faculty on the whole had mixed feelings about the Free Speech Movement, a select group was unequivocally hostile to the student radicals. What was notable about this antipathy, aside from the nontrivial fact that many of the professors in question were sociologists, is that some of them had built their careers in part on a certain appeal to progressive dissent. Though FSM adversary Seymour Lipset may have been (in Hal Draper's phrase) "an academic entrepreneur of notable talent," his colleagues Nathan Glazer and Lewis Feuer had published work vital to the New Left at its founding.[1] Glazer coauthored *The Lonely Crowd* (1950), and Feuer edited *Karl Marx and Friedrich Engels: Basic Writings on Politics and Philosophy* (1959), an anthology that was required reading for campus activists. Yet both men, following many of their peers in the shift from radicalism to conservatism, wrote books at the end of the 1960s that gave the student movement most of the credit for their political conversion.

However self-serving these books may have been, Feuer's *The Conflict of Generations* (1969) and Glazer's *Remembering the Answers* (1970) were as interested in settling old scores as in offering a defense, along traditional disciplinary lines, of a school culture threatened by what Feuer called the "authoritarianism of the student intellectuals."[2] Yet the inescapable irony of these rearguard apologies for the school was that neither Feuer nor Glazer held any real brief for disciplinary traditions. Feuer was as much a philosopher as a social scientist, and Glazer (like his mentor David Riesman) fit uneasily in the harness of mainstream sociology. In strictly disciplinary terms, these thinkers steered a course far removed from the hard-science aspirations of quantitative sociologists and the equally self-enclosing disciplinary impulses associated with Parsonian theory. As Riesman points out in a 1959 essay, "The sociologist is often at a loss to say clearly what it is that he does, what it is that distinguishes him from other academic people."[3] This generic blurriness frustrates what he calls the "search" for "unequivocal identity" that he observes among his students, for whom he considers it "tempting to provide the symbols of belongingness by insistence on a single pattern of methodology" ("AC," 163).

Tempting though it may have been, this was a lure he refused. Riesman suggests that the associative nature of modernity, with its lack of unifying norms and its drift toward anomie, is reflected in the epistemological curvature of sociology as a discipline. As an instance and not merely an analysis of gesell-schaft, sociology thus denies Riesman's students the satisfactions of together-ness. In another 1959 essay, Riesman argued against the view that the sexual precocity allegedly rife among college students marked a decline of moral stan-dards, suggesting instead that "routinization is too quickly reached" by the ten-dency of the young to pair off in "steady relationships, . . . with stability quickly achieved."[4] For Riesman, the campus does not promote enough promiscuity. Noting that "compartmentalizations remain very important in our culture in spite of greater freedom and permissiveness" ("PSR," 216), he ascribes the "routinization" of gender roles to the college's "implicit statements about ideas as 'feminine' or 'masculine'—statements which are carried in the language or texture of the discipline, and in the tone and attitudes of its professors" ("PSR," 215). If the school helps implement gender roles, then "the problem remains of providing young people with . . . a moratorium in which their identity can be at large and open and various" ("PSR," 217).

The student-teacher relation epitomizes what Riesman conceives as the si-multaneous inertia and dynamism of the school. Riesman singles out "the col-lege professor who devotes himself uninterruptedly to his students" and who, as a result of this undue devotion to the young, "is likely to end up either very dry or very damp. As he ages, while of course his students do not, he may have less and less to give them in terms of intellectual leadership and grasp of the world we live in" ("AC," 98). As a model of how not to teach, Riesman's "very dry or very damp" professor fails to see that the crucial relation the school transmits is not harmony but conflict, the model of which Riesman perceives in cross-generational antagonism. In the 1968 book *The Academic Revolution* (coauthored with Christopher Jencks), Riesman sees the structure of conflict as permanent ("the lack of intimacy and harmony between young and old is hardly a twentieth-century novelty") at the same time as he understands the content of that conflict to be impermanent (since newer generations with different values always supplant their predecessors).⁵ In *The Conflict of Generations*, Feuer likewise notes "the de-authorization of the old out of which every student movement is born."⁶

Like the ship of Theseus, the school's identity from one generation to another depends on a continual replacement of personnel, and the professor who "ages" in place while his clientele perpetually turns over has missed the intellectual boat. The "academic revolution" of Riesman and Jencks's title refers not only to the professionalization of disciplines after 1945, then, but also to the business as usual of the university. For this reason Glazer likens the student revolt to the "predictable . . . departmentalization" that brought "the great experiments in liberal education of the 1920s and 1930s . . . to a close."⁷ In their desire for what Riesman calls "unequivocal identity," student radicals join forces with administrators and trustees in trying to set mission statements and objectives. "Neither the right of the university to determine its nature," Glazer argues, "nor to determine the conditions that foster it was respected by the FSM." Rejecting the academic's opinion that determination is a project best left deferred, the FSM "had decided to impose its views as to what was important on the university and accept no limits on the means it would use to compel the university to accept its views" (111).

The tension between the tenured professoriat and the doctrine of impermanence it chiefly values forms a staple of the academic style whose vicissitudes during the 1950s and 1960s the previous chapters have somewhat compulsively pursued. The defense of sociology as an antisystemic endeavor, a method that eschews method, recalls the similar repudiation of "system" in postwar literary criticism, just as Riesman's effort to turn his students away from the "unequivocal" toward the "various" evokes English 1's ideal of instrumental subjectivity. Appealing as it may be to write off their comments on the college as a willful blindness to the happy conditions that enable their privileging of the rootless academic, I argue that the postwar sociologists offer more than hypocrisy regarding the challenge they infer from the loose parameters of their discipline. And I want to consider the challenge in turn that this inference offers to some of the New Left's basic assumptions. Our own challenge consists in differentiating the views of sociologists and student radicals in light of their shared vocabulary. In observing that "colleges will continue to turn out people capable of exploiting their own and others' 'needs' on behalf of an endless race of production and consumption," Riesman could be channeling Tom Hayden or Herbert Marcuse.[8] Likewise, when Glazer (citing his colleague Erving Goffman's work on mental hospitals) observes that "any institution that must process large numbers of people tends to develop an institutional style in doing so" (101), he sounds like Mario Savio, who saw the college precisely as a processing plant, "a factory that turns out a certain product needed by industry or government."[9]

Despite the obvious overlap of their concerns, what separated postwar sociologists from the student radicals whom they frequently taught was a series of assumptions about the social world that did not translate readily to the culture of the New Left. Whereas Riesman admits in *The Academic Revolution* that he and his coauthor "are ambivalent or uncertain about many issues," which "leads to a good deal of irony" (xiii), the student Left opposed irony and detachment as insufficiently outraged (and thus more or less complicit) responses to the moral failings of the national security state. Yet as much as it names the affect central to the professoriat, Riesman's was not an irony of detachment. Detachment was precisely what the permeability of modern institutions revoked. "In an industrially advanced society," Glazer writes, "change is continuous," and "no solution is ever complete or final, and consequently there is no alternative to bureaucracies, administrators, and experts" (178). Far from conceiving of change as an unalloyed virtue, the sociologists were aware of how frequently it served to justify ever more manipulative programs of adjustment and accommodation. "It is possible," Glazer observes of Berkeley, "that this huge and on the whole practically oriented university has no basis on which to set any standards" (97). The absence of standards accounts in Glazer's view for the revolt of the students, who refuse the opaque mandate that is the academic's occupational hazard. Because that mandate dictates that we must have standards but that we cannot know in advance what they are, "intellectual work is never done," according to Riesman, "and it is certainly never done to one's own satisfaction" ("AC," 161).

This perpetual dissatisfaction with the voluntary society reverses the high praise Seymour Lipset (Glazer's Berkeley colleague) and Clark Kerr (Berkeley's former chancellor) conferred on voluntarism as a hallmark of the multiversity. For these thinkers, as suggested earlier, the university's elective structure, in creating a space where all acts and roles would be freely chosen, embodied the ideal of liberal pluralism. If this vision was unrecognizable to figures like Riesman and Glazer, it was not because they believed that the university was other than voluntary but because they did not concede a strict opposition between voluntary and compulsory acts. As their work sought to demonstrate, no hardened lines could be sustained between these poles in regard to the operation of power. In his critique of FSM, Glazer argues that the students "do not see that the power to regulate on the basis of standards appropriate to a university also increases the potential scope of their activity and protects them from the civil arm." Glazer treats institutional power as what Foucault would call *productive*, generating as well as constraining possibilities for action: "It is much easier to hold a meeting on the Berkeley campus than on the city streets" (97). Unlike Foucault, however, neither Glazer nor Riesman sees the power of institutions like the school as particularly strong, especially when compared to what Glazer calls "the involuntary organization" of "the state" (121).

The defining feature of contemporary society, Glazer argues, is the absence of "bound institutions" whose "limits and bonds" can be "burst." "The tension between inside and outside" what he calls "the system" has "relaxed" or "loosened," giving rise to "more interchange between those inside the system and those outside" (55). Riesman and Jencks specify their choice "to speak of established institutions, not of 'the establishment,'" because they decline "to see America as ruled by an interlocking directorate" (11) even as they acknowledge "the hegemony of institutions" (12). Institutional America in the sociologists' view is weakly rather than strongly hegemonic. Rather than "interlocking" with the smooth functionalist precision envisioned by Foucault (or by C. Wright Mills, the target of Riesman and Jencks's aside), the gears of the social machinery have slipped their bearings. And the fact that institutions don't know their own bounds threatens to dismantle what Glazer calls the already "fragile thing" that is "organized society" (109). The result is an endless series of territorial skirmishes—or, according to Glazer observing campus unrest, a perpetual civil war.

We might refine the contrast between the sociologist's and the radical's view of the social machine by looking at Glazer's example, adopted from Goffman, of the mental hospital, which "processes all those who come into contact with it in specific ways," as "any institution must" (101). "Processing" recalls the FSM's chief complaint about Berkeley's mission, but Glazer and Goffman give it a meaning somewhat different from Mario Savio's. Midcentury sociology was uninterested in the solution to processing that Savio and others demanded. Juxtaposed to FSM activist Michael Rossman's plea that "it must stop," we find Glazer's apologetic admission that "any institution must." Whereas radicals insisted on the need of the processed to undo their own manipulation, Glazer claims that "processing" is best understood as forming persons rather than undoing them. And if processing is just a synonym for the making of persons, the question for the sociologist is whether the processing is good or bad.

"Whether a particular total institution acts as a good or bad force in civil society," Goffman writes in *Asylums* (1961), "force it will have." As "forcing houses for changing persons," each of the "total institutions" that Goffman's book surveys "is a natural experiment on what can be done to the self."[10] Though he is well aware that institutions manipulate persons, Goffman does not share the New Left view that they turn persons into objects. Institutions transform persons into other kinds of persons. Like Glazer, for whom the student activist mistakes the "voluntary organization" of the university for the "involuntary" institution of the state, Goffman is leery of drawing spurious analogies between distinctive institutions. "A university is a place to pick up your mail," Goffman told his student Gary Marx.[11] Reminiscent of Clark Kerr's definition of the multiversity as a "series" of buildings "held together by a central heating system," Goffman's statement reflects the professorial detachment that FSM despised.[12]

Yet this is not to say that Goffman believes institutions as unlike as the school and the prison have nothing in common. His argument is that the practices they share will have importantly different consequences based on the degree to which membership in them is elective or compulsory. In Goffman's well-known view, all institutions function as dramaturgical spaces, organized around the performance of ritualized roles and expectations. If total institutions sanction the bare minimum of deviance from social roles, even this enjoinder can be thwarted by the inmate who manages to put "a distance" between himself and "the attachment the inmate is expected to manifest to his iron home" (*A*, xiv). This is the reason that Goffman calls the "social reality in a total institution . . . precarious[:] . . . the more profound the drama of difference between staff and inmate, the more incompatible the show becomes with the civilian repertoire of the players, and the more vulnerable to it" (*A*, 111).

The use of his infamous dramatic conceit in the analysis of the total institution raises a striking point about Goffman's approach to that institution's shortcomings. Though he hardly ignores the total institution's questionable objectifying practices, Goffman's view of what such objectification denies to inmates is rather different from the account to be found in the antipsychiatry movement with which his writings on the asylum are often grouped. "In the total institution of the 'mental' hospital," R. D. Laing writes in *The Politics of Experience* (1967), the individual is "invalidated as a human being."[13] Yet where Laing speaks in the idiom of "alienation" (13) to assert that the asylum poses a threat to "authentic possibilities" (xv), Goffman assumes that the total institution deprives persons not of their "true selves" (xv), as Laing would say, but rather of their ability to execute the roles they would like to present to the world. In fact, the worst thing about the total institution is its willful "disruption of the usual relationship between the individual actor and his acts" (*A*, 35). The "loss of identity equipment" that occurs on admission to the asylum is intended to "prevent the individual from presenting his usual image of himself to others" (*A*, 21). And this drastic minimizing of the props and tricks of the individual's "presenting culture" corresponds to an equally severe reduction in the range of roles the inmate is permitted to enact (*A*, 4). What is denied in the total institution is not the individual's essence but rather the opportunity to improvise that persons enjoy in their "home world" (*A*, 67). Defining autonomy as the access a person gains or loses to the "informational preserve regarding self" (*A*, 23), Goffman passes judgment less on the institution's reification of persons than on the specific form it takes: a blanket injunction against role-playing.

The claim about the nature of personhood advanced in Goffman, we should observe, inverts the account of personhood as core identity privileged by the New Social Movements. If the New Left conceived of persons as essences whose expression was thwarted by the institutions that confined and deformed them, the postwar sociologists figured personhood as both the object of processing in particular (in the sense that an institution channels its members along specific paths) and the result of *process* in the abstract. "The individual" is "a stance-taking entity," Goffman avows, "a something that takes up a position somewhere between identification with an organization and opposition to it, and is ready at the slightest pressure to regain its balance by shifting its involvement in either direction. It is thus *against something* that the self can emerge" (*A*, 320). That is an unusually indefinite definition of the self, an imprecision that derives in no small measure from the reiteration of the word "something." Goffman assumes a lack of specificity worthy of Robert Frost because, like Frost, he owes his central propositions about the self to the pragmatist tradition.

This was the lineage Goffman's teacher Herbert Blumer, the originator of "symbolic interactionism," explicitly claimed for that method by way of George Herbert Mead. And like Mead, who was equally dubious of essences, postwar sociologists shared a belief in the process-centered self. Their work repeatedly imagined identity as contingent on unstable interactions. In *Stigma* (1963), Goffman calls this "the infinite regress of mutual consideration that Meadian social psychology teaches how to begin but not how to terminate."[14] "I do not myself assume," Riesman writes in a 1967 essay, "that there exists a basic human nature, potentially benign, which needs only to be liberated. But the perhaps characteristic fear of being fenced in may lead many Americans to overemphasize the despotism of socialization."[15] This claim accords with Goffman's point that even the most despotic total institution never wholly realizes the "despotism" to which it aspires. Given its "permeability" (*A*, 119) by the outside world, "neither the stripping processes nor the reorganizing processes" the asylum uses to recast individuals "seem to have a lasting effect" (71).

This is a less optimistic conclusion than it seems, for Goffman maintains that just as total institutions are less all-encompassing than they appear, so open institutions are less elective than we assume. Goffman and his colleagues were acutely aware that strong constraints on interactions predominated outside the asylum's walls. Thus, he cautions in *The Presentation of Self in Everyday Life* that the modern trend toward informality should not be mistaken for a liberalization of society itself. What he discovered in postwar culture was a collapse of the traditional distinction between "front" and "backstage" such that all social space (including those precincts of private life imagined as inviolate) had become a proscenium for a performing self who was now always on call.[16] Even the recital of casualness required a "bureaucratization of the spirit"—the hard labor persons must continually undertake to give their roles "expressive coherence" (*EL*, 56). Likewise, responding to the perception that the affluent society made it imperative for its members to treat identity as a continual dress rehearsal, Riesman argued that the practitioners of such self-staging—identified in *The Lonely Crowd* with the notorious label of "other-directed people"—had "an exceptional sensitivity to the actions and wishes of others," whom they treated less as equals than as audiences.[17] As a result of these changeable spectators, "the other-directed person tends to become merely his succession of roles and encounters" (*LC*, 139). Yet whatever their misgivings about the pressurized performances in midcentury culture, none of these sociologists took the view that the self existed somewhere apart from its roles.

In *Symbolic Interactionism* (1967), Blumer thus refuted the notion that social interaction is "merely a means or a setting for the release of human conduct" because he denied that the self came endowed with "pre-existing factors" that required "expression."[18] And Goffman considered it a mistake to imagine that persons had authentic selves that drove their performances, when in fact the reverse was the case: "A correctly staged and performed scene leads the audience to impute a self to a performed character, but this imputation—this self—is a *product* of a scene that comes off, and is not a *cause* of it" (*EL*, 252). Indeed, far from grounding a liberationist politics, Goffman argued, the mistake of treating the self as cause rather than effect was itself a powerful ruse of social control. The universal requirement to "express possession of the standard subjective self" (*S*, 116) signals the tyranny of what Goffman provocatively calls "the expressive order."[19] That a person "cathects his face" (*IR*, 6) serves to "make of every man his own jailer; this is a fundamental social constraint even though each man may like his cell" (10). His disdain for the "expressive order" explains Goffman's admiration for the "discreditable" actor capable of "dividing the world" (*S*, 95) into various segments and parceling the "information" available about himself across discrete audiences. "If role and audience segregation is well managed," Goffman writes, "he can quite handily sustain different selves and can to a degree claim to be no longer something that he was" (*S*, 63). If impression management is risk management, the canny social actor spreads out the liability of a devalued social identity by assuming not one essential but many improvised roles.

It should be obvious from these examples that postwar sociologists had little interest in stigmatizing the instrumentalist nature of performed identity as a political demerit and even less interest in mobilizing authentic identity as a political virtue. Midcentury sociology did not confront the problem of a compromised autonomy by appealing to an inner reality or an individual's rightfully self-determined essence.[20] In response to the notion of autonomy as what Laing called "the search . . . for what we have all lost" (34), the sociologist answered that there was nothing to be found in even the deepest excavation of the self's interior. The social performance went all the way down. Thus, the performing self's authenticity or lack thereof was incidental to Goffman, who considered performance an "amoral issue" (*EL*, 251). The problem with performance was not its artfulness but its restrictiveness. The authoritarian currents that had seemingly ebbed in the wake of society's easement of status distinctions resurfaced in the limits the "expressive order" placed on both the number of roles it allowed persons to play and the amount of improvisation it permitted within those roles.

Like Goffman, Riesman had no ethical stake in the dichotomy of role and reality and was less interested in role-playing as a problem in itself than in the coercion embedded in the outwardly liberating openness of the affluent society and its "cult of effortlessness" (*LC*, 157). In reference to the blurring of work and leisure signified by the ubiquity of casual clothing, Riesman writes that "most men today simply do not know how to change roles, let alone mark the change by proper costuming" (*LC*, 157), and contrasts this confusion of dramatic spaces with the inner-directed man's capacity to "put on whatever mask he cares to" (158). It is not performance that presents a crisis for autonomy in other-directed society; it is instead the inability to choose which disguise one would like to assume. "For us, at any rate," Riesman notes in "Some Observations on Changes in Leisure Attitudes" (1952), "there is nothing easy about effortlessness."[21]

Method Acting's Natural Motives

In *Mythologies* (1957), the inaugural text of modern semiotics, Roland Barthes dissects the "capillary meanings" of Joseph Mankiewicz's *Julius Caesar* (1953) and concludes that various "signs" deployed by the film make "legible" particular identifications: forelocks mean "Roman-ness"; sweat on the face means "moral feeling."[22] Uneasy with this coding, since it "remains on the surface, but does not for all that give up the attempt to pass itself off as depth," Barthes nonetheless takes the sword-and-sandal epic as the occasion for reflecting on "an ethic of signs" (28). Committed neither to the "total artifice" of the sign ("as in the Chinese theatre, where a flag on its own signifies a regiment") nor to the "simple reality" of the sign (as in "the art of Stanislavski," for whom a sign, "revealing an internal, a hidden facet," is "indicative of a moment in time, no longer of a concept"), the Hollywood film prefers "the intermediate sign," and this choice results in "the degraded spectacle" (28) that we see in Mankiewicz's on-screen rendering, and rending, of Shakespeare's play.

There are no doubt many points to quarrel with in Barthes's ethic of signs, not the least of which is his peculiar charge that Mankiewicz's film dishonors the spirit of a Shakespearean original whose own commitment to reality is rather sketchy. But one way to read Barthes's commentary productively is to note that what he is faulting is the Hollywood product's too-successful execution of conventional realism, its ability to quell its viewers' doubts that these conventions are anything other than the real thing. Authentic realism would seem to inhere for Barthes in a more proper alignment of surface and depth, where the elements on the body's surface could be understood as pointing to internal experience or emotional states rather than confirming a superficial concept (a cliché "Roman-ness"). In this regard it is telling that Barthes singles out Marlon Brando's "naturally Latin forehead" as dressed with the one "fringed" hairdo in *Julius Caesar* that "impresses us and does not make us laugh" (27). For in addition to his "plausible" (26) Mediterranean physiognomy, Brando is the iconic practitioner of Method acting, the American remake of "the art of Stanislavski."

Barthes's praise of both Stanislavski and Brando for their ability to divorce the sign from concept shares in a certain wariness, originating in twentieth-century dramatic theory but not exclusive to it, toward the referentially ambiguous signage that postwar sociology made its privileged topic. The ethic of signs that Barthes attributes to Stanislavski entails an antisymbolic naturalism, a relation to signs that (unlike the conventional realism of narrative cinema) does not rely on the beholder's willingness to treat gestures and actions as symbols that require decoding. Discarding the layers of apprehension that the sociologist interposes between persons and their surroundings, Stanislavski's actors pursue a stance akin to the one favored by New Left activists: what is hidden is destined for expressive exposure, and the actor's job is to rid a performance of all stage tricks and gimmicks in order to clear the way for revealing. Whereas the role obliges Stanislavski's actor "to crystallize its essence" and distill the "quintessence of its contents," the "symbol" by contrast aims to "synthesize feelings and life."[23]

Stanislavski's is an antitheatrical theater. Replacing a drama of symbol with a drama of quintessence, it refuses the indirection of the conventional stage in favor of the unmediated expression of what Barthes calls "simple reality." Such antitheatricality informed the work of Stanislavski's American adapters. "The theatre was created to tell people the truth about life," Stella Adler lectured her students, adopting a view that blithely contradicted the normative identification of drama with artifice.[24] Whereas sociologists saw performance as a means to fashion claims about the improvisational nature of modern authority, the Method's pioneers saw performance as an end in itself. Against Goffman's notion of "self" as "*product*," Method teachers sought to ground identity less in a shifting series of contexts than in a bounded and embodied individualism. The goal of the Method was to instill in its practitioners an awareness of their own coherence across time, a prospect on which the sociologists had cast some doubt. In *An Actor Prepares* (1936), Stanislavski called this sense of coherence "emotion memory," and while his successors were divided over the term's interpretation, they agreed that both emotions and memory were sacrosanct.[25] "You can borrow clothing, a *watch*, things of all sorts, but you cannot take *feelings* away from another person," Stanislavski declared. "My feelings are inalienably mine, and yours belong to you in the same way" (191).

In addition to sharing Stanislavski's view that acting could achieve uniqueness by virtue of an actor's sole ownership of her feelings, the Method's founders—Adler, Lee Strasberg, Sanford Meisner, Robert Lewis—saw performance as capable of attaining an authenticity that sheer self-identity could not produce. Where sociology's focus on impression management raised the question of the degree to which we perform according to the opinion we want others to have of us, the Method appeared to resolve this question by claiming that the inner truth of a performance mattered more to an actor than any audience attending to it. "The basic problem for the actor is not how he deals with his material in terms of his audience," Strasberg observed, "but how he begins to make his material alive to himself."[26] Confirming the revolt against theatricality as a revolt against entrapment by the audience, Stanislavski's 1898 production of *The Seagull* opened on a stage where the actors sat with their backs to the house.

It is no small irony that the triumph of Method acting has had the effect of turning into formula what its creators understood as a dismantling of theatrical conventions. Yet this tension existed from the Method's beginning. Just as the Method exalted authenticity in performance, so the deeply contentious history of its founding generation, all of whose members eventually broke with one another, distilled to a contest over authenticity itself. From the moment Adler denounced Lee Strasberg's "misusing" of Stanislavski in front of their fellow Group Theatre members, the Method would foster in its adherents a perpetual incentive to fix its truth value.[27] "Most Method teaching is corrupt," Elia Kazan told Paul Gray in 1964. This debasement flowed from its having been left to its mercenary teachers, who "become showhorses of authority in order to establish the reputation necessary to draw students" ("SA," 57).

Kazan's appraisal reveals the primacy the Method conferred on the school as its theater of operations. In "Stanislavski and America" (1964), Gray noted that the "success of the Studio," supervised by Strasberg, "was soon followed by Method schools" headed by "Adler, Meisner, [Paul] Mann, and [Joseph]

Anthony," who had by 1956 "flooded the field with actors all trained in varying degrees and shadings of the Method" ("SA," 44). "A cult had been formed," as Gray suggests, "not of Stanislavski, . . . not even of Strasberg—just of something called the Method" ("SA," 51). In Gray's account, the Method had acquired the sort of charismatic authority that sociologists from Weber to Claude Lefort have observed in bureaucracies. If sociologists like Riesman and Glazer were leery of ascribing a method to their discipline, the "master teachers," as Foster Hirsch calls the Method's founders, "passed on to their students" both "a deep regard for the actor's art" and a strenuous fidelity to technique.[28]

In fact, the production of authenticity demanded instruction in not just one but many methods, from traditional voice training to the psychoanalysis that Strasberg recommended to his students. "Although our actors are in the main experienced," Actors Workshop founder Paul Mann told Richard Schechner in 1964, "we recognize the need for constant study."[29] For Mann and his colleagues, there was no contradiction between "being *natural*" (88) and aspiring "to regularize and standardize actor training" (95). And like Kazan's, Mann's target was less bad acting than bad schooling: "It's terrible to see gifted artist-teachers become charlatans because they have to support a physical plant by enrolling enough students to pay the bills" (85). In place of such "an idiotically competitive and chaotic set-up" (95), Mann proposed "full-time professional schools" with "a four-year course" (85). The way to save the Method from the internecine struggles of artist-teachers was to give it the structure of a university discipline.

Of course, not even the treatment of acting as an undergraduate major could satisfy the need for constant study that the Method required. Proponents of the Method thus adopted a pedagogy like that of B. F. Skinner, in whose *Walden Two* we find a similar disgust with the business as usual of teaching and the promise of an "education" that "goes on forever."[30] As we have seen, Skinner's utopia promoted a ceaseless experimentalism in reaction to the finite experimentalism of the college. And just as Walden Two enabled its members to carry on "the experiment with your own life," so the Method's practitioners shared Skinner's view that one's own life was the ideal subject matter for research.[31] The student of the Method, Charles McGaw notes in *Acting Is Believing* (1955), "will become involved in a process that may be described as *an exploration of yourself*."[32] Much of the Method's rhetoric appears to have been lifted from Skinner's midcentury renovation of behaviorism, which aimed to ground psychic events in the measurable reality of the sensory environment. Joseph Roach has shown the extent to which Stanislavski relied on Pavlov's theory of conditioning in the design of his system.[33] We might say that in adapting Stanislavski for the American context, the Method derived its performance vocabulary from an equally homegrown behaviorism.

The Method's advocates were drawn in particular to behaviorism's transposing of cause and effect in matters of expression. Skinner rejected as "prescientific" the belief that "inner" motivation was "responsible for the behavior of the external biological organism."[34] "Emotions," he insisted, "are not causes."[35] And while this claim suggests a continuity between Skinner's behaviorism and symbolic interactionism, which also reversed the intuitive account of cause and effect in regard to subjectivity, Skinner's goal was not to deny causality but to relocate it from the hopelessly fuzzy domain of "consciousness" to the body at large. Embracing this logic, Actors Studio cofounder Robert Lewis considered it "a mistake to wait to act until you feel," arguing that "you must act and feeling will come."[36] And Adler pronounced to her students, "Feeling comes from doing" (93). Method teachers shared a Skinnerian belief in physiological authenticity. The body would reveal its secrets once enough pressure was applied, in the form of drills or other forms of conditioning, to soften the boundary between inner life and outer world. "You do exercises," Sanford Meisner told his students, "to train yourself to follow the truth."[37]

"An all-or-none subject matter lends itself only to primitive forms of description," Skinner writes. "It is a great advantage to suppose instead that the *probability* that a response will occur ranges between these all-or-none extremes."[38] Whereas behaviorism encourages us to see a likeness between "conditioned reflexes" and the conditional tense, the Method places this verb form at the center of its body language. Stanislavski thus describes the "peculiar quality" of the word "'if' . . . as a lever to lift us out of the world of actuality into the world of imagination" and singles out its importance for producing an "inner stimulus" (49): "With this special quality of *if*, nobody obliges you to believe or disbelieve anything. The secret of *if* lies first of all in the fact that it does not use fear or force, or make the artist do anything. On the contrary it reassures him through its honesty, and encourages him to have confidence in a supposed situation" (50). "If" statements allow Stanislavski's actors to avoid the all-or-none choice between reality and falsity by orienting them instead to the "honesty" of *suppositions*. Yet even more provocative than this elevation of persuasiveness over actuality is the implication that the Method is understood to induce a reorganization of the performer's very psyche. Method actors are thus most successful when they "achieve such a similarity to life that it is easy to believe in what you are doing" (57), when, in short, they manage to convince themselves of their authenticity.

"The Method," according to David Savran, "attempts to foreclose the endless chain of deferral that constitutes theatrical performance based on a written text by denying the actor's contingency."[39] Yet in Method discourse, the greatest contingency the actor faces is not from the playwright but from the audience. The disdain for the audience found among the Method's practitioners mirrors their critique of Method pedagogy. "Enrolling enough students to pay the bills," as Paul Mann says, is no more conducive to the teaching of acting than a full house is to the execution of a successful role. For Goffman, the audience is the key institution of contemporary life, since its continuing (and continually shifting) presence compels the self to make a good impression. The school functions in Method discourse as a means of expelling the audience from consideration, since (unlike the commercial theater) it allows for both failed and successful experiments. And the chief lesson the Method's schools teach is to act as if no one is there. Strasberg's "Private Moment" exercises were designed to foster just such inattention. Here is Paul Gray on a "well-known Actors Studio improvisation": "Enter two actors, one male, one female, both dressed in abbreviated attire. One property—talcum powder. Action—they powder each other, oblivious to their audience, for nearly a half-hour" ("SA," 49). Strasberg insisted on a shameless expression designed to "release the actor," as Hirsch claims, "from any obligation . . . to an audience."[40]

"The interpenetration of the formerly fairly discrete fields of theater studies and the social sciences," Marvin Carlson notes in an analysis of the rise of performance studies since the1960s, "has not been without cost."[41] That cost has been the adoption by performance studies of the "resistance to theatricality" that Carlson attributes to the social scientist's "negative association of theatricality with rigidity and empty repetition."[42] Though Carlson is right about the prevalence of an antitheatrical bias in postwar culture, he is mistaken about its provenance. It was not sociology but rather the acting profession that found theatricality wanting. Whereas teachers like Adler urged their students to turn the "job" of acting into the search for essence (144), a "tearing open of the truth" (155), teachers like Goffman were inclined to imagine that no deeper motive impelled a social actor than the desire to sustain a well-constructed front.

This is the reason that Riesman speaks of a "moratorium" in which "identity can be at large and open and various": identity is always a fugitive substance in the sociologist's view not because it hides within the self but because it has no reality aside from its social entailments. The idea that identity ought to be "various" is no less a utopian conceit than the Method's idea that it should be recoverable at the self's core. But Riesman's utopianism is of less interest than the specific shape it takes. If the notion of an identity at large suggests a vaguely criminal idea, the moratorium opens an idyllic window in the individual's career when the refusal of the demands of what Goffman calls the "expressive order" do not carry the usual risks or penalties. I next turn to Patricia Highsmith's *The Talented Mr. Ripley* (1955), a text whose effort to flout the demand for motive that Method teachers make central to their account of identity results in its author's refusal to hold her unlawful protagonist accountable for the very bad acts he performs.

Patricia Highsmith's Method

In Patricia Highsmith's "The Middle-Class Housewife," one of the stories in her *Little Tales of Misogyny* (1975), Pamela Thorpe attends a "Women's Lib rally, . . . mainly to amuse herself," only to learn that she dislikes "what the younger generation had to say."[43] In reply to a call for "the abolition of alimony," Pamela protests that such a move will "destroy a woman's *meal ticket*," and though she immediately realizes that this is an "unfortunate phrase," its effect is irreparable. The room turns "nasty and hostile," with "armies . . . ranging themselves in groups" and making a "din that resembled the loud cackling of hens" (46). Because "many of the women had their shopping bags," the combatants hurl their purchased foodstuffs, in addition to "hymnals" (the rally takes place in a church) and "a sturdy faldstool" that serves as Pamela's projectile of choice. Despite ducking "in time to avoid being hit by a cabbage," Pamela succumbs to a "tin of baked beans" that, hitting her "smack in the right temple," kills her "within a few seconds." Thus the story ends, with her "assailant . . . never identified" (47).

It would not be untoward to identify this slender vignette's sexist conceits about female unreason, and its generally dim view of female collectivity, with Highsmith's own violent antagonism toward "Women's Lib" and the other "silly protest movements" (45) that shaped the era during which she wrote much of her fiction. Even were this story only satiric, it remains the case that Highsmith conducts her satire through a layering of stereotypes with little to suggest that these various parcels of conventional wisdom about how women behave (like a gaggle of "hens," like perpetual shoppers, like a "mob" [46]) are meant to refute one another. The pleasure Highsmith takes in the stereotype is a feature of her work that readers have found hard to recuperate for a progressive agenda. Consider the most prominent example: *The Talented Mr. Ripley* appears to revel in stereotypes of gay male villainy that a homophobic world has long presupposed. Given its author's penchant for equating homoerotic and homicidal tendencies, one might reasonably ask whether this book can be rehabilitated for gay studies and (more to the point) what such rehabilitation would confer.

If we look to Highsmith's personal views, the reply to such concerns does not appear promising. Her one-time lover Marijane Meaker describes Highsmith's "hatred of all Jews" as "an obsessive-compulsive disorder."[44] Her biographer Andrew Wilson also portrays Highsmith as woefully benighted, her politically incorrect views hardening over time. "When Highsmith was questioned about her attitude toward women," Wilson notes, "she confessed that she loathed the feminist movement."[45] Readings of *The Talented Mr. Ripley* address these uncomfortable facts about its author by positioning Highsmith as either symptomatic of the Fifties repression of sexual nonconformity or as queer *avant la lettre*, having preemptively dispatched the normalizing pieties of contemporary identity politics. The first approach submits the novel to the Whiggish narrative that chronicles our progress from a repressive to an open society for gays and lesbians. The second does not place the book in history at all. But the anachronistic "queering" of Highsmith has one advantage over the Whiggish view. Its acknowledgment of her preference for the bad guy over a yet-to-be-conceived "good gay" at least takes note of her delight in Tom's exploits and her insistence that readers likewise root for his getting away with murder. Critics who claim that Highsmith replicates Cold War culture's demonizing of the sexual other can hardly square this aspect of her novel with that charge.

The effort to parse Highsmith's intentions is further complicated by her work's singular hostility to explanations. Though she occupies that subliterary ghetto of genre fiction known as "suspense," it is one of the peculiarities of Highsmith's work that it marshals the paranoid structure of detective fiction while perennially deferring the moment of exposure. Her novels are distinctive less as mysteries than for what sorry specimens of the genre they make. This shortcoming owes a great deal to their habit of denying their readers a verifiable motive. "The 'who-dunnit,'" Highsmith confessed, was "definitely not my forte."[46] Such an escape clause is necessitated by the fact that she wrote formula novels most formulaic in their reliance on parallel but discrete events and unrelated phenomena. "Two crimes are strikingly similar," she writes of the "germ" for *The Blunderer* (1954), "though the people who commit them do not know each other" (*PW*, 2). That sentence appears in *Plotting and Writing Suspense Fiction*, a book whose self-canceling lessons rank it among the least helpful manuals ever composed: "I see my characters and the setting, the atmosphere, and what happens in the first third or quarter of a book, let's say, and usually the last quarter, but there is apt to be a foggy spot three-quarters of the way through" (*PW*, 53). Highsmith comes close to asserting here that she knows how to establish both exposition and denouement but not how to get her characters from one to the other. Yet rather than a failure of imagination, her habitual swerve toward the aporetic might be seen as the governing impetus of a poetics that insists on undoing patterns and severing motive from action. In *Strangers on a Train* (1950), Bruno imagines a "pure murder" as "without personal motives."[47] The purity of the crime resides in the inability of anyone to infer why it was carried out.

Paying no heed to her claim that "insight is not something found in psychology books" (*PW*, 144), Highsmith's critics often shift to a psychological idiom when filling in the blanks where her characters' motives should be. This is an understandable move. Because her "fond[ness] of coincidences" (*PW*, 51) and her sense that "the only good parts of a book are the explanations that are left out" (87) lead Highsmith to disregard realism's implicit yet emphatic demand for causality, it has been hard for critics to locate the motives in her novels without resorting to the history of postwar America's repressive conformism and its consequent psychic toll. Tom Ripley thus kills because he can't express himself in healthier ways. Or as Chris Straayer puts it, "Tom is a psychopath."[48] Far from stabilizing authorial intention, such a diagnosis inevitably draws attention to the critic's own motives. Transferring the onus of negativity from Highsmith to Tom, the critic strives to distance Highsmith from her creation and to share custody with her in the dual role of Tom's judge and analyst, as when George Haggerty asserts that Highsmith is "intent in looking into his motivations and explaining his behavior."[49] But the author, disclaiming such separation, was fond of signing her autograph "Tom Ripley" and frequently confessed to being in love with him. "I often had the feeling Ripley was writing it," she said of her most famous novel, "and I was merely typing" (*PW*, 69).

The existential primacy Highsmith accords Ripley not only makes it hard to foster the dissociation necessary to a criticism founded on the revelation of motive but also confirms the suspicion that Highsmith believed performance and surrogacy more than adequate proxies for reality. When he sheds his masquerade by "identifying himself as Thomas Phelps Ripley" to the police in Venice, Tom predicts it will be "one of the saddest things he had ever done in his life."[50] Yet far from steeped in pathos, the moment of his disclosure turns out to be "a very boring little scene" (202). Highsmith in turn construed authenticity as a dull way of being in the world. "I create things," she observed, "out of boredom with reality" (*PW*, 46). This attitude has made her intractable to a queer criticism whose heuristic is almost without exception embedded in gay liberation's specific revolt against artifice, the exodus from the closet.

This is not to say that Highsmith categorically embraces the excitements of role-playing. Adrift on the crosscurrents generated by the dueling notions of performance in postwar culture, *The Talented Mr. Ripley* finds its title character caught between the impression management that sociologists saw as inescapable in contemporary society and the motivated expressivity that the Method's teachers saw as an antidote to the corrosive and alienating effects of other-direction. As though taking his cues from Adler or Strasberg, for example, Ripley understands the relays between somatic responses and mental states as wholly commutative. "If you wanted to be cheerful, or melancholic, or wistful," Tom reflects, "you simply had to *act* those things with every gesture" (193). Both the content and the construction of this sentence reveal the debt Highsmith owes to a narrative of acting derived from the Method and its emphasis on the conditional tense—what Stanislavski called "the magic *if*" (50). But Tom is incapable of dismissing the audience whose shaming power the Method actor is taught to abjure. Tom thus combines the self-consciousness and internal distance that Goffman saw as basic to the performing self with the "belief in what you are doing" (14) that Stanislavski and his American adopters conceived as prerequisite to the performance of authenticity.

The Method's treatment of self-conviction as the measure of a good performance helps us make sense of one of Ripley's more flagrant pathologies: his habit of staying in character even when he is offstage. After disposing of Dickie

Greenleaf's bludgeoned body off the coast of San Remo and moving to Rome in order to assume Dickie's identity, Tom resumes his study of Italian. "After the sixth lesson," Highsmith writes,

> Tom thought his Italian was on a par with Dickie's. He remembered verbatim several sentences that Dickie had said at one time or another which he now knew were incorrect. For example, "Ho paura che non c'e arrivata, Giorgio," one evening in Giorgio's, when they had been waiting for Marge and she had been late. It should have been "sia arrivata," in the subjunctive after an expression of fearing. Dickie had never used the subjunctive as often as it should be used in Italian. Tom studiously kept himself from learning the proper uses of the subjunctive. (136)

The question raised by this passage concerns the matter of audience. For whom would Tom need to avoid "the proper uses of the subjunctive"? If it is to persuade those so close to Dickie that they realize he misuses the subjunctive, the avoidance is futile, since their intimacy with Dickie would preclude their being fooled by even the most careful imitation. If it is to convince those who have never met Dickie, Tom's solecisms are irrelevant, since anyone who doesn't know Dickie presumably also doesn't know that he couldn't master the subjunctive.[51]

Yet to put the problem with Tom's audience expectations in these terms is to exhibit a certain obtuseness about the dexterity behind his performance, which consists in the ability "to maintain the mood and temperament of the person one was impersonating" (131). Maintenance is key to a performance that in order to be plausible must be ongoing. It is thus less important for him to "artificially change his appearance" than to assume Dickie's "very expression" (92). Such expressivity requires Tom less to bear a physical resemblance to the person for whom he is passing than to be able to suppose, even when alone, what that person might think or do. The adoption of another's "mood" thus appears to provide Tom with an "unassailable" disguise (256). "Mood" is the operative word here, and it is significant not just because it is such an intangible quality of persons (harder to detect and thus to expose than a wig or false mustache) but also because it is, grammatically speaking, what the subjunctive is: a verbal mood, as the *OED* lets us know, "employed to denote an action or a state as conceived (and not as a fact) and therefore used to express a wish, command, exhortation, or a contingent, hypothetical, or prospective event." This is a mood Tom has mastered even as he vows to disown it in the effort to embody Dickie's resolutely sanguine "temperament." The reason Dickie lacks fluency in the subjunctive, of course, is that he rarely finds cause to use it. Blessed with looks, money, and a lifetime of ruling-class entitlement, Dickie has as little to doubt about the world as he has to desire from it. No "expression of fearing" is necessary.

Though he seeks to curtail his use of it in order to rein in his own status anxiety, his command of the subjunctive leads Tom to negotiate the world less by means of Dickie's style of certitude than through the Method's logic of prolepsis, which partitions experience into what Adler calls "smaller actions" (145) and requires the actor to treat those increments as links in a probabilistic chain. "When the inner world of someone you have under observation becomes clear to you through his acts," Stanislavski advises, "follow his actions closely and study the conditions in which he finds himself. Why did he do this or that? What did he have in mind?" (102). It is hard to ignore Tom's virtually clairvoyant ability to anticipate what other people will do based on his inferences about their "conditions." When Dickie's mother sends Tom to Brooks Brothers to buy a robe for her son, "Tom chose a dark maroon flannel" that "he felt . . . was exactly what Richard would have chosen" (28), and "as Tom had anticipated, Dickie was extremely pleased with the bathrobe" (55). Later, in need of lodgings in Rome, Tom selects a "hotel near the Via Veneto, because the Hassler was a trifle flashy, . . . the kind of hotel . . . where Freddie Miles, or people like him who knew Dickie, would choose to stay" (121). Sure enough, when Van Houston phones Tom after the police find Freddie's body, he is indeed calling from "the Hassler . . . going over Freddie's suitcases with the police" (161).

Yet these feats of predication uncannily mirror Tom's bouts of panic, also notable for their strident marshaling of the conditional tense:

> He was trying to figure out what would logically happen if he did nothing, and what he could make happen by his own actions. Marge would very likely come up to Rome. He mustn't see Marge, that was all. Everything would go haywire if he saw her. It'd be the end of everything! But if he could only sit tight, nothing at all would happen. . . . Absolutely nothing would happen to him, if he could keep on doing and saying the right things to everybody. (165)

Inhabiting a world saturated by "if" statements, Tom continually resorts to suppositional grammar to generate convincing performances. As the teeming conditionals in this passage indicate, the probabilistic mode is inescapable, since it does not really yield to completion. It only leads to further suppositions. Although it seems indistinct from what critics have diagnosed as his paranoia, Tom's relentless consequentialism is hardly an idiosyncrasy of his person. It is the preferred form of ratiocination in the culture Highsmith transcribes. It is thus more important for Tom to convince people that he "may be" than that he is Dickie. He belongs to a fictive world whose inhabitants are given to second-guessing their own perceptions. Highsmith's is a world suffused with the subjunctive, the mood of maybe.

In keeping with his compulsive recourse to doubt and expectation, Tom's inability to relax into a settled role (because the same people likely to take him for Dickie then again might not) suggests an equally pronounced focus on a future understood as perpetually deferrable. For this reason "his anticipation was more exciting," Highsmith writes, "than his experiencing" (180). While endemic to the subjunctive mood, which subordinates the present world to one that might be hoped into being, Tom's inexorable sense of anticipation also resonates with the vicariousness that comes standard on the model of Cold War homosexuality whose stereotypes Highsmith is often accused of exploiting. Yet it would be a mistake to treat Tom's anticipative pleasures, any more than his conditional logic, as the exclusive property of his queer person. For such vicarious speculations are more aptly seen as the ready currency of Eric Larrabee's "self-conscious society," which represented a seamless dovetailing of New Critical close reading with the anxious lay heuristic of Riesman's "other-directed" Americans, busily decoding the social text and tracking the ever variable tokens of what their fellows "may be." As Larrabee puts it, "The discoverer of a new status symbol can live off it conversationally for weeks."[52]

While New Critics and their lay counterparts both prized ambiguity, the latter sought this quality not in lyrics that were irreducible to paraphrase but in the *mystique* of persons who would not submit to reciprocity. Leo Braudy suggests that this social style was a "hallmark" of midcentury culture: "Many individuals of essentially solitary nature could nevertheless draw vast audiences by both the alluring mystery of their aloneness and their seeming obliviousness to the audience's attention."[53] "Restrictions placed upon contact," Goffman likewise notes, "provide a way in which awe can be generated and sustained in the audience." The value of such "mystification" (*EL*, 67) suggests itself to Tom when he secludes himself on his transatlantic voyage: "His aloofness, he knew, was causing a little comment. . . . He imagined the speculations of the other passengers: Is he an American? I think so, but he doesn't act like an American" (40). This passage both depicts Tom doing what he does best (imagining what others might imagine) and introduces a structure of incitement through concealment that rivals his more earnest poses. The most attractive role one can play from this standpoint, as Tom starts to grasp, is an act that keeps its motives ulterior, just as the "honest" performance of the Method actor is typically produced in tandem with its impassive counterpart, the performance of celebrity.

Indeed, despite their uncanny physical resemblance, Tom could not be more unlike Dickie in one respect. Whereas Tom is always at risk of exposure (showing up on the beach, for instance, in a "very revealing" [46] "yellow and black G-string" [44]), Dickie never really gives anything important about himself away. Put differently, whereas Tom possesses a knack for conjecturing motives, Dickie is equally adept at finessing his own. "The Italian police could never get to the bottom of Signor Greenleaf's emotional involvements," Tom muses. "He hadn't been able to himself" (207). Simultaneously reminiscent of phallic prowess and schoolboy innocence, Dickie's very name suggests both a permanent child (and thus a kind of emotional blank) and a supremely virile adult. When Tom arrives at Mongibello, Marge shows him Dickie's boat, the *Pipi*, which Tom finds "indiscernible" from the boats docked around it. "The boats looked very much alike, but Marge said Dickie's boat was larger than most of them" (48). While it may be "short for Pipistrello" (48), Highsmith assures us, there is nothing diminutive about Dickie's *Pipi*.

The point is not to dwell on the faintly puerile wordplay Highsmith nevertheless compels us to ponder regarding Dickie's sizable boat but to underscore how the novel's other characters fixate on Dickie's impressive endowments, which are so obvious that he need not take any pains to show them off. In addition to veiling his status the more forcefully to project it (the "Greenleaf" of his surname implying a fig leaf that conceals and so magnifies the potency behind his vaguely salacious sobriquet), Dickie has the enviable capacity to conceal any hint of the stigma that Tom finds himself routinely confronting. It is Tom who unwittingly "outs" himself on the beach in Cannes when he shouts "bravo" to a band of acrobats, attired (like Tom earlier) in "yellow G-strings" (98), while Dickie calls them as he sees them, or rather implies their homosexuality in the simultaneously erudite and juvenile rhyme he misquotes from "I Wandered Lonely as a Cloud." "Ten thousand saw I at a glance," Dickie recites, "Nodding [sic] their heads in sprightly dance" (98). Dickie deflects stigma with a retreat into the markings of his class. His "coldly" *haut bourgeois* "distaste" for what Tom refers to as the "fairies" (99) seems so pervasive that he cannot bring himself to say the word, only to gesture toward it via a detour through Romanticism. In Wordsworth's poem, "Ten thousand" refers not to fairies but to daffodils. Either Tom doesn't know the poem and thus mistakes the referent or he fills in the referent with the only term he can intuit. In any event, he implicates himself in both a class and a sexual lapse. He is not schooled enough to know Wordsworth; he is all too familiar with fairies.

It is worth calling to mind how Wordsworth's lyric proceeds in light of Tom's embarrassment in this scene. "A poet could not but be gay," he writes, "in such a jocund company." Even if his recall of the poem is imperfect, Dickie demonstrates through its invocation his superior aptitude for concealment, while also offering an implicit rationale for the benefits of deniability. It is in the lyric speaker's interest to separate himself from the "ten thousand" even as he might delight in a "company" best sampled from afar: "when on my couch I lie / In vacant or in pensive mood."[54] If familiarity with the "gay" spectacle entangles the observer in its compromising mise-en-scène, Dickie's feat is to make his mood appear more vacant than pensive, more in line with an absence of affect than with the self-consciousness crucial to the subjunctive, the novel's other privileged mood. Daffodils and fairies have in common that their multitude effaces the singularity (what Wordsworth calls "the bliss of solitude") that individuals of Dickie's class enjoy as their due.[55] Dickie recognizes the fairies only to disown them; Tom, too late to catch himself, ends up indistinct from them.

This is only to say that in the maybe world of Highsmith's novel, Tom tends to fall on the side of *probably*. Despite his protestation that "I'm not queer" (80), he has not mastered Dickie's ability to camouflage whatever motivations he may have. Because the substance of Tom's sexuality is subordinate to the perception that characters routinely have of what he possibly is, it is crucial for Tom to keep people guessing. When they settle on certain knowledge of him, they tend to end up either dead or (what is scarcely less tragic) no longer interested in Tom as an erotic prospect. Dickie is both an object of desire and an elusive catch in part because he never professes to leaning one way or another. And Tom's own manner of inciting desire is not very different from—albeit far less adroit than—the elaborate mesh of speculations Dickie knits around himself. When we first meet Tom in the novel, he has been living a transient life as a kept boy in a series of abodes whose owners' queer identity is not open to debate even if Tom's seems to be. Tom trades on being "trade," both purveying and with-holding his sexuality in the effort to string out his welcome for as long as his hosts are willing to support him. Inevitably this guessing game tires its players, as in the "humiliating moment" when Tom's friend Vic "had said, *Oh, for Christ sake, Tommie, shut up!* when he had said to a group of people, for perhaps the third or fourth time in Vic's presence, 'I can't make up my mind whether I like men or women, so I'm thinking of giving them *both* up'" (81). The statement's rote theatricality denotes Tom's failure to cultivate mystique. By overacting the sexual ambivalence Dickie easily radiates, Tom loses erotic credibility.

Highsmith's novel presents us with a conflict not between truth and im-posture but between two overlapping models of performance: Tom's "honest" impersonation and Dickie's habit of concealment. "It's just the way you act," Dickie tells Tom when confronting him with the suspicion that "Marge thinks" he is "queer" (80). Tom does not readily grasp that acting connotes queerness, and not just in the sense of "acting-out," as when he first wins Dickie over with a draggy "pantomime" of "Lady Assburden sampling the American subway" (58), but in the sense that both acting and queerness subject their practitioners to the logic of the spectacle, to imagining oneself at the mercy of a presumptuous or hostile audience. It is as if, despite his otherwise flawless embodiment of Dickie, Tom has failed to imbibe the Method's deeper lesson that the audience is not his friend. To the extent that he is better at playing Dickie than Dickie is, Tom becomes overly invested in his character: "He had let his imagination run away" (167). This equivocal sentence captures the essence of Tom's dilemma. While it signifies his habit of "pretending, uncontrollably" (153), his insistence when alone in his room of moving "as Dickie would have done," thinking "about what Dickie would be thinking about" (167), turns Tom into the "dull" (182) Dickie and so causes his imagination to run away in another sense. Total accession to the Dickie persona, full of "negligence and unconcern" (183), leads Tom to cede his own instrumental self-consciousness. It is only when he returns to his for-mer role that his acting becomes more or less perfected, since that reentry finds Tom armed with the trappings that allow for the social distance and occlusion of motive that Dickie has naturalized. "Tom behaved in a reserved but friendly manner appropriate for a young man in his position," Highsmith writes after he reassumes his identity, "a sensitive young man, unused to garish publicity" (219).

Dickie's veiled aloofness, however, is not just a presentation of self in Goff-man's sense but a way of inhabiting the closet that Highsmith declines to render pathological. Whereas the Method seeks to authenticate performances according to behaviorism's logic of conditioning, the closet furnishes Highsmith with a means to preserve a domain beyond the reach of both spectacle and reflex. It becomes the site of self-determination. And this endorsement of the closet aligns Highsmith with postwar sociologists whose project concerns the effort to make performances not more authentic but less coercive—pursued not on behalf of an "inner nature," to borrow Charles Taylor's phrase, but in the service of different scripts.[56] Whereas postwar sociology equated revising official scripts with reforming official institutions, Highsmith by contrast had an interest in what amounts to *preserving* the unofficial institution of the closet. Yet if *The Talented Mr. Ripley* turns out to be deeply invested in the pre-Stonewall closet, it also severs the association between the closet and queerness while universalizing the link between closeting and desire. Rather than the privative space from which individuals struggle to emerge into full-blown authenticity, the closet materializes in this novel as an erotic nexus that saturates postwar culture irrespective of individuals and their orientation.

According to Eve Sedgwick's justly influential model, the closet cannot be thought apart from "the reign of the telling secret."[57] Thus, "*anyone* who witnesses and identifies the invert," she says of the "ironclad epistemological receivership" to which the closet remits its casualties, "feels assured of knowing more about him than he knows about himself" and benefits from "an empowering and exciting specular differential of knowledge."[58] Insofar as it assumes an opposition between an active subject-supposed-to-know and a passive object of that knowledge, this view of the closet as a structure of cognitive dominance is incomplete. Highsmith shows us that a crucial supplement to its design would have to be the subjunctive tense, the tense play of maybes, built into the edifice of postwar sociability. The resident of Highsmith's closet is neither walled inside against his will nor seeking a shelter purchased at the cost of self-denial. Tom instead treats the closet as an elite pleasure club, entrée to which is all the more coveted by virtue of its exclusive door policy. Despite the interest many people have in making his acquaintance, Tom "never asked anyone up" to his apartment in Rome, "with the exception of one attractive but not very bright young man" (136).

We can measure Highsmith's idiosyncrasy with regard to the closet by comparing her novel to another text that stands close to it in time if not exactly in sensibility. The hyperactive consciousness that Highsmith treats as both Tom's curse and saving grace also characterizes David, the tortured protagonist of James Baldwin's *Giovanni's Room* (1956), who maintains a firm divide between himself and the *folles* (fairies) with whom he nonetheless cannot help associating. David's greatest fear is to be taken for one of the "old theatrical sisters" who "looked like a peacock garden" as they flock around Guillaume's Paris bar.[59] Like the "specialists in self-deception" he derides, practiced in "elaborate systems of evasion" (20), David goes to great lengths to execute a precisely machined illusion. After a brush with a "sailor [who] gave me a look contemptuously lewd and knowing" (92), David seduces an acquaintance named Sue, a woman to whom he is not attracted and who thus furnishes a sort of stress test for keeping his "manhood unquestioned" (104). Taking note of her "cries" and "fists on my back," David "realized that [his] performance with Sue was succeeding even too well" (100). The clinical attention to the "performance" while it occurs, "as though she were a job of work" (100), both confirms David's queerness and grants an almost foolproof means of denying it. Contrary to gender expectations, David is able to gratify Sue even as his own pleasure is brilliantly faked.

Baldwin's larger point of course is that such performances are never as successful as David would like to imagine. He has no recourse to the Method when it comes to acting the part of a heterosexuality he does not own. And his attempt to reduce his "idyll" with Giovanni to "something that happened to me once, . . . that happened to a lot of men once" (94), is thwarted by the indelible imprint of that youthful romance. "Now, as though I had been branded," David notes, "his body was burned into my mind, into my dreams." Yet this branding only spurs David to more elaborate flights of self-protection: "I had to get out of there for my face showed too much, the war in my body was dragging me down" (144). Giovanni's "abject" example provides a rationale for that escape's urgency; for, in the aftermath of their breakup, Giovanni has "affected . . . a fairy's mannerisms" (147) and, "like a falling movie star, has lost his drawing power. Everything is known about him, his secrecy has been discovered" (156).

That Baldwin keys the narrative of Giovanni's decline to a movement from a "secrecy" that confers a certain inescapable allure on its possessor to an "outrageous" effeminacy is not incidental (128). We could say that his book proceeds in the opposite direction and arrives at a rather different account of the closet from the one that Highsmith pursues. Highsmith plots Tom's movement as a social ascent that begins with his discovery of the arts of secrecy crucial to a certain glamorization of the closet. Whereas Giovanni ends up like the *folles*, in a state of "humiliation" (147), Ripley unlearns the bad habit of exhibitionistic self-display in the effort to cultivate a mystique that is both sexually charged and class distinctive. Yet Highsmith doesn't harbor the contempt for fairies that Baldwin appears to hold. For Ripley, the salient choice is between becoming a distinguished rich man and remaining an obscure poor one, not (as it seems to be for Baldwin) between two equally intolerable erotic alternatives: the contemptible fairy and the self-loathing closet case. Baldwin insists that, despite their seeming opposition, the closet case will inevitably shape-shift into the drama queen, as conspicuous to others as he has been in denial to himself. Giovanni, David tells us, "seemed to find my face as transparent as a shop window" (158). Baldwin confronts David with this impasse because he holds performance in deep suspicion in whatever form it takes—either the excessive acting out of the "theatrical sisters" or the unrelenting private spectacle of sexually paranoid men.

In this opinion, as we have seen, Baldwin would find many compatriots among gay liberationists who likewise condemned the confinement to role that plagued the prepolitical queer world. Highsmith was not one of them. By contrasting *Giovanni's Room* and *The Talented Mr. Ripley*, I mean to stress how deeply we misread Highsmith's novel if we assume its author shares our view of the closet as the sine qua non of conformity to repressive sexual values. For the role-playing that Baldwin treats as a perpetual imprisonment Highsmith treats, finally, as a kind of qualified freedom. Rejecting the expressive authenticity that would prove central to the politics of New Left radicals, Highsmith insists on picturing the closet as a subjunctive space that may provoke the doubtful or expectant among her readers not just to anticipate the world as it probably is but to imagine how things may be otherwise. Prioritizing the self's instrumentality, Highsmith forfeits a claim to the self's authenticity, its being an end rather than a protracted albeit versatile means.

Yet it may be premature to find in these subjunctive gestures a utopian antiessentialism, a way of salvaging the political utility of *The Talented Mr. Ripley* after all. Tom's simultaneous departure from and parodic conformity to rigid social conventions seem to make him an ideal recruit for such recuperation if we agree with Judith Butler that antiessentialism's real point of attack is less identity as such than the "regulatory norms" whose "forcible reiteration" legitimizes some identities by rendering others "uninhabitable."[60] Yet it is hard to believe that even the most fervent antiessentialist would admit the blithely murderous Tom into the ranks of abject subjects who should be accorded the same footing as hegemonic ones. Ripley's chief misgiving with regard to homicide, after all, is merely that corpses are messy.

The more serious point to make is that the political project grounded in the performative, which strives for social change by emphasizing the derivative nature of identity, is somewhat compromised by a text that, like Highsmith's, equates a disregard of authenticity less with a radical upheaval of society than with an embrace of social privilege in which the status quo is left affirmatively intact. And just as the book challenges our efforts to infer from it a politics of what Butler calls the "critically queer," so Highsmith's determination to eroticize the closet as a locus of mystique likewise presents us with the uncomfortable question of whether such an outrageous fantasy of the closet's sexual appeal could ever be defensible.[61] I argue that it is precisely on the plane of fantasy, which often thrusts against the bounds of decorum, that her work is most suggestive, in part because Highsmith herself seems entranced by the ideal of radically unencumbered self-closeting *The Talented Mr. Ripley* entertains.

We might get at her complex attitude toward the novel's presiding fantasy by noting the simple fact that even as Highsmith may glamorize the closet in this novel, it was a space she resolutely declined to inhabit even if her critics cannot seem to help situating her there. There is much in her biography to indicate why this gesture has seemed so expedient. When late in life she republished her lesbian pulp classic *The Price of Salt* (1952) under her own name, Highsmith flouted the many requests to divulge the novel's "personal" meaning. Andrew Wilson writes that her decision to lay claim to the book "did not mean . . . that Highsmith felt comfortable enough to talk about her sexuality in public."[62] Inferring from this occasion that Highsmith evaded public admission of her lesbianism, Wilson seems oddly imperceptive to the qualms Highsmith might have felt about airing her sexual past in the promotion of her early book. It seems more likely that, for Highsmith, casting the reissue of *The Price of Salt* as what Wilson calls a "literary coming-out" was beneath contempt, hence her rebuffing of interviewers intent on posing questions whose answers they already knew.[63] From a woman who insisted, as Meaker recalls, on "holding girls' hands on the street, in the supermarket, in restaurants" in pre-Stonewall New York, Highsmith's refusal to respond to the question of her sexuality implies less a fear of being exposed than an indignation with a prurience masquerading as human interest.[64]

Opposed to the presumption of such interpellations, Highsmith inhabits not the closet exactly but the fantasy that she can be unknowable to her audience, that she can (like Ripley, like strangers on a train) maintain the mystique of anonymity or perpetual role reversal. Across Highsmith's fiction, persons are not only attracted to strangers but also drawn to the idea of being strangers. During sex with his wife, Heloise, who debuts in *Ripley under Ground* (1970), Tom feels "as if he derived his pleasure . . . from a body without an identity," a sensation that corroborates both our intuition about Tom's steadfast queerness and Highsmith's commitment to eroticizing impersonality even in the midst of a relation as intimate as the conjugal tie.[65] What engrosses readers in *The Talented Mr. Ripley* beyond its Cold War moment is its willingness to fantasize a world without determinate identities or their consequences, a fantasy all the more enticing in the context of the novel's imagined social order, which treats as compulsory the need to anticipate and follow up the implications of every presumption. Yet we cannot ignore the peculiar fact that this fantasy of an untraceable erotic life embraces what is a male-identified erotic mode: the sleazy and anonymous pleasures of cruising. Highsmith lets us know that Ripley is likewise partial to cruising's pleasures and locales. When he is touring Paris, he notices with palpable glee the city's readily accessible "public urinals" (125).

5 Deviant Ethnographies

Impersonality and the Postwar Toilet

Highsmith's identification with Tom's desire for impersonal sex—or more specifically, with what the sociologist Laud Humphreys called "tearoom trade" in his 1970 book of that name—suggests another angle from which to consider the models of performance and social structure that find or lose their way into the New Social Movements. One development to which the work of the 1950s sociologists lent itself was what we might call the "deviant ethnography" that flourished in the wake of the dramaturgical approach to society. Unlike the sociology of deviance that preceded it, deviant ethnography was a social science not only of but *by* deviants. While Goffman was leery of the prestige accorded to the "term 'deviant,'" observing that "there are categories of persons who are created by students of society, and then studied by them," the queer social scientists who came of age during the 1960s were drawn as much to the notion of deviance as to the heuristic possibilities of "role" for the study of sexual subcultures.[1] Deviant ethnographers like Humphreys and the anthropologist Esther Newton studied social groups who even into the post-Stonewall present continue to challenge the limits of pluralist tolerance: closeted men who have sex with other men in public (in Humphreys's case) and men who dress as women (in Newton's case). It is as though Tom Ripley, with his fondness for public toilets and drag improvisation, were their informant of choice. Whereas Humphreys's straight-acting men underplay the homosexual stereotype and Newton's drag queens overplay it, both miss the mark of the "real" homosexuality that was beginning to make itself known under the auspices of gay liberation at the moment these scholars were publishing their fieldwork.

What Gayle Rubin calls the "repositioning" of deviance as an analysis of social hegemony rather than a diagnostic taxonomy came about by and large through the work of Howard Becker, whose "labeling theory" shifted the focus on deviance away from deviant populations and toward their observers.[2] Like Goffman, Becker understood deviance as a concept that arose in a culture in which impressions—and the risk of their being discredited—were among the dominant mechanisms of social control. And like Goffman, Becker took an interest in how much distance an agent could put between himself and his permitted roles. Deviance was both the name of a system of social labeling (what Becker called "a hierarchy of credibility") and the name for any act of deviating from script.[3] The "deviant" as a type did not exist apart from the "injunction to believe the man at the top" of a status hierarchy.[4]

Following Becker's lead, Mary McIntosh begins her classic essay "The Homosexual Role" (1968) by noting that "homosexuality . . . is still commonly seen as a condition of certain persons in the way that birthplace or deformity might characterize them," with the consequence that students of homosexuality pay undue attention to "its etiology" rather than to the proper "object of study . . . the practice of social labeling."[5] In shifting her discussion from the labeled to the labelers, McIntosh sought to displace both the view that homosexuality developed from behavioral circumstances and the view that it surfaced from the self's inner depths. This effort ran counter to the position taken by the advocates for gay liberation. "We reject society's attempt to impose sexual roles and definitions on our nature," read the Gay Liberation Front's (GLF) "Statement of Purpose" (1969). "We are going to be who we are."[6] Touching on McIntosh's concern with role as an imposition from a hostile world, the GLF and other groups nonetheless repudiated McIntosh's claim that since "much homosexual behavior occurs outside the recognized role" (182), the role itself indicated the fallacy of a distinct homosexual body. Indeed, for GLF founder and "Gay Is Good" (1969) author Martha Shelley, speaking on behalf of "homosexual bodies," bodies "consubstantial with homosexuality," the goal of gay liberation was obvious: "no roles."[7] Addressing her ostensibly straight readers, Shelley invokes the self-evident body that served figures from Mario Savio to Norman Mailer as the testament of meaningful politics. Crucial to this politics is a commitment, which GLF shared with other New Left groups, to the sanctity of the person who exists outside the role. Thus, Shelley declares: "When I am among gays or in bed with another woman, I am a person, not a lesbian" (31).

McIntosh had little interest in such declarations of personhood or the distinctions that ostensibly turned on them. For her, it was not the "person" but the category that mattered. Although this is the implicit premise of all social scientists, indifference to the person forms the explicit subject of Laud Humphreys's *Tearoom Trade*, a subject made evident in its subtitle: *Impersonal Sex in Public Places*. That book began life as a Washington University sociology dissertation on the mostly married men who cruised public toilets. Taking up the role of "watchqueen," Humphreys bore witness to "hundreds of acts of fellatio" in "nineteen different men's rooms in five parks."[8] Humphreys focused on figures who all but defied the basic prerequisite of sociological inquiry: a self-conscious group identity. His "informants" not only were unapproachable but also wanted it that way, preserving strict silence both in the ritual of the tearoom and in their disavowal of gay subculture. This problem led Humphreys to develop a series of "oddball tactics" (12) to contact a sampling of the men whose behavior he had observed. He tracked down the names and addresses of a number of them through their license plates and then posed as a health surveyor to gain access to their homes. The method and topic of his fieldwork were so scandalous that Washington University almost revoked his doctorate, while a contingent of the sociology department led by Alvin Gouldner tried to suppress his dissertation. Humphreys later came out during a heated debate with a homophobic colleague at a meeting of the American Sociological Association in 1974.

It is tempting to read this later event back onto *Tearoom Trade* and to see its author as the tortured creature of the closet who, married with children and under the pretext of scholarly inquiry, took an even more degraded solace in the tearoom than its already abject clientele. This is a narrative that *Tearoom Trade* gives us good reason to resist, for the aim of the book is not to extract from its subjects a retroactive truth about their desire. Humphreys is interested not in what social conditions these men had to come from in order to want to practice such a desperate form of erotic exchange but what features of the larger social world they model in the pursuit of sexual contact. Humphreys argues that the risks attached to the tearoom constitute a fully anticipated dimension of the experience of impersonal sex. In this environment, the only stable thing is the cruising man himself, drawing on an elaborate set of rules to negotiate the contingencies of what Humphreys calls the tearoom's "interaction membrane" (54), a space endlessly susceptible to intrusion. These rules are "noncommittal" and "noncoercive" (60). Humphreys claims he never witnessed a forcible sex act or even an aggressive advance; everyone who plays the tearoom game appears fluent in its contractual syntax. Consent and equality here approach something like their Enlightenment ideals.

Humphreys has frequently been charged with romanticizing the tearoom environment, seeing in it a Whitmanesque democracy of the flesh where lines between classes break down. This critique is both justified and incomplete. Humphreys does in fact idealize the tearoom, but the ideal he locates there is not utopian. The tearoom is neither a site for the redistribution of power nor a site for the release of simmering urges (nor even a site for the recruitment of unwitting passersby to the lure of instant sex). Instead, the tearoom social game faithfully reflects the conventions that regulate ordinary life. Humphreys insists on the continuity between the tearoom's anonymous theater and the spheres of home and family, work and leisure, from which its frequenters arrive and to which they return. These are men who have mastered their parts in the tearoom script because of their schooling in what Goffman calls the "techniques of impression management" requisite for other-directed society.[9] They are so fluent in the navigation of fractured social roles that the performance of yet one more is hardly a stretch.

But of course it *is* a stretch, since the risks of embarrassment Goffman locates at the heart of all interactions take on a different magnitude in the context of an action that is both illegal and universally taken to be depraved. Even beyond their ostracism by law-abiding society, those who flock to the tearoom find little common cause with the New Social Movements. Their facility with tearoom etiquette renders Humphreys's cruising men no less suspect than Highsmith's Ripley, for they have realized an impersonality held in contempt not only by the New Left radicals whose indictment of the "noncommittal" we have previously observed but also by gay liberationists like Shelley, whose "Gay Is Good" censures "the homosexuals who hide, who play it straight or pretend that the issue of homosexuality is unimportant" (32). But the men depicted in *Tearoom Trade* are not hiding behind "cardboard characters" in order to "cut off" their homosexuality (33). They execute some parts flawlessly (husband, father) to earn the privilege of acting badly in another (anonymous fellator). Both in the carefully choreographed scene of the tearoom and on the stages of private life, their role-playing serves a calculated sexual opportunism as much as a hegemonic sex-gender system.

The "true identities" that Shelley wants to "shout out" (32), then, are somewhat beside the point for Humphreys. For the sociologist, persons are dependent on their roles, which are far from incidental. For the gay liberationist, by contrast, persons exist apart from their roles, which thus serve only to distort their true expression. Method antitheatricality reappears in gay liberation's resistance to role, understood now as an intolerable bargain with a "straight society" that wants to keep homosexuality "*secret.*" Thus, any act the closeted homosexual performs is undertaken in the spirit of what Shelley calls "self-deceit" (32). *Tearoom Trade* reaches a different conclusion. Humphreys argues that persons who engage in what looks to be the most compromising behavior do so not as the pawns of their innermost drives, nor even as the victims of straight society, but in keeping with the norms of rational choice. Humphreys's object in writing *Tearoom Trade* is not to reclaim the "true identities" of men who have sex in public but the more modest goal of getting police to stop arresting them. The book does not aspire, in other words, to get them to stop performing their roles.

Tearoom Trade appeared at the end of a decade whose major novelists took no small interest in the relation between sex and toilets. Among the numerous bathrooms Oedipa Maas visits in the course of *The Crying of Lot 49* is a "latrine" on whose wall "she noticed the following message: '*Interested in sophisticated fun? You, hubby, girl friends. The more the merrier. Get in touch with Kirby, through W.A.S.T.E. only.*'"[10] W.A.S.T.E. is the novel's subterranean information network, and we are incapable of missing its resonance with the excremental domain of the tearoom and the men who circulate there for all the wrong reasons. In another bathroom, Oedipa finds "an advertisement by AC-DC," the "Alameda County Death Cult" (122) whose members "choose some victim from among the innocent, the virtuous, the socially integrated and well-adjusted, using him sexually, then sacrificing him" (123). These invitations to ritual slaughter and group sex, AC-DC or otherwise, suggest that bathrooms provide the setting for acting badly under cover of the anonymity that, as we observed through the "effeminate" assassins in "The Courier's Tragedy," Pynchon insistently links to male homosexuality. This is to say nothing of the motel bathroom Oedipa enters after Metzger dares her to a game of "Strip Botticelli," a bathroom that "happened to have a walk-in closet" in which she "began putting on as much as she could of the clothing she'd brought with her" (36). The bathroom that begins as the backstage for her striptease ends as the site of a burlesque showstopper involving a runaway aerosol can and a sound track from the television—as well as an audience, the Paranoids and their dates, one of whom calls the scene "kinky" (38).

There is likewise a moment in Saul Bellow's *Herzog* (1964) when Moses watches a young German intern stand before a night-court judge on charges of "indecent solicitation" in a men's room under Grand Central Station. "You don't destroy a man's career," Moses thinks, "because he yielded to an impulse in that ponderous stinking cavern below Grand Central . . . where no mind can be sure of stability." Yet Herzog's apologia obscures the larger context of this scene in Bellow's novel, which plots the men's room as a venue for impromptu theater. The toilet in Grand Central functions as a proving ground for managing the provisional surfaces the self presents to its audience of strangers and intimates alike. Hence, the most interesting figure in this scene is not the unnamed German medical student but the "androgyne number, . . . Alice or Aleck," a "dream actor" who mingles feminine and masculine physical traits— long dyed hair with bulge-revealing jeans—in order to ply his trade as a hustler whose best asset is the flexibility of his gender.[11]

The most famous incident of postwar American toilet theater occurs in Philip Roth's *Portnoy's Complaint* (1969), the second chapter of which chronicles Portnoy's remembrance of his compulsive "whacking off" behind the locked bathroom door in his parents' Newark apartment.[12] With their endless banging on that door, these parents form a sort of unwitting audience for the young Portnoy's masturbation. "What is this, a home or a Grand Central Station?" (20) asks his father (channeling Herzog). The rapt attention Portnoy pays to himself makes him actor in and voyeur of his own peepshow, replete with a series of props (his sister Hannah's bra, a cored apple, a milk bottle, and a piece of liver). When later he accompanies his father to a public bath, Portnoy is "hypnotized" by the sound of masseurs pounding old men's backs, a noise he likens to an "audience applauding the death scene in some tragedy." "They slowly twist their limbs," Portnoy observes, "as though to remove them in a piece from their sockets" (48). The bathhouse doubles as a realm of Bacchic transformation; one thinks of the Maenads rending Pentheus in the hills outside Thebes. Like that Attic predecessor, the bathhouse invites a shedding of the diurnal world's roles. It is a place in which men "can be natural," regressing to a state "before there were toilets and tragedies" (49).

This is surely an ironic statement, given that the license to playact naturalness arises precisely because of the link between "toilets and tragedies"—that is, because Roth's culture insists on turning the bathroom into an amphitheater. For Roth, as for Pynchon and Bellow, the bathroom marks a crisis space where doing one's business cedes to show business, where persons deny their expected behaviors and cultivate or conceal illegitimate ones. It thwarts the demand for *expression* associated with the toilet in the most visceral sense: the flushing out of excess, the purging of waste. Far from shedding the body's surplus (clothing, dirt, shit) and granting it immunity from the rigors of performance, the postwar bathroom foists the individual into a complex theatrics in which one must redouble that body's encumbrances. Catching them in the bathroom, Pynchon, Bellow, and Roth situate their characters between the dramaturgical approach to society and the antitheatricality of the Method and the New Social Movements. The mediation of erotic acts by the logic of performance raises the problem of authenticity in those domains where the realist novel traditionally intervenes: in the phenomenology of embodied experience and in the possibility of interpersonal intimacy.

That the novel retained the power to make such interventions was decidedly unclear in postwar culture. In "Everybody's Protest Novel" (1949), his cri de coeur for a revival of the novel's aesthetic autonomy, James Baldwin describes the crisis facing the genre in terms of the hegemonic triumph of sentimentality, "the ostentatious parading of excessive and spurious emotion," which unites such incongruously paired "pamphleteers" as Harriet Beecher Stowe and Richard Wright in their "aversion to experience."[13] Wright's fiction "aim[s] . . . to reduce all Americans to the compulsive, bloodless dimensions of a guy named Joe" (20). Despite its altruistic intentions, the protest novel destroys the very point of the novel in its embrace of a sociological standard of reality. "The failure of the protest novel lies in its rejection of life, the human being," Baldwin thus concludes, "in its insistence that it is his categorization alone which is real" (23). "The tendency to divorce sex from the other manifestations of life is a strong one," Lionel Trilling wrote the year before in a review of Alfred Kinsey's *Sexual Behavior in the Human Male.*[14] Spelling out the dire consequences that follow from Kinsey's "absorbing study of sex in charts and tables" (122), Trilling seeks to reassert the "authority" of "literature" over "sociology" (123) in assessing the "morality" of "sexual conduct" (121). What literature grants to sex for Trilling is "the idea that sexual behavior is involved with the whole of the individual's character" (132). For both Baldwin and Trilling in the late 1940s, the chief antagonist to the literary artist is not mass culture but academic social science. "Literature and sociology are not one and the same," Baldwin writes. "It is impossible to discuss them as if they were" (19).

Just as sociology appeared in postwar America as a byword for impersonality, so the sociological standard of sex appeared to observers like Trilling as an embrace of *standardization*. In studying "impersonal" sex, of course, Humphreys sees its participants not as other than persons but merely as anonymous. Like the Free Speech Movement, however, the postwar novelist tends to equate impersonality with the absence of any humanizing identity. "Impersonal" means not anonymous but "nonperson." This is the word Kurt Vonnegut uses in the introduction to *Slaughterhouse Five* (1969), where he notes how missing a transatlantic flight turned him into "a nonperson in the Boston fog," a status ratified by "Lufthansa," which "put me in a limousine with some other nonpersons."[15] As with Mario Savio's implacable "machine," faceless bureaucracy sorts everyone into nonpersons. Billy Pilgrim is considered "a repulsive nonperson" (245) by Bertram Rumfoord, the man in the hospital bed next to him, a libertine Harvard professor who has spent his career writing the official history of the US Air Force.

But impersonality also manifests for Vonnegut as a state of indistinctness, a blurring of the boundaries between persons that Vonnegut understands as threatening their moral integrity by relaxing the constraints of a culture that has given way to a kind of ambient anonymity. Dissolution breeds dissoluteness. The "nonperson" is Goffman's name for the "categories of persons . . . servants, the very young, the very old . . . who are sometimes treated in their presence as if they were not there" and who thus "have some license to commit gauche acts."[16] Vonnegut refutes this depersonalization by means of the ethics of naming consolidated by the FSM and other New Left groups. "That was I," he writes at one point. "That was me. That was the author of this book" (161). Vonnegut's jarring first-person intrusion serves a purpose similar to that of Mailer's third-person narration in *The Armies of the Night*: a way of keeping the author's presence before the reader as an unassailable fact.

Yet what is most striking about this insertion of the author in the novel is that it occurs in a latrine in the German prisoner-of-war camp to which Billy Pilgrim has been sent. Vonnegut's self-identification takes as its foil the theatrical toilet whose frequent cameos in the novels of the 1960s we have just glimpsed. At this point in *Slaughterhouse Five*, the American POWs have been given a generous welcome by the British veterans of the camp, who have provided them with a festive meal and an evening's entertainment—an all-male revue of *Cinderella*. The "welcome feast," Vonnegut writes, "had made them sick as volcanoes," and "an American near Billy wailed that he had excreted everything but his brains" (160). This American turns out to be "the author of this book." It is important for Vonnegut to declare himself engaged in the proper business that a latrine occasions: taking a crap, as opposed to acting out the indecent script that all-male environs make possible and to which (on the evidence of their gender-bending theatricals) the British POWs have succumbed.

Excretion becomes for Vonnegut a powerful form of purgation. It is expressivity, we might say, in its most embodied form: pressing out matter from the body. If *Slaughterhouse Five* is rife with scatological imagery, from "the farts of people eating wartime food" (161) to Billy's father-in-law's "favorite song" ("In my prison cell I sit / With my britches full of shit" [197]), the reason is that the act of shitting is the antithesis of anal penetration. "Human beings in there were excreting into steel helmets which were passed to the people at the ventilators," Vonnegut says of the train cars that carry him and his fellow prisoners to the camp. "Out came shit and piss and language," as though the fact that bodily function can be preserved in such circumstances is enough to ward off the suspicion that anything in the train car is going where it shouldn't be or that the "sleepers who nestled like spoons" on its floor do anything but sleep (90). Turning the car into a toilet preserves the sanctity of persons by saving them from the indignities of nonperson status and the sexual license it permits. "When food came in," Vonnegut notes, "the human beings were quiet and trusting and beautiful. They shared" (90).

Ostracized from the train car floor because "nearly everybody . . . had an atrocity story of something Billy Pilgrim had done to him in his sleep" (100), Billy is sacrificed to the homosocial collective's need to maintain its integrity by expelling the taboo it most enables. As if to fit him to the part, Vonnegut dresses Billy in "a little overcoat" (114) that "became a fur-collared vest" (115) and, later, "a lady's muff" (182) to which he has added the "silver shoes" (202) from the British POWs' *Cinderella* show and "a piece of azure curtain which he wore like a toga" (188). The coat is "a *joke*" and "an *insult*," a "deliberate attempt to humiliate" Billy by turning him into "one of the most screamingly funny things they had seen in all of World War Two" (115). The "atrocity stor[ies]" of Billy's nocturnal escapades are thus paired with the equally "abominable . . . sight" of Billy in drag, the "star" who "led the parade" (191) of American soldiers marching through Dresden. Just as his night terrors are mistaken by his fellow prisoners for clumsy seductions, so is it "supposed that Billy had gone to a lot of trouble to costume himself just so" (193). Billy's status as victim registers most saliently in the fact that he has no control over how others register him. And the unwitting exhibitionism of his POW role structures the fantasy world to which Billy escapes from the catastrophic horrors of war or the quotidian drudgery of his marriage: confined to an "artificial habitat in a zoo on Tralfamadore" (97), Billy is forced to have sex with Montana Wildhack in front of an audience of aliens. Even in the recesses of his inner life, he cannot escape the trauma of a depersonalization that negates heterosexual intimacy.

Esther Newton and the Prepolitics of Drag

Vonnegut tells us that after serving in World War II, he "went to the University of Chicago" (9) as "a student in the Department of Anthropology," where "they were teaching that there was absolutely no difference between anybody" (10). This statement might be said to reintroduce the quarrel between literature and social science that Trilling and Baldwin announced around the time Vonnegut was enrolled at Chicago, where a number of social theorists during the 1940s and 1950s were apparently "taught" to believe, as he puts it, "that nobody was ridiculous or bad or disgusting" (10). Vonnegut treats social science as the engine of a depersonalization that, in ignoring "difference," both deprives persons of individualism and disables moral valuations. If persons are interchangeable, they have no obligation to be other than "ridiculous or bad or disgusting" since, without individual accountability, anything goes. Although Vonnegut of course did not become an anthropologist, he admits with a certain ruefulness that the lessons of Chicago were hard to disengage: he "never wrote a story with a villain in it" (10).

Yet Vonnegut seems not to have been a very good student of social science at Chicago. For the lesson of those who taught or trained there at midcentury was that we should *not* take pity on the deviant. In fact, Howard S. Becker critiques sociologists who, because of their "deep sympathy with the people [they] are studying, . . . neglect to ask those questions whose answers would show that the deviant after all has done something pretty rotten and, after all, deserves pretty much what he gets."[17] Whereas Vonnegut feels bemused disbelief toward the social scientist's allegation that persons have no differences, his attitude toward the "villain" is a "sympathy" tempered by the conviction that such figures, like Billy Pilgrim, are (in Becker's words) "more sinned against than sinning"—victims rather than agents.[18] Thus, *Slaughterhouse Five*'s prologue ends with Vonnegut, after perusing the Bible on the lookout for "tales of great destruction," ironically referring the fate of Sodom and Gomorrah to the "vile people in both those cities" (27). It is ironic because Vonnegut doesn't buy this explanation; rather than reject the sinner, he takes on the role of Lot's wife, "told not to look back," and thus becomes "a pillar of salt" in his own rearward glance at life during wartime (28). Vonnegut's regretful pose—"my war book," he writes, "is a failure, and had to be" (28)—derives from his sense that there are no good explanations for war because there are no "vile people" to blame. There are only victims.

But this is not the opinion that social scientists at Chicago were taught either in the 1940s, when Vonnegut was a student, or in the 1960s, when Esther Newton did her graduate work there. In fact, "vile people" were thick on the ground of virtually every ethnography that might be grouped under the rubric of "deviance," since the implication of the view that "there was no absolutely no difference between anybody" as Becker and his colleagues understood this claim was that deviants were no less competent than what Goffman calls "we normals" in having mastered the skills of role distance and impression management that came with the territory of everyday life.[19] Unlike Billy in accidental drag, a spectacle Vonnegut uses to reject the notion that persons are responsible for their misconduct ("It was Fate, of course, which had costumed him" [193]), the drag queens studied by Newton or the drug users studied by Becker are not merely ascribed their status. They have also achieved it. It is not that there are no villains in the sociology of deviance; it is rather that whatever villainy deviants might harbor is never strictly a function of their deviation. And one thing Newton makes clear in *Mother Camp*, the most important deviant ethnography of the 1960s, is that a lot of drag queens are jerks.

In Newton's book on "female impersonators in America," as its subtitle reads, the drag queens all use aliases because male drag performers require female stage names, of course, and also because "the limiting condition on drag," as Newton points out, "is its illegality."[20] The phrase "female impersonators" is itself something of an alias "for the benefit of the straight world" (3) made uncomfortable by the in-group label "drag queen." It is helpful to compare naming in *Mother Camp* to naming in *Slaughterhouse Five*. Real names abound throughout Vonnegut's novel—from its dedicatee, Mary O'Hare (who "didn't want her babies or anybody else's babies killed in wars" [19]), to Vonnegut's agent, Seymour Lawrence, whose "friends . . . call him Sam" and whom Vonnegut addresses directly: "And I say to Sam now: 'Sam—here's the book'" (24). If that novel's title furnishes a visceral index of what lies between its covers,

Newton's title functions by contrast like the Times Square porno shop Billy visits, where the Kilgore Trout novels in the window serve as pretext for the store's more profitable wares: it is a face-saving front for a less savory (if more intriguing) content.

Indeed, where the term "female impersonators" aims to console "the straight world" of academic readers, the phrase "Mother Camp" inflects the book toward a subcultural vernacular whose usages oblige Newton to explain herself in a footnote: "'Mother Camp' as an honorific," she writes of her "idiosyncratic" title, "implies something about the relationship of the female impersonator to his gay audience. . . . He himself is a magical dream figure: the fusion of mother and son. All this lies behind the terrain covered in this book; the title simply points hopefully in that direction" (xx). A different onomastics is thus in force in the drag world from that in Vonnegut's novel or, for that matter, in the 1960s at large. Naming functions not as an ethics but as a code ("To get in" to a gay bar in Kansas City, "you must be recognized by the man at the door . . . or at least produce a name that is known to him" [115]). The consequence is that efforts at labeling in both drag culture and its scholarly treatment begin to look like evasive maneuvers. The drag world's habitués, like those of the tearoom, are strategically hard to pin down.

Then, too, the possibility of finding "unison" among "people who define themselves as 'gay'" (22) is sabotaged by the invidious distinctions the gay world's inhabitants make among themselves. Between the "covert" gays, for whom the distinguishing mark is the "double life" (32), and the "overt . . . street fairies" (8), defined by "immersion in the gay world" (34), Newton locates both the "street impersonators" (street fairies who have made a go of professional drag by lip-syncing to records onstage) and the "stage impersonators" (7) (live entertainers who perform as women yet segregate "work and private domains" [17]). Stage impersonators interest Newton because they are neither fully discredited like the street fairies nor subject to the risks of discrediting (loss of job or status) faced by respectable gays. They achieve a "socialization of private deviance" (41), using drag both to acknowledge and to quarantine the stigma of effeminacy. Doing drag for a living keeps it from defining their life.

One way of looking at the distinction between "street" and "stage" impersonators is to reprise the dueling accounts of performance canvased previously: the dramaturgical approach of postwar sociology and the Method acting of the postwar stage and screen. Where the dramaturgical approach saw social life as a theater in which the individual continually negotiated the assumptions of an audience, the Method saw its task as training the actor to deny any appeal to the audience. Goffman's actors are instrumentalist and oriented to the impressions they make; Strasberg's actors are antitheatrical and oriented to the expressions they make. In their commitment to showmanship, stage impersonators might be understood to favor the dramaturgy featured in midcentury sociology: role distance, the dominion of the audience, the view that performance sustains a front rather than reveals an essence. The best drag acts involve "putting on a good show while indicating distance" (104). Their accommodation to perceptions explains the stage impersonators' interest in "lighting and make-up and stage effects" (98). Theirs is an aesthetics of concealment. Stage performers rely on "impressions" (98), moreover, both in the sense of currying favor with an audience and in the sense of imitating celebrities. In fact, the impersonation of Judy Garland or Carol Channing guarantees ovations, on the principle that people applaud most loudly what they already know.

In contrast to the stage impersonators, fluent in the "subtleties of relating to various types of audiences" (17), as well as in the finer points of role segregation, the street impersonators appear to borrow the Method actor's disdain for both audience and role distance and to favor a strategy of expressivity. They don't manage their identity with special effects; they embody it with their being. Even when not "openly contemptuous of the audience" (11), Newton writes, "they often seem wrapped in a trance-like state, never looking at the audience" (12). Moreover, street performers live their parts full-time. Yet the street impersonator's contempt for the *inauthentic* is what finally resonates with the Method's precepts. This category includes all gay men "who emulate straights," what one street impersonator refers to as "phony pink tea fairies" (15). When Newton asks an informant "why he had to ask for trouble on the street," the man suggests "sarcastically" that he should "get a crew cut and buy a sweatshirt" (9). It is in the "sartorial system" that the essence of the part is revealed (101), just as the Method taught that authenticity necessitates conformity between the internal and the external self. For street performers, dressing the part is the necessary but not sufficient condition of owning it.

No sooner have we imposed these accounts of performance on different drag styles, however, than the scheme begins to unravel. Although the Method values performance as an end in itself, the street impersonators by and large "view work instrumentally, that is, as a way of making money" (11). And whereas street impersonators are instrumentalists, their stage counterparts are the guardians of a certain authenticity by virtue of their commitment to the audience. If "there is no drag without an actor and his audience, no drag without drama (or theatricality)" (36), as Newton categorically states, then the stage performer alone earns the right to call himself a real drag queen. In either street or stage attire, then, drag thwarts the dichotomy of essence and artifice as those concepts were being imagined and exercised by sexual liberation movements. What counts as "authentic" drag—"the necessity to play at life" (109)—is not what gay liberationists mean by authentic. For this reason Newton feels the need to "stress" that "camp" is "pre- or proto-political." Since the real drag queen is committed to playing to audience expectations, "he agrees with the oppressors' definition of who he is" instead of "saying that the oppressors are illegitimate" (111).

Newton makes this comment in a footnote from 1972, at the height of gay and women's liberation. Her ambivalence toward this definition of politics as identity driven makes itself apparent in another footnote, where she observes that "politically militant homosexuals are now overt as a matter of principle," by which she means that "they wear homosexual lapel buttons and/or verbally announce their homosexuality publicly" but "are not overt in the older sense: they don't look or act like homosexuals" (24). This is a peculiar distinction. For overt homosexuals, like street fairies, Newton tells us, do not care what the audience thinks about them and feel only hostility for "the oppressors' definition." The difference between the overt homosexuals "in the older sense" and the "politically militant homosexuals" cannot be reduced to the issue of resistance. It is rather the difference between what it means to "look or act like homosexuals," the difference between wearing a wig and wearing a button.

Drag entails a political conundrum for Newton because its internal assumptions bring the politics of expressive authenticity to an impasse. The drag queen is simultaneously a figure whose efforts to grab attention tend to repel the audience at large and a figure who understands his social role as fundamentally a put-on that can be manipulated instrumentally to get what he wants. The drag queen fuses the role distance and impression management of the dramaturgical sociologist with the confrontational attitude of the Method actor, the attitude that featured prominently in the New Social Movements as they sought to repeal what Newton calls "the oppressors' definition." As I have implied, Newton was somewhat skeptical of this account of politics even as she enacted its tensions in framing her book's argument. *Mother Camp*'s preface describes Newton's conversion from middle-class graduate student to radical academic: "Now I think that anthropology and the other social sciences are the ideological arms of sociopolitical arrangements." The sorts of truth that "scholarship" could only intimate are now confirmed by "Liberation," which "has led me to *experience* the arbitrariness of our sex roles" and to "*know* now (rather than *think*) that the structure of sex roles is maintained by the acquiescence of *all* the participants who accept their fate as natural and legitimate" (xvi).

The movement from merely *thinking* to *knowing* something should be familiar to us as the hallmark of the expressive model privileged in the Method, which also equated conviction with an actor's unflagging confidence in her "experience." Yet Newton hardly abandons the ironic style of the academy for the revealed self of "liberation movements" (xvi). She continues to insist not on essence but on the distance from role that, according to Goffman, all social actors feel. Even in the midst of an embrace of the politics of experience, Newton revives the Cold War liberal's argument against the true believer who cannot distinguish between the fantasy and reality of a dramatic role. If what liberation reveals to her is not identity but its "arbitrariness," then the goal of a just society is not more acceptance of true roles but more disbelief with regard to the roles we already play. But Newton's uneasiness with the drag queen's prepolitical stance has another dimension that cannot be escaped, and it has to do with her own acquiescence to a role she maintains even in the teeth of gay liberation's call for "no more roles." If Newton has become a politicized academic, the stress falls on the *academic*. Though she makes it clear that her radicalization has taken place in the interval between the writing and publication of *Mother Camp*, she is less forthcoming about an aspect of her own self-identification that she will later make central to her work: her strong commitment to the butch persona. Explaining the ease with which informants opened up to her, Newton notes, "My status as a bookish female enabled me to present myself as a relatively asexual being" (135).

In this and other instances in *Mother Camp*, Newton might be seen as practicing a kind of deflection. She never lets readers "*know* . . . rather than *think*" that her "familiarity with drag" derives from anything other than a bookish interest (133). In playing down the butch, she plays up the academic, though *Mother Camp* provides enough clues to suggest that its author is more than simply asexual. Attending a drag show with a straight couple at a "tourist club" in New York, Newton mentions that "the other woman wore a simple dress and high heels," while Newton "wore a suit" (89). In such asides, the asexual academic permits a glimpse into a set of commitments other than those to the school. The point is not to "out" Newton as a butch lesbian, a task rendered superfluous in any event by her 1996 memoir, "My Butch Career," where she writes: "Butch is my handle and my collective name."[21] It is to suggest why the distinction between the prepolitical acquiescence to an external standard of identity and the liberationist's enlightened self-expression cannot be sustained. For even in the midst of her strongly worded confession of politicized consciousness in *Mother Camp*'s preface, Newton might be charged with holding something back. Of course, such strategies of evasion reveal themselves only retrospectively. Knowing Newton is a butch licenses the search for evidence of it in places where she thus appears to be concealing it. But such a search is of less interest than the fact that *Mother Camp*'s author appears to retain a queer stylistics even as she recognizes, and at times endorses, the intensive liberationist pressure to let role-playing go.

Given Newton's appreciation of role's nuances, an appreciation that includes what looks like a wily act of self-closeting, it is a bit curious to find *Mother Camp* willing to sacrifice the drag queen to an ideal of the self that he cannot possibly admit on the terms that gay liberation requires: the replacement of style by substance. One effect of gay liberation was to transform the virtuosity of the drag queen (for whom "speed and spontaneity are of the essence" [110]) into a habit over which the drag queen has no control. If the prepolitical homosexual world shunned drag queens because they willfully acted out their deviance, the post-Stonewall world treats drag queens as "untouchables" (129) because they are the victims of a "progression toward greater effeminacy" (77) whose gravitational pull they are unable to withstand. What seemed like a bad choice now appears a pitiable compulsion. And where drag's skill set was once synonymous with improvisation, drag after Stonewall assumes the narrow dimensions of a rote performance: "If you work in a club where you are a female impersonator," an informant tells Newton, "you're still stuck with each other, still stuck with the audiences you're going to perform to" (131). While this particular informant's testimony again raises the question of the difference between "homosexual performers" and "performing homosexuals" (7), between approaching a role with distance and irony and earnestly believing it, it also seems to answer that question in a way that decides the case against the drag queen on the terms of gay liberation's rejection of roles. Vonnegut's narration of drag as something that happens to Billy Pilgrim against his will turns out to be farsighted. Just as Billy is "costumed" by "Fate" and destined to a circular and alien temporality, "having come unstuck in time" (32), so drag really is a fatal curse: "You're going to have to ride this ship," Newton's informant says, "the rest of eternity. Just back and forth" (131). *Mother Camp* ends with the pathos of the queen whom drag consigns to a time warp.

Newton likewise suspends her own commentary because she is unsure, finally, about drag's contribution to the cause of liberation. While she may see camp as prepolitical, she betrays strong misgivings about the politics that has displaced it. Admitting a distaste for the "male worship among gays" (xiv) that has arisen in the decade since she published *Mother Camp*, Newton archly notes in the book's preface: "Sissies are out" (x). But then again sissies have always been out, both in the liberationist sense of "out loud and proud" and in the pejorative sense of "out of fashion." Gay liberation has never overcome the impasse between these forms of "overtness" (25). It has embraced the expressive authenticity of object choice with the same zeal that it has disclaimed the expressive authenticity of the sissy. No statement has become more indicative of liberated gay men than the mantra of *ordinariness*: "Just because I desire men doesn't mean I'm different from any other man."

If *Mother Camp* implies that this utterance is no more plausible than the drag queen's assumption that men who desire men act more like women than like men ("the covert homosexual must in fact impersonate a *man*" [108]), the book remains on the fence about the drag performance that the normative liberationist seeks to override. Both positions seem, in Newton's view, to catch their practitioners in a tension between role distance and audience expectation that no resort to expressive authenticity can resolve. Gay male activists have long assumed that there is a political advantage in insisting that there is no "real" difference between men who want men and men who want women. Reading *Mother Camp* through the lens of the dueling accounts of performance in postwar culture suggests a much less charitable view of this assumption. Though the prepolitical drag queen can be charged with a failure to "disagree with the oppressors" (with pandering to the audience), this claim is no less true of the "straight-acting" gay man who denies the sissy in the name of a homoeroticism wholly compatible with a virility determined by popular demand. Whereas the drag queen managed the stigmatized role of "feminine man" through the saving grace of camp humor, post-Stonewall gay man has no such recourse. His insistence on the lack of incongruity between his object choice and his embodied behavior must be taken entirely on faith.

From Dramaturgy to Performativity: Butler without Goffman

If *Mother Camp* has enjoyed a longevity beyond its (liberationist) time and (disciplinary) place, this is partly the result of its walk-on role in Judith Butler's *Gender Trouble* (1990), which makes Newton's research the starting point for its own widely debated musings on gender parody. In treating Newton's work as evidentiary rather than theoretical, Butler manages to tip her hat to the deviant ethnography of the postwar period without having to engage the conceptual framework from which that ethnography emerged. In "Performative Acts and Gender Constitution" (1988), the earliest mention of her influential thesis about the constructedness of gender, Butler distinguishes her project from Goffman's by claiming that he "posits a self which assumes and exchanges various 'roles,'" in contrast to her own claim that "this self is not only irretrievably 'outside,' constituted in social discourse, but also the ascription of interiority is itself a publically regulated and sanctioned form of essence fabrication."[22] Given a statement like the following, typical of Goffman's thought at every stage of his career, Butler's description of his work as positing an original, interiorized self can only be strategic misreading: "Individuals do not merely learn how and when to express themselves, for in learning this they are learning to be the kind of object to which the doctrine of expression applies, if fallibly; they are learn-ing to be objects that have a character, that express this character, and for whom this characterological expressing is only natural." "The notion of essence," as Goffman makes clear, "is social."[23]

In the more substantial argument she evolves in *Gender Trouble*, which absorbs most of "Performative Acts and Gender Constitution" into its third chapter, Butler drops the reference to Goffman, whose name does not appear in that or any of her subsequent books on gender.[24] This is an odd omission. If Butler's account of antiessentialism is rather precisely foreshadowed in the work of the postwar sociologists, it seems worth asking why she has shown so little interest in taking up those predecessors. Butler insists that the perfor-mative is not identical to (or even analogous with) the theatricality on which Goffman's work consistently alighted. Yet her writing is somewhat cagey with regard to the connection between performativity and performance (as is made obvious by the publication of "Performative Acts and Gender Constitution" in *Theatre Journal*). Though Butler asserts in *Bodies That Matter* that "the reduction of performativity to performance would be a mistake,"[25] her earlier essay is sanguine about the conflation of performance and performatives: "Gender is an act which has been rehearsed, much as a script survives the particular actors who make use of it, but which requires individual actors in order to be actualized and reproduced as reality once again."[26]

Nor is it the case that Goffman seemed unduly impressed by the sort of distinction between self and role that Butler imputes to him. "Goffman argues that human activity cannot be divided up into realms of authentic action and stereotyped or conventional behavior," Heather Love has observed; "he refuses to represent people and their activities in the sacralizing terms in which they see them."[27] It is interesting to speculate on what Goffman would have made of Butler's star had he lived to see its rise (he died in 1982, eight years before *Gender Trouble* was published). The argument Butler took up in her breakthrough monograph shows strong parallels with his own critique of gender's "doctrine of expression" in *Gender Advertisements* (1976), which assails the notion that "various 'expressions' of femininity (or masculinity)" indicate "something biological or social-structural that lies behind or underneath these signs." His dismantling of such "naturally indexical signs" bears the signature of the unapologetic constructionism that we have observed in his work: "That a multitude of 'genderisms' point convergently in the same direction might only tell us how these signs function socially, namely, to support belief that there is an underlying reality to gender. Nothing dictates that should we dig and poke behind these images we can expect to find anything there—except, of course, the inducement to entertain this expectation."[28] It is characteristic of Goffman that he appears to draw no broader lesson from the artifice of gender than the sly point that it reveals our own eagerness to "entertain" essences.

Toward the end of his career Goffman became interested in the Austinian performative that Butler makes the centerpiece of her critique of gender essence.[29] More precisely, he became interested in the philosophy of language as part of his career-long cannibalization of other thinkers, whose ideas he habitually pressed into service as confirmative restatements of his own. A more generous take on this point is what Eliot Freidson has in mind when, in a 1983 obituary, he praises Goffman for "employing with imagination and passion any resources that seem useful to illuminate aspects of human life that most of us overlook."[30] Goffman's lavish borrowings account for the frequency with which commentators like to point out his "literary" sensibility. If he never goes so far as to turn the approaches of other disciplines into sheer metaphor, he also never quite rises above treating, say, game theory or speech act theory as sheer *analogy*. In line with the midcentury humanist discussed previously, whose penchant for analogical thinking was subject to anxious ridicule in the postwar campus novel, Goffman's chief interest in the social world was working out the terms for "what it is like."

It would be overstating matters, but not by much, to say that Goffman gravitated toward other disciplines with no larger goal in mind than the effort to vary the forms of description that could be brought to bear on the social world. The eclecticism that is the keynote of his style can also, as his devotees sometimes inadvertently acknowledge, betray a static indifference. Here is Dell Hymes, resorting to metaphor (of the kind often employed by Goffman himself) to sum up his colleague's method in a memorial essay published in 1984:

> Twenty years ago it was easy enough to think of his work as a kind of anthropology or psychology; later it could be thought of as a kind of linguistics, ethology or communication science. That's what can happen to a diamond in the rough. As it polishes each facet in turn, different segments of the environment are caught in its gleam. . . . From the point of view of the diamond, of course, it is in the same place, simply adding to its ability to illuminate.[31]

Hymes all but admits that as brightly as Goffman could shine, there remained a kind of obdurate fixity to his thinking, an endless polishing of the same albeit multifaceted exterior. Hymes's figure ends up paying tribute less to Goffman's genius than to a familiar pattern in Goffman's work: its view of the "interaction order" as a sort of continuous surface that seems boundless only because it actually forms a circle. The oracular force with which Goffman aphorizes tautologies is in keeping with this circularity: "We are socialized to confirm our own hypotheses about our natures."[32] Goffman's style is no less compelling for its tendency to recast self-evident claims as lightning strikes of epiphany. This is only to suggest, however, what Goffman himself sometimes leads readers to suspect: the language of demystification in which he is so obviously fluent amounts to an elaborate joke.

Like the postwar humanist pedagogy lampooned by McCarthy and Nabokov, his commitments appear to lead Goffman away from rather than toward the values of humanism itself. If it is true that he represents a vigorous "anti-humanism," as Love suggests, the power of this stance resides in its disconcerting refusal to save anyone or anything.[33] This accounts for much of the ambivalence his career and writing have inspired. While no one denies that he was a brilliant writer, few social theorists have actually been drawn to adopt what Michael Schudson calls his "miniaturist" style, partly because that style seems relentlessly to parade its own inconsequence, to vaunt the finitude of its reach.[34] Hence the confession at the end of *The Presentation of Self in Everyday Life*: "Now it should be admitted that this attempt to press a mere analogy so far was in part a rhetoric and a maneuver, . . . that it is not to be taken too seriously."[35] In such self-canceling gestures, Goffman is almost a parody of the Cold War ironist, the relic of a bygone era of arch posturing. If his method has proved hard to reproduce, the reason is not merely that it flaunts its own antisystemic bona fides, nor that he is a stylist of great originality, but that he sets such little store by his own model, has such apparent contempt for the "applicability" of his claims to anything beyond the contexts that occasion them. Goffman sets a *bad example* all around.

Virtually the opposite is true of Judith Butler's example. For Butler has nothing if not followers. Measuring influence is always an inexact science, but it is arguable that what accounts for the wide influence, understood as imitation, of Butler's theoretical model is her explicit politicization of imitation itself.[36] Where Goffman's antihumanist vision tends toward a sometimes nihilistic complacency with the world as it comes, the vision that has informed Butler's work from the early 1990s onward provides an elemental building block in the research programs of a great many scholars precisely because it marries its anti-humanism to a "constructive" agenda (one way of understanding the prestige that the term "constructionism" has accrued in the last generation). Whereas Goffman's project is description, Butler's is "reconceptualization." "The reconceptualization of identity as an *effect*, that is, as *produced* or *generated*," she writes, "opens up possibilities for 'agency' that are insidiously foreclosed by positions that take identity categories as foundational and fixed."[37]

This statement is hedged with qualifiers that exempt Butler from charges of naïveté. In particular, the word "possibilities" provides Butler with a canny exit strategy for disclaiming (or deferring) the political work of her critique via a signifier of such indeterminacy that it deprives us of any claim on what such political work might look like. "Reconceptualization" nonetheless bears more than passing resemblance to the consciousness-raising techniques of the New Social Movements, albeit with a critical reversal of emphasis. For Butler, the object of reflection is uncovering artifice and effects rather than essence and expressions. But to call this a reversal of emphasis is somewhat misleading, for the key move in Butler's early work on gender performativity is surely the recasting of critique as a political gesture. What is especially noteworthy about this shift is the assumption underlying both Sixties radicalism and contemporary academic radicalism that one advantage of "the political" over "politics" as such is the promise of a more authentic politics than what transpires on Capitol Hill. The political is politics purified. Whereas politics means "compromise," the political means "possibilities."

In drawing out this distinction, I am concerned with neither the leftist lament regarding "the notion that poststructuralism has thwarted Marxism," as Butler puts it, nor the liberal lament that the postmodern academic has abandoned traditional politics at the cost of any direct or meaningful effect on the social order.[38] What interests me in the move from politics to the political is its having been repeatedly staged as a passage from unreality to a more direct and more meaningful reality. When academic theorists invoke the *truly political* as an honorific, for example, they are not referring to voter drives or ballot measures or, for that matter, picketing the Democratic National Convention. They have in mind other possibilities beyond the vestiges of civics or civil disobedience. And as if to confirm this assumption that politicization happens all around us (except perhaps in the sphere of politics "proper"), the debates that Butler's work has invited rarely center on a clarification of what Butler means by the political. They ask whether the approach for which Butler argues—parodying performatives—is a useful way of theorizing the political. When her critics accuse Butler of not being political enough, they are really impugning the authenticity of her theory. The terms of this accusation replicate those of *The Port Huron Statement*, which makes what its drafters imagine is the urgent point that "the moral clarity of the civil rights movement has not always been accompanied by precise political vision, and sometimes not even by a real political consciousness."[39]

This is only to observe that Butler and her critics discard the Sixties ideology of expressive authenticity while retaining the equation that the Sixties forged between authenticity and action. Hence, even while it rejects the gender politics of the manly New Left or the cult of true womanhood that dominated second-wave feminism, Butler's work reconstructs the Sixties appeal to an authentic politics as a politicization of authenticity itself. "To be called unreal," Butler writes in *Undoing Gender*, "is thus one way in which one can be oppressed."[40] This book makes explicit *Gender Trouble*'s earlier intimation that an antiessentialist politics is valuable not exactly for the abolition of "identity categories" but on behalf of their radical pluralization. "The conception of politics at work here," Butler writes, "is centrally concerned with the question of survival," and one answer she gives to this question entails validating "forms" of gender that "the norms governing reality have not admitted . . . to be real."[41] This construal of authentication as a tool of distributive justice might be said to rank chief among the "political possibilities" enjoined by "a radical critique of the categories of identity."[42]

The language of "political possibilities" suggests, then, a reason for Butler's reluctance to engage dramaturgical sociology. For what is irksome in Goffman's discourse is akin to what is irksome in drag life (and then in academic life) for Esther Newton: it is prepolitical at best and apolitical at worst. For drag to do the political work that Butler asks of it, she must discount the sociological insistence that performance is not a political matter but simply a way of life that always leaves the world intact. Goffman posits that persons are already attuned to the fictive quality of their identities and that self-consciousness merely compounds rather than extenuates what are hopelessly inconclusive performances. In contrast to Butler, who suggests that the performance of gender as naturalized norm is a problem that can be mitigated through a reflexive attention to "the hyperbolic status of the norm itself," Goffman takes such reflexivity as a by-product of a social order whose members are already in the habit of continually monitoring identities that have ceded any meaningful claim to essence.[43]

For Goffman, reflexive awareness does not constitute "distance" in the reparative sense of opening a space of possibilities between the agent and her domination. It is just another word for alienation. As if to make matters worse, at least for political possibilities, such alienation is requisite for the observation Goffman values—the "value-free" description of the social sciences. Descriptions can facilitate the right picture of a society, but they cannot induce the right relations people in a society ought to have. Insofar as it aspires to be purely descriptive, Goffman's work is thus also *purely academic*. It is instructive to recall the special resentment between the Berkeley students and the sociologists who kept their distance from the Free Speech Movement in view of what many of them took to be the FSM's confusion of politics and academics. Goff-man took as given that not much followed from the recognition of the roles we play beyond the recognition itself. This may account for his sniping remark during the FSM crisis: "When they start shooting students from the steps of Sproul Hall I guess I'll get involved, but not until then."[44]

My point is not that Goffman's politics were essentially quietist but that however we choose to interpret his politics, Goffman made it very difficult to read off his academic work a transformative program. This point can be seen even more clearly by recalling that while Goffman may have been a catalyst for the work of deviant ethnographers like Esther Newton, even she finds it hard to move from a theorization of camp to a political program in which camp might be a surrogate or analogue for *consciousness raising*. In order to "do" politics, after all, Newton feels a need to announce politics as separate from the academic milieu, which—with its institutional commitment to bad faith and its playing to the expectations of its composite audience of students, faculty, and admin-istrators—bears a striking resemblance to the "acquiescen[t]" scene of the drag show. Newton appears to have learned from Goffman, in other words, what we might call the limitations of knowingness: her drag queens, like her academics, know better than they act. Armed with an awareness of the oppressive inconsis-tencies of their environments, they nonetheless choose to remain inside them.

Mean Camp

This is a somewhat troubling account of knowingness in the era of the New Social Movements. It obliges us to see anew not only the proximity of camp sensibility and academic irony but also, and more to the point, the discontinu-ity between camp and the consciousness raising at the heart of Sixties activism. The effort to gloss over this discontinuity, to save camp for a transformative project, partly motivates Susan Sontag's effort to distinguish "naïve" camp from its unregenerate double, the "manufactured, calculated" camp that betrays the spirit of the sensibility with its archness.[45] Yet as much as it conforms to the reg-nant opposition within the New Social Movements and the politics of authen-ticity, Sontag's influential effort to parse "pure" camp from "deliberate" camp (282) poses its own problems for any attempt to recuperate a camp style for a consciousness-raising agenda. If naïve camp's purity is a measure of its un-knowing, after all, it cannot exactly deliver itself up to the cause of social change on the grounds of its privileged relation to knowledge.

One way into this set of concerns might be to speak less of a pure and an impure camp than what, in contrast to Sontag's description of camp as a "tender feeling" (290), we might call "mean camp," the goal of which is to appropriate camp itself for decidedly impolitic ends. Camp has always had a dark side, to be sure, a hint of cruelty nowhere so visible as in the presumed misogyny with which female impersonators have undertaken their caricature of femininity. Much ink has been spilled by those either making or defending against this charge. But camp's misogynistic or minstrel impulses are not what I have in mind. Mean camp does not deride womanhood or normative gender roles; its chief target is the camp sensibility itself. Mean camp does not see the charm in incongruity; it sees only contemptible inconsistency.

In the effort to get a handle on this concept, let us take an example from a film beloved among queer theorists not least because of its camp credentials: Paul Morrissey's *Trash* (1971). *Trash*'s final scene finds Holly Woodlawn's character refusing to give up her shoes to a social worker, even though he won't approve her welfare claim without this bribe and, as he tells her, with welfare she "could buy twenty pairs of shoes." The social worker wants the shoes to "make a lamp out of them," a refurbishing that puns on the equation, already a cliché by 1971, between camp's transvaluing aesthetic and political enlightenment. This commitment to remaking, as well as to conceiving of objects as interchangeable (he sees the shoes as a "fair trade" for welfare), marks the social worker as a suspect figure. Depicting his social worker as a camp aficionado, Morrissey announces a recognizable collusion between bureaucracy and queerness in securing the liberal compact.

Morrissey is a self-described "reactionary conservative," who once claimed that he made *Trash* to demonstrate that "there's no difference between a person using drugs and a piece of refuse."[46] Although these facts might make us question the embrace of the film among critics who see it as redemptive and transgressive in equal measure, the film alone suffices to show that it has almost no interest in any narrative of transformation. "It is not that human beings become as worthless as trash," Jon Davies argues in *Trash: A Queer Film Classic*, "but that trash becomes as precious as human beings."[47] This is, I would hazard, a wildly imprecise description of *Trash*. For whatever his political allegiance, Morrissey's object is not to reverse the terms society uses to classify things into useful and useless. Trash in Morrissey's *Trash* is a mechanism of de-creation, a figure of failed transformation. The film enlists the assumption many critics of

Trash have of trash—that its goal is to be redeemed or salvaged—in order to demonstrate that the process of redemption does not take.

In *Trash*, recirculation does not equate with renewal no matter how much work one puts into the act of salvaging. We can get a sense of this defeat most clearly in the kind of trash Holly gathers. As viewers are well aware, Holly tends to collect a lot of beds: a "mattress" for "my sister," whose baby Holly plans to raise; a "bassinet" for the baby itself, which is really "just a drawer"; "nice garbage" up on 24th Street, which includes yet another mattress. This partiality for beds reveals a common feature of Holly's finds: whether or not they started out that way, they are repurposed for sitting or lying, for containing the body in a state of proneness. The dirty mattress or drawer relaxes the prostrate body into a state of fixed matter and thus concretizes the passivity that *Trash* ascribes to Holly's compulsive need for welfare. Like the drug use that figures as the film's signature motif, welfare allows for a repose that stills the body without expending its energy. The pleasure of heroin in the film is the reward of immobility. In a scene that finds her climaxing with the aid of an empty bottle, Holly shouts, "Oh God I want welfare," as though sexual release were a direct result of going on relief. Yet it would be more appropriate to say that the desire for welfare doesn't bring on sexual satisfaction so much as replace it.

Trash stages a face-off between a camp sensibility that can turn anything (like shoes) into an object of desire and a camp sensibility that uses trash or "junk" to turn the self away from desire. The fact that the representative of the latter position is a drag queen is surprising if only because the drag queen, as Esther Newton shows, is widely praised (or condemned) for his knowingness; and Holly is too obtuse to work out that her garbage cannot be recycled, too obtuse to grasp the basics of exchange or the difference between worth and waste. "Once in a while I do her a favor and clean up the place," Joe tells a teenager Holly has brought home. "It's all garbage. She doesn't even know when you throw it out." Like Divine, the star of the early films of John Waters (another practitioner of mean camp), Holly Woodlawn practiced a specific type of drag: what Michael Moon and Eve Sedgwick call, specifically in reference to Divine but evocative of Holly's unrecyclable litter, "unsanitized drag."[48] This is not the female impersonation of the stage illusionist, whose success is determined by mimicry of Judy Garland or Bette Davis, but an acting out much closer in spirit to that of the street performer, who is often a poor illusionist because he neglects to observe the boundary between life and stage, identity and act.

My point is not that Divine and Holly fail to pull off "successful" performances as women but rather that, however convincing they may be as women, the characters they play are nevertheless marred by an insurmountable crisis of self-transformation elsewhere: in Holly's case, an inability to convince us that the trash she collects is salvageable and, in Divine's case, an equally dramatic failure to convince the world that her self-proclaimed attributes are objectively shareable. The Waters repertoire is powered on the electric tension between its characters' delusional speech acts and the unreceptive contexts in which they are uttered ("I still am the top model in the country," insists *Female Trouble's* Dawn Davenport [Divine], her face ravaged by acid scars).[49] Both Waters and Morrissey exploit the spectacle of delusional queens whose gestures of self-determination inevitably run aground on the disbelieving contempt of both on-screen and off-screen audiences.

We would be remiss in not attending more closely to the laughter occasioned—or, more accurately, *demanded*—by the defective self-perceptions to which such characters are prone. The disconnect between intention and execution (or between subjective impression and objective reality) is central to the camp aesthetic, which prides itself on paying close attention to the way its favored objects fail precisely because of their overambitious aims. The camp product is by definition an overextended undertaking. But in Morrissey and Waters, camp's fondness for such dissociation is subject to a mean-spiritedness that we overlook because of our penchant for seeing their works as politically consoling (if only because they fluster a normative sensibility). When Frank O'Hara's speakers muse about their desires ("I am the least difficult of men," notes the speaker in "Meditations in an Emergency." "All I want is boundless love"), they are never unaware of the discrepancy between their limitless appetites and their finite circumstances.[50] Morrissey and Waters turn away from this equation of camp sensibility with the recognition of limits by making their drag protagonists seem oblivious to the constraints on their own self-assertion and self-perception. Holly and Divine are in this respect anomalous creatures: while they traffic in the camp logic of possibility, they appear ignorant of camp's ironic retrenchment in the face of impossibility. They fail to be in on the jokes they make of themselves.

These performers appeared in films made during a period when sentience was increasingly coming to seem a determinant of entities beyond the human vessel, from animals to intelligent machines to the earth itself. Gary Snyder's

1972 essay, "Energy Is Eternal Delight," urged his readers to take a cue from "Pueblo societies," for example, where "a kind of ultimate democracy is practiced" in which "plants and animals are also people."[51] Given the prevalence of what environmental historian Roderick Nash calls the "ethical extension" in the post-1960s milieu, the withholding of a basic self-awareness from their characters is worth some attention in a discussion of Waters or Morrissey.[52] Like Morrissey, whose shoe-obsessed social worker wears a peace button and dutifully asks Joe and Holly whether they prefer to be called "hippies" or "flower children," Waters was disdainful of the counterculture and the culture that had appropriated the counterculture. "Sitting in the mud with a bunch of naked hippies and their illegitimate children," Waters writes of Woodstock, "was hardly my idea of a good time."[53]

Divine's obtuse characters, like *Trash*'s naïve Holly, appear as rebukes to the counterculture's fascination with expanded consciousness in its manifold forms, from Aquarian philosophy to deep ecology. To be sure, it was a favorite sport of pundits in the late 1960s to find in Jonathan Livingston Seagull's flights of self-actualization, say, a camp spoof of New Age enlightenment. ("He took in new ideas," Richard Bach writes of his titular bird, "like a streamlined feathered computer.")[54] The rejoinder to the ersatz transcendentalism of the counterculture from artists like Waters and Morrissey was not a smug knowingness, however, but a more disconcerting embrace of a state awfully close to stupidity, an anti-intellectualism that was in deep respects antisocial. There is no brighter proof of the disdain for consciousness raising in the mean camp repertoire than the moment in *Female Trouble* when Dawn Davenport strangles her daughter to death after the latter has become a Hare Krishna.

Whereas Divine and Holly Woodlawn are its warped embodiments, mean camp's program text is Gore Vidal's *Myra Breckinridge* (1968). Like Morrissey's *Trash*, Vidal's novel takes aborted transformation—in this case, from the male Myron to the female Myra—as its central topic, a theme it pursues through a relentless focus on the gap between Myra's self-perception and the world outside her head. The dissonance between Myra's view of things and the external account is reminiscent of that in *Pale Fire*'s Kinbote. Both characters are fugitives of a sort, recording their thoughts from the dubious sanctum of a motel room; both take up asylum in the school; and both are consumed with nostalgia for a halcyon past. For Kinbote it is prerevolutionary Zembla; for Myra, it is the Golden Age of Hollywood cinema, "if only because *in the decade between*

1935 and 1945, no irrelevant film was made in the United States."[55] Finally, both fashion themselves as scholars on a mission: Kinbote seeks to bring out Shade's posthumous "Pale Fire," and Myra has devoted herself to finishing her dead husband's book, *Parker Tyler and the Films of the Forties; or, the Transcendental Pantheon* (17).

It is in the choice of subject matter, however, that Vidal departs from his predecessor. Whereas Nabokov's hero is devoted to the highbrow canon, a taste his creator finds unimpeachable, Myra's adulation of *"blessed* celluloid" (5) mirrors her overweening self-regard, and there is no doubt that Vidal holds both styles of mythmaking—the Hollywood version and the glamour girl version—in contempt.[56] Yet this is only to note that Myra is a camp diva in the passé mode. Identifying with a burnt-out star system, she is a throwback to an earlier camp dispensation. Like Divine in most of her roles, Myra is utterly convinced of—and just as mistaken about—her own godhead: "Alone of all women, I know what it is like to be a goddess enthroned" (185). At the same time, we are unsurprised to learn that while living in New York, Myra "appeared in a number of underground movies," which gave her a "sense of what it must be like to be a star" (28), a sensation that would have been familiar to any drag queen who happened upon Warhol's Factory circa 1968.

Vidal bestows on his heroine the obdurate denseness with which *Trash's* Holly Woodlawn is endowed. Just as Holly refuses to believe that her garbage cannot be recycled, so Myra is never so gullible as when she professes her heightened consciousness: "My own uniqueness is simply the result of self-knowledge" (135). But more to the point, her counterfeit consciousness raising takes a singularly unsociable form, a parody of the millenarianism to which some New Left revolutionaries were given. "Death and destruction, hate and rage," Vidal writes, "are the most characteristic of human attributes, as Myra Breckinridge knows and personifies" (142). Entertaining a giddy Malthusian fantasy in which rampant heterosexual intercourse "has so filled up the world with superfluous people that our end is now at hand" (234), Myra eagerly welcomes "war and famine and the physical decadence of a race whose extinction is not only inevitable but also desirable" (234). In giving vent to her all-consuming narcissism ("After me what new turn can the human take?" [234]), Myra thus betrays (or, for the campus novelist, confirms) the school's governing pedagogy: all experience except her own is irrelevant. Because "these young people are a new breed who have gone beyond linear type in their quest for experience," she observes of her charges at Buck Loner's Academy of Drama and Modeling, "I find it extraordinarily difficult getting through to them even the simplest thought" (47). Committing what the progressive educator might consider a deadly sin, Myra concludes that her students are unteachable because they substitute experience for knowledge. Myra has a zero-tolerance policy with regard to the postwar humanist's pedagogy of analogy. She insists on "an exact, literal sense" (5) of the self-identity she is chronicling and declaims her abhorrence of "metaphors," since "nothing is *like* anything else. Things are themselves entirely and do not need interpretation, only a minimal respect for their integrity" (8).

This might well be the mission statement of the student movement, and its invocation here reveals not only the obvious incoherence of Myra's theory of education but, much more interestingly, the rather cynical view that Vidal insists on taking toward both midcentury school culture and the radicals who rebelled against it. In Vidal's account, neither the cultural institution of the school nor the countercultural attack on the school can do more than default to the status quo ante. Just as she travesties school culture's most sacred lessons, so Myra's epic struggle to remake gender definitions is "demented" (261) and "pretentious" (262), according to Myron, who has resumed his identity by the novel's finale. *Myra Breckinridge* ends on the most banal of anticlimaxes: Myron weds Mary-Ann (a student from Buck Loner's Academy) in a Las Vegas chapel and sets up a suburban idyll in the San Fernando Valley. Its heroine's reversion to her quondam identity would seem to confirm that Vidal's novel preempts any gesture toward renewal or metamorphosis. While Vegas may be the final frontier for a certain revisionist upheaval of modernist space, as in Robert Venturi's influential *Learning from Las Vegas* (1972), it is also, as Myron and Mary-Ann's nuptials attest, a place to get married.

Such reversion to the norm is the point of Vidal's novel and the derisive sensibility it typifies, for the exemplary practitioners of mean camp seek to negate the equation of camp's "solvent" (290) effect (Sontag's word) and a politics of social transformation. This undertaking assumes various strategies, from the ambiguously mean-spirited casting of a protagonist as hopelessly obtuse to the overt scorn for camp affect itself. But the most dramatic implication of such assaults on camp in the guise of camp is twofold: on the one hand, a disdain for what Leo Bersani has dubbed the "culture of redemption"; and, on the other hand, a disdain for the New Social Movements, as though it were incumbent upon mean camp artists to denounce the culture of redemption through an equally withering dismissal of any effort to reframe the world.[57] Yet it cannot escape our notice that the myriad offenses perpetrated across the mean camp repertoire against the culture of raised consciousness assume as their privileged form the compromised drag queen (Divine or Holly Woodlawn) or transsexual (Myra). These figures are compelling precisely because they fail to transition, to make the exchanges—surgical, sartorial, intellectual—that are basic to the culture of redemption.

Mean camp's characters often speak in the language of revolution, but their rhetoric belies a will to power no less aggressive for the ease with which their delusions are foiled. That will to power returns us to the lesson that Vonnegut found in sociology classes at the University of Chicago, which taught him that "nobody was ridiculous or bad or disgusting." The goal of social theorists from Becker to Newton was to argue precisely the opposite. There were many such "villains" in the subcultures to which deviant ethnography turned its gaze; moreover, the study of such baddies could lead to real knowledge. Morrissey, Waters, and Vidal seem to arrive at yet another conclusion. Theirs is a world made up largely of villains, like those characters in *Pink Flamingos* who vie for the title of "filthiest people alive."[58] But their villainy teaches us no lesson. Newton comes close to a version of this recognition when she admits in *Mother Camp* to a certain impasse between her own understanding and the camp attitude: "One of the most confounding aspects of my interaction with the impersonators was their tendency to laugh at situations that to me were horrifying or tragic" (109). From the vantage of mean camp, the queer subculture begins to look less like the "proto-political" vanguard of liberation, clearing a path for a critical mass of gay persons by "neutraliz[ing] moral indignation" (290), as Sontag puts it, than like a terror cell dedicated to the triumph, as Waters "fantasized" it, of the "hate generation."[59] But if it is obvious that camp seen in these terms does not favor redemption, it makes even less sense to impute to it a policy of what Newton calls "acquiescence."

Mean camp takes the off-putting laughter of Newton's informants even further, defeating the social-scientific aim of "knowing the other" by turning out others who are themselves unknowing, whose cluelessness makes them permanently resistant to conversion. Thrown back on the status quo ante, such characters exhibit nonetheless a consoling obliviousness. When Dawn Davenport is executed at the end of *Female Trouble*, she goes out of the world delivering her acceptance speech at what she thinks is the Oscars. Is there finally, surreptitiously, a drive toward redemption in work that pursues the singular aim of having no redeeming qualities? Mean camp tries hard to answer this question in the negative. But the very labor to condemn all institutions as unredeemable itself betrays a kind of wishful thinking not far removed from what we might see as mean camp's "consciousness-lowering" agenda: a desire for an alternative state beyond the reach of institutional frameworks. The notion that consciousness can be lowered, after all, is no less seductive than the idea that it can be raised.

6 Feminism, Meritocracy, and the Postindustrial Economy

Frigid Women and Single Girls

In *Slaughterhouse Five*, the only "book in English" Billy Pilgrim's alien abductors deem worthy of collecting is Jacqueline Susann's *Valley of the Dolls*, a book that Billy (having read it on the voyage to Tralfamadore) "thought . . . pretty good in spots" despite the fact that "the people in it certainly had their ups and downs."[1] While Vonnegut doubtless intends this reference as a throwaway joke, or a nod to the blending of high and low genres prized by postmodernists and camp followers alike, it's possible to detect an oblique logic in his enlistment of *Valley of the Dolls* as a text that might speak to the indignities befalling his protagonist. One of the basic "ups and downs" in *Valley of the Dolls*, after all, concerns the rise and fall in reputation that its principals—like Vonnegut's beset POW—must face at every juncture. The difference between Vonnegut's hero and Susann's heroines is that Billy seems incapable of escaping the rumors that eddy around him, whereas Susann's characters must fuel the rumors about themselves on behalf of their nonstop promotional campaigns.

Susann herself shared Billy's unlucky tendency to run afoul of gender ascription, presenting her femininity in ways liable to call the wrong kind of attention to its owner. In a *Tonight Show* appearance, to take one notorious example, Truman Capote called her "a truck driver in drag."[2] That Capote took a fiendish delight in seeing through her makeup to its unprepossessing foundation appeared intolerable (Susann threatened a libel suit) because it implied an assault on the vigilantly maintained product of her life's work. Susann had long imagined herself an adept in the arcana of feminine allure. Her biographer, Barbara Seaman, notes that while she may have been shortchanged of physical gifts, Susann had a talent for capitalizing on the ones she had. "Jackie was truly beautiful for about five minutes when she was very young," one "friend" informs Seaman, while another concedes, "She used to get a fantastic makeup."[3] After

Valley of the Dolls exposed her to the spotlight of celebrity, Susann's facade was much harder to sustain. The journalist Sara Davidson began a 1969 profile by describing Susann with "a mask of makeup—black penciled brows, heavy false lashes, orange lipstick, and a black shoulder length fall made of Korean hair."[4]

While there are no drag queens in *Valley of the Dolls*, strictly speaking, there are numerous characters who perform femininity for a living, whether as models or actresses or starlets or Broadway divas. There is also a good deal of innuendo about their sexuality and that of the men who gather around them. In Susann's novel, where the women make the money, the men in their lives stand accused of being "faggots."[5] Just as the book insists that the woman who succeeds in show business can never escape the gossip mongering that feeds into the manufacture of celebrity, so the threat to her reputation appears nowhere so lurid as in her guilt by association with the queer. Queerness has a fundamentally suppositional aspect in *Valley of the Dolls*. Anne Welles's boss says that perhaps her unrequited love, Lyon Burke, "could turn into a fag" (56), and Neely O'Hara speculates that the theater legend Helen Lawson is "maybe . . . turning queer in her old age" (89). Meanwhile, Neely's "double-gaited" husband, Ted Casablanca, tells her in the midst of their breakup, "You almost made me think I *was* a queer" (260). A relentless hypothetical, queerness rolls onstage whenever Susann needs an objective correlative for the sort of chin-wag that arouses without exhausting speculation.

This claim is actually somewhat ungenerous to Susann, whose most famous novel contains a more intricate meditation on the "ups and downs" of reputation than I have thus far implied. Its own curiosity regarding sexual matters is certainly more pluralistic. Though *Valley of the Dolls* makes much of the specter of homosexuality, it is just as interested in the specter of "frigidity," a condition that should pose some interest for the student of sexuality. "She knew the truth now," Anne Welles thinks on her way home from dinner with the secret millionaire Allen Cooper, who has given her an unwelcome marriage proposal. "She was frigid. That awful word the girls at school used to whisper about" (29). Susann's novel is keenly aware of the ways in which frigidity, like faggotry, operates as a shaming device, a threat wielded by men against women who resist their advances, as when Allen tells Anne that she's "afraid of sex," that "most girls of twenty aren't virgins," and that he wants "to see if I can't rattle some feeling into that perfect face" (106). Like queerness, frigidity is less an open than a muttered secret in *Valley of the Dolls*, its "maybe" status always a lively topic of debate.

In this regard at least, Susann's book reads less like escapist potboiler than documentary record. *Valley of the Dolls* takes place over a span of time, from the late 1940s through the mid-1960s, in which the proliferation of "the frigid type" (326) had become something of a national catastrophe. "True frigidity in women" turned out to be not only "one of the most common problems in gynecology," as Charles Freed and William Kroger observed in a 1950 paper, but one of the most eclectic. Its victims ranged from the repressed woman who withholds sex entirely to the nymphomaniac who is "in search of satisfaction which is never achieved."[6] One of the challenges frigidity appeared to present to the diagnostician indeed arose from the enormous frequency of sexual activity among those who suffered from it, a situation that allowed for such seemingly oxymoronic figures as Freed and Kroger's "extremely promiscuous and totally frigid woman" (530) and for Edmund Bergler's assertion that "nine-tenths of all cases of infidelities on the part of the woman are traceable to frigidity."[7]

If its manifestations were hard to sort, its epidemiology was even more of a puzzle. For Freed and Kroger, frigidity derived from "narcissism, and too much self-love" (532); whereas for Clark Vincent, "frigidity is symptomatic behavior in women who have lost or who lack basic self-respect and self-love."[8] Vincent further claimed that an "overemphasis on technique" paved the way for frigidity by turning "the sexual relationship" into "a chore which loses the spontaneity of a love relationship" (357), while Lena Levine and David Loth held that "problems of technique" often forced women to endure the clumsy groping of their partners, from whom they garnered so little pleasure that they came to dread sex altogether.[9] Such women "are inclined to attribute the greatest delight to chance . . . without really trying to remember the exact sequence of stimulation and reaction" (116). Too much repression or not enough, too much sex drive or not enough, too much self-love or not enough, too much technique or not enough: The "problems" of "frigidity," as Vincent puts it, "entail many variables" (360).

Just about the only thing most observers of frigidity agree upon is that it manifests across the gamut of its patients as an unbridgeable distance between what they feel and what Levine and Loth call the "spontaneous affection" they are supposed to feel (49). Spontaneity proves the holy grail in frigidity discourse, a quest object rendered even more elusive because it demands both a capacity for and surrender of self-control, a dynamic that recalls the paradoxical yielding of Method actors who must work themselves up into a state of self-abandon. If frigidity can be distilled to a single complaint, it would be a variant of the grievance that the Method's advocates brought against theatrical conventions that had become so formulaic as to lose all credibility: its victims do not feel like women even as they endlessly perform their femininity. The diagnosis of frigidity routinely arises when performances of conventional womanhood are understood no longer to convince either their actors or their audiences.

Although it afflicts the vast majority of women, frigidity's most hazardous effects transpire in the marriage bed. Wives face a burden that single women are spared; when the latter fake it, there are no husbands to judge them against past performances. The difference between the single woman and the wife is the difference between a woman who has to perform as though her livelihood depends on it and a woman who, once she becomes a spouse, must leave performance behind. Lack of spontaneity in the marriage bed derives from an inability to stop "indulging in" what Freed and Kroger call the "masquerade" (527) of innocence or allure that landed the husband in the first place. According to frigidity's experts, then, the feminine wiles brought to bear in a successful courtship must be suspended on a woman's wedding day. It is no wonder so many women come to feel that marriage is a bore. The performance that was essential to becoming a wife is now a liability, since marriages aren't intended to involve the stagecraft that gives courtships or romances their flirtatious kick. Glamour—the ability to cast a spell, to engender mystique—is the prerogative of unmarried women.

The single girl, the "newest glamour girl of our times," Helen Gurley Brown writes in *Sex and the Single Girl* (1962), "lives by her wits"; self-supporting in the corporate rat race, "she has had to sharpen her personality and mental resources to a glitter in order to survive in a competitive world and the sharpening looks good."[10] Brown's book might rank alongside *The Feminine Mystique* as a foundational text of women's liberation were it not for its resolute insistence that women ought to work, finally, to make themselves more marriageable. Yet if marriage was hardly incidental to her brand of self-help, the path Brown recommended wasn't exactly a straight shot. Drawing on the example of her own work ethic, she encouraged women to stave off marriage until "you have both jelled," on the assumption that it is "much safer to marry with part of the play out of his system *and yours*" (5). As though mindful of the pitfalls that await the overactive single girl in the staid marital bower, Brown offers a way out of the double bind of female performance that frigidity's experts caution against. Her working woman doesn't frost over after her wedding day so much as coagulate with her husband into a wedlock imagined as a somewhat temperate zone to begin with. Spontaneity pays no dividends in *Sex and the Single Girl*, which instead places a premium on "potential" (66). Through painstaking effort, Brown—who was "not beautiful or even pretty, . . . not bosomy or brilliant"—"worked hard" for "seventeen years . . . to become the kind of woman" who landed the rich husband she "deserved" (4). In *Sex and the Single Girl*, womanhood is a meritocracy.

By way of the prestige the meritocracy confers on "potential," we can approach female frigidity as other than merely a symptom of Cold War repression. While frigidity makes its awkward appearance in the nation's marriage beds during that postwar retrenchment in American culture when gender roles become both polarized and constricted, we might also attribute its rise to a certain, albeit contradictory, appeal to equal opportunity. Whereas its experts agree that frigidity names the gap between spontaneity and conduct, they also conclude that nearly every woman is capable of feeling sexual pleasure if she is just willing to exert herself. The frigid woman may suffer not from trying too hard, it would seem, but from not trying hard enough. From this angle, frigidity reveals the meritocracy's quintessential binary: the tension between who you are and what you do, between what you are given and what you can earn on your own. Midcentury accounts of merit seemed to settle on grace over works: the rise of standardized testing as the chief metric in sorting the college bound from everyone else implied the triumph of a culture in which "native ability" irrespective of social position allegedly determined merit. But even the nascent Educational Testing Service felt obliged to market its SAT as a tool for bringing the innately talented and underprivileged to the College Board's attention in order for the latter to make it possible for high-performing students to *realize their potential.*[11] In evolving a narrative whereby women could overcome their condition by an effort of the will, the discourse of frigidity privileged an extreme but not atypical account of the biopolitics of merit, in which the conflict between the given (female embodiment) and the achieved (female pleasure) was finessed with appeals to improvability.

This was a conflict that Jacqueline Susann—not quite pretty or tall enough to model, not quite charismatic enough to be a television personality—endured on a virtually daily basis over the course of her life. In one sense, Susann personified Brown's bootstrapping ideal. As with her self-administered makeovers, she compensated for her pronounced lack of writerly talent with a tireless enthusiasm for marketing her work. *Valley of the Dolls*, a book not so much composed by its author as wrestled into being by its embittered line editor, Don Preston (who told Barbara Seaman that Susann "almost wrote free association"), might rightly be understood as having become a bestseller through its creator's sheer pluck and determination.[12] Susann and Brown became friends through their publisher, Bernard Geis, but Susann's real kindred spirit at Geis was Letty Cottin Pogrebin, who was made its director of publicity in the early 1960s. At Geis, Pogrebin helped launch Brown and Susann to stardom; after Geis folded in the early 1970s, she became a founding editor of *Ms.*

Brown, Susann, and Pogrebin occupied what we might call the "parafeminist" milieu, a bridge between the mass-cultural discourse of positive thinking and the New Left discourse of consciousness raising. In Pogrebin's *How to Make It in a Man's World* (1970), the opportunistic glad-handing of Dale Carnegie is a cornerstone of empowerment; "realizing your potential" means "reacting like a seismograph to everything around you."[13] For Pogrebin, however, the obligation to be "malleable and available to adjustment" (66) is less a brief for conformism than the opening wedge in an antiessentialist critique of workplace bias. The constructionist terms of the corporate personality seep into a reconsideration of labor as artificial, chosen, or voluntary. "I work because I want to, not because I have to," she claims. A good deal of Pogrebin's advice for women in the workplace consists of encouraging her readers to land "a position that allows you to think up a party, plan it, and then go to it" (185). Shifting labor from the realm of necessity into the domain of desire, Pogrebin treats "the 'need' standard for job filling" as the most insidious form of employment discrimination. Against the "primitive" view that "a man *needs* a job even if a woman *deserves* it" (200), Pogrebin argues for a gender-blind meritocracy in which applicants compete solely on the basis of ability.

Pogrebin describes herself as a "chameleon" and insists that "the real you is what you are at any given moment, . . . the phony is as 'real' as the honest woman, . . . the surface is as real as the contents" (251). These are not axioms we tend to associate with the self-actualized person. Yet as the concept of "self-actualization" was gaining traction in the 1960s (182), it made its most important headway in the precincts of the corporate culture to which Pogrebin's ideas pay heed. Parafeminism's antecedents were located not only in the ruminations of managerial theorists but also in the self-help crusade that by the early

1960s was coalescing into the "Human Potential Movement." Business gurus and countercultural enthusiasts alike took to the "humanistic" psychology of Abraham Maslow, a fixture at the Esalen Institute and the proponent of the view that psychologists needed to focus less on sickly psyches than on the "positively healthy."[14]

A brief detour through Maslow's thought reveals a likely provenance for the heady cocktail of self-actualization and other-direction Pogrebin mixes. Maslow counseled that "identification with important causes, or important jobs," provided a means of "enlarging the self and making it important."[15] The conflict between autonomy and heteronomy that sociologists like Riesman saw as basic to midcentury culture was vastly exaggerated, according to the view set forth in Maslow's *Toward a Psychology of Being* (1962). Indeed, "self-actualization," he claims, "makes it *easier* for the person ... to merge himself as a part in a whole larger than himself." And the converse is also true: "One can attain to autonomy only via successful homonomous experiences" (232). In Maslow's view, spontaneity and other-direction are of a piece because each involves a kind of "absorption." Successful organizations allow workers to develop such strong "ego-centering" that the self can be "transcended" (42) without any risk to core identity. Potential is as crucial to Maslow as spontaneity, and we pay no small tribute to his ambition when we note that he turns these arguably contrary values into isomorphic ones, making "purposeful and pragmatic striving" (158) and "openness to experience" (156) entail each other. For Maslow's self-actualized worker, "the distinction between work and play" has become "shadowy" because "pleasure" is "merged with duty" (155). Or as Pogrebin puts it, a fulfilling job is "a position that allows you to think up a party, plan it, and then go to it."

In a formulation that has proved deeply amenable to upper-management types, Maslow equated what he famously called "peak experiences" with winning performance—or, put less facetiously, with the definition of "performance" furnished by Douglas McGregor, who called it "actions relative to goals."[16] Adapting Maslow to management theory, McGregor's influential *The Human Side of Enterprise* (1960) defined successful business leadership as "a process primarily of creating opportunities, releasing potential."[17] It is not hard to see how Maslow's theory of peak experience might lend itself to the vertical scale fundamental to the meritocratic climbers of the corporate ladder. And it is by way of the peak experience, defined as "completions-of-the-act," or as "closure," "discharge," or "finishing" (122), that we can also bear witness to the intensive preoccupation with frigidity that swept the postwar medical establishment, given that its experts repeatedly posit frigidity as an act that refuses to end, an act rehearsed by wifely performers who neglect to bow out gracefully from a feminine staging rendered unnecessary by their having achieved the "goal" of marriage. While Maslow doesn't explicitly invoke the frigid woman, he seems to have her in mind when he observes that "one must be a healthy, femaleness-fulfilled woman . . . before general-human self-actualization becomes possible" (50). Since there is for Maslow no more obvious "peak experience" than the "Reichian type of complete orgasm" (122), it is unsurprising that such experience proves unattainable to "the obsessional person, flat, tight, rigid, frozen, controlled, cautious" (157).

Maslow's peak experiences bring to mind the ups and downs Billy Pilgrim identifies in *Valley of the Dolls*, which is prefaced with this bit of doggerel: "You've got to climb to the top of Mount Everest / To reach the Valley of the Dolls." Yet in Susann's novel, peak experiences don't leave their partakers with the sense of "culmination" that Maslow descries in Reichian orgasms. They are the very definition of an anticlimax: "You stand there, waiting for / the rush of exhilaration / you thought you'd feel— / but it doesn't come." We might thus conclude that Susann's characters are not "self-actualized" in Maslow's sense; expecting to "hear the applause / and take [their] bows" (3), they somehow miss the point of getting to the top, which for Maslow is to bask in the wonder of the view. They are, to use the terms that Michael Fried generates as the governing dichotomy of post-Enlightenment aesthetics, too beholden to "theatricality" to give way to what Fried and Maslow both call "absorption."[18]

Susann's frustrated mountaineer treats the arrival at the summit like another part of the show (instead of its finale). And in this regard, *Valley of the Dolls* offers both a cautionary tale for the psychologist of self-actualization and an object lesson in the poetics of ambition as determined by the gender meritocracy, that special corner of midcentury culture where the discourse of female striving meets the discourse of human potential. Whereas Maslow holds that fulfillment in "femaleness" comes prior to self-actualization, Susann argues that womanhood is precisely what can never be fulfilled, since a woman can always improve her prospects even by a gesture as minor as changing venues. This is why marriage is the great career killer in *Valley of the Dolls*: yoking her to a husband, it limits a woman to an unchanging audience of one. Marriage preempts the experience Susann ascribes to Helen Lawson: "love on a mass scale" (114). Maslow's project of "overcoming . . . existential shortcomings" would seem to find no better avenue to success than through the impersonal vehicle of stardom.[19]

Such a claim might test our patience, since however intimate its ties to the performing arts, stardom is intuitively just what cannot be performed as a kind of goal-oriented labor. Celebrities are chosen; they do not make themselves. Yet it is a striking feature of *Valley of the Dolls* that, notwithstanding their typically fortuitous success, its principals operate on the assumption that their stardom is *earned*. While Jennifer's mother insists that her daughter has no talent, just the "luck" of "a gorgeous face and the kind of body men go for" (169), she works to perfect these God-given immutables by doing nightly bust exercises and, when it is time for her to return to America after ten years in Europe, by getting a face lift so that her image can stand up to the paparazzi's flash bulbs. And while Neely is blessed with strong lungs and enviable dexterity, she works tirelessly to hone these gifts into powerful weapons for laying siege to Broadway and Hollywood. The goal of Susann's characters is to work hard at becoming better women, worshiped for their specialness. In *Valley of the Dolls* the work is all about making the ordinary into the extraordinary, the inconspicuous into the "conspicuous" (41).

Yet read from a certain perspective, *Valley of the Dolls* amounts to a critique of both Maslow's version of self-actualization and Brown's version of the gender meritocracy, the refrain of both of which might be "having it all." In the book's reckoning, there are ultimately no exceptional women—only women who think they can pass as such. Susann suggests, moreover, that such delusion is a liability that no woman can escape. Thus, the dual specters of the queer and the cold woman hover constantly just beyond view in *Valley of the Dolls*, reminding us that stigma can come at any juncture. For all their rewards, Susann's characters seem paralyzed by their never-ending and never-successful-enough impression management. They are trapped between accusations that they might be frigid, might be lesbian, or might like sex too much.

Given the rigors of a sex-gender system that keeps its would-be beneficiaries on their toes, it is no wonder that Susann's characters put their hopes for rehabilitation in a rejuvenating sleep cure. "You see the brain has little niches," Jennifer's Swiss doctor explains. "Each niche is a thought or memory. If we think of the same thing repeatedly, the niche grows deeper and the thought is engrained. It is the way an actor learns his lines. But when the thought stops, the niche begins to fill in like a cut. And in time it is erased. Three weeks of the sleep cure will help a gash to heal over" (314). Like frigidity, the sleep cure might be seen as a solution to a problem that scarcely counts as such in the gender meritocracy's economy of striving: the continuous need to be in a state of satisfaction, as in Letty Pogrebin's commitment to a "fulfilled, satisfied, accomplished female all rolled into one pretty package" (256). To hear the doctor describe its curative effects, the "sleep cure" abides by the Method's version of physiological authenticity. But where the Method teaches an actor to follow routines in order to access her real self, understood as a stable compendium of otherwise untapped emotional memories, the sleep cure reverses this logic. It returns its beneficiary to herself by taking her thoughts from her, leaving a blank where there had been a too-consistent and recursive mentation.

In this regard the sleep cure functions less like Method-style consciousness raising than like a fancier (or at least more expensive) version of the junkie's stupor in *Trash*, a way of erasing thought on the assumption that thinking is the problem for which a kind of blankness is the solution. Susann accompanies her novel's fixation on a hypothetical homosexuality that postwar culture routinely associates with the subjunctive mood with mean camp's consciousness-lowering agenda and its effort to undermine the New Left gestalt of self-transformation. No less than Vidal or Waters, she refuses the conversion narrative that equates hyperactive knowingness with a privileged access to identity in the era of the New Social Movements. Giving narrative flesh to the abstract capacity for "potential" that writers like Pogrebin and Brown make the centerpiece of their how-to books, Susann also reveals the limits to that capacity. If in *Valley of the Dolls* there is no end to either what you can achieve or want—"nothing in the world you can't get if you want it badly enough" (58), as one character puts it on behalf of all the characters—this principle turns out to leave a lot to be desired, since even wanting turns out to be a full-time job.

Underperformance in the Separate Sphere: *Play It As It Lays* and *The Bell Jar*

Although my discussion of the gender meritocracy is guided by the midcentury accounts of performance introduced in Chapter 4, another notion of performance I have been implicitly drawing on is as much a product of the theater department as the engineering or management school, as when we speak of "high-performance" cars or portfolios or, with Douglas McGregor, of "actions relative to goals." These meanings connote one another, particularly in the corporate workplace's cult of maximum efficiency, where a mastery of role-play is understood as tantamount to the finely tuned precision of the business machine. These connotations are likewise reciprocal in parafeminist discourse, wherein a woman can succeed—can "realize potential," a phrase favored by or-ganizations—only by working at being a woman. It is in this fraught context that Susann's toying with frigidity and sleep cures is most illuminating. For Susann alerts us to the value stillness might accrue in the face of a performance style that, despite Pogrebin's assurance that "a consistent outflow of the best that's in you is not as depleting or as enervating as it may sound" (123), seems always on the verge of burning its actors out.

In the remainder of this chapter, I consider some of the other spinoffs of the gender meritocracy in postwar fiction by women, a canon of mostly popular novels that turn to nearly the opposite problem faced by Susann's overworked women. I first focus on Joan Didion's *Play It As It Lays* (1970) before tracking back to Sylvia Plath's *The Bell Jar* (1963). Then I focus on Erica Jong's *Fear of Flying* (1973). These novels are preoccupied with the question of what hap-pens to women whose capacity for performance dwarfs the conditions in which they are allowed to perform, women whose energy is thus not discharged or expended. The short answer such novels give to this question is that they go insane. I hasten to add that to pose and answer the question in these terms is to perceive in midcentury women's fiction an old-fashioned thermodynamics of gender, something like a holdover from the naturalist moment. (What I have just described is the plot, for example, of Charlotte Perkins Gilman's "The Yel-low Wallpaper.") In fact, in *Getting Yours*, the 1975 sequel to *How to Make It in a Man's World*, Letty Pogrebin speaks (now in the more enlightened cadences of a properly feminist agenda) of "a growing need to slow down," which means declining the rigors of the gender meritocracy and its insistence on making a woman pleasing to men.[20]

Even though the discourse of female overwork in the context of insufficient outputs has much in common with its Progressive-era forebear, the postwar narrative of female institutionalization differs in one obvious way from that proposed by "The Yellow Wallpaper." In that text, there is little doubt that the heroine's condition is exacerbated by her confinement; the cure is merely an extension of the disease. But in the novels with which I am concerned, what Goffman calls "total institutions" are less the enemy of self-actualization than the crucial means to its pursuit, because total institutions promote an ideal of impersonality that appears to conform to the meritocracy's insistence on achievement over ascription. Thus, Plath's Esther Greenwood must submit to the ascribed identity of mental patient in order to arrive at the possibility of meritocratic success, which depends on what Pogrebin calls "well-defined standards of performance where your expertise can be clearly measured and evaluated."[21] Plath's and Pogrebin's affirmation of institutional standards shows us something interesting within the era of the New Social Movements: a scarcely permissible penchant for the *organizational* in a context that sees bureaucratic processing as a form of slavery. Charting the shift from parafeminism to feminism by way of the various postwar discourses of performance obliges us to register how feminism reclaims some key features of the Cold War social style. Basic among these are a retrieval of strategic make-believe, particularly as that attitude became synonymous with gaming the system of institutional attachment, and a reprise of the era's queer demonology, which saw the true believer as an emblem of unchecked deviance.

Given the bleak moral landscape women's fiction surveys, it seems merely contrarian to argue that it upholds rather than condemns the total institutions of the postwar establishment. *Play It As It Lays*, after all, reads like *Valley of the Dolls* without the "ups and downs." In Didion's novel, there are only downs. Its protagonist, Maria Wyeth, is a has-been actress married to a film director named Carter Lang, and—as though to drive home her lack of resolve—she cannot even kill herself. It is BZ, the bisexual producer of her husband's latest film, who ends up dying of a Seconal overdose while Maria lies in bed holding his hand in a Nevada motel room. Maria's unraveling is explicitly referred to the derailing of her career; she can no longer get any recognition except as "Carter Lang's wife."[22] In the course of the novel she has multiple affairs, is forced by her husband to abort a pregnancy resulting from one of these liaisons, and finally lands in the "Neuropsychiatric Institute." One objective of *Play It As It Lays* is clearly to deglamorize what *How to Make It in a Man's World* calls the "glamour fields" (19), an exposé that appears to align Didion with the demystification practiced by Betty Friedan.

But the novel's investment in the asylum as a regenerative space makes it hard to follow up on any proposed alignment of Didion's narrative with the feminist critique of institutionalized gender differences. Friedan not only treated female subjugation as a mental illness but also saw institutions like the asylum as part of the problem rather than the solution to female "unreality." "The mystique," she writes, forces women "to deny reality, as a woman in a mental hospital must deny reality to believe she is a queen."[23] *Play It As It Lays* by contrast conceives of the mental hospital not as the engine for perpetuating delusions but precisely as the site of forging a connection to reality. In Maria's case, the institution assumes the task of reassembling a selfhood that the culture industry has dismantled. And it succeeds by steering Maria away from her bad habit of acting like a "queen," which is to say, engaging in the sort of subcultural behavior anatomized in deviant ethnographies like Laud Humphreys's *Tearoom Trade* and Esther Newton's *Mother Camp.*

It ought to be noted that Didion had a pronounced hostility toward the women's movement. Whereas many of its participant-observers were keen to distinguish parafeminism (the inauthentic discourse of "having it all") from feminism proper (the authentic discourse of emancipation), Didion allowed for no such distinction. As detailed in "The Women's Movement" (1972), feminism's chief policy statement was that girls just want to have fun. "Eternal love, romance, fun," Didion writes, "are relatively rare expectations in the arrangements of consenting adults, although not in those of children, and it wrenches the heart to read about these women in their brave new lives."[24] Given her dubious pity for what she considers feminism's infantile delusions, it is thus strange to find *Play It As It Lays* rather heavily invested in the catastrophic view of the middle-class housewife set forth in *The Feminine Mystique.* In diagnosing that titular malaise, Friedan unearths "a link between what is happening to the women in America and increasingly overt male homosexuality" (274), which has become widely publicized through films like *Suddenly Last Summer.* As we have had occasion to observe, Friedan's wives ("sex-seekers" [370]) are forced into a compulsive reenactment of sexual fantasies scripted for the female masses by gay men like "Tennessee Williams," for whom "no reality remained . . . except his sexual perversions" (371).

Rehearsing this drama of female subjugation to gay male caprice, Maria Wyeth takes her cues from that demimonde for which Williams might be the cultural attaché: "I knew a lot of Southerners and faggots," she tells us about her brief modeling career in New York, "and that was how I spent my days and nights" (8). Though Maria no longer keeps such poor company, her endless drives on Los Angeles freeways afford Didion an apposite figure for the cruising to nowhere inextricable in postwar culture from anonymous man-on-man action. In keeping with such aimless motion, Maria finds it hard "to keep" her sexual relations "distinct" (68), "as if . . . her life had been a single sexual encounter, one dreamed fuck, no beginnings or endings, no point beyond itself" (69). And while her confrontation with "some boys in ragged Levi jackets" (129) in Oxnard merely hints at a reenactment of her performance as "the girl who was raped by . . . a motorcycle gang" (19) in her husband's film *Angel Beach*, that real-world encounter involves a "total complicity" between Maria and her would-be rapists, a "scenario" she starts to "replay" in her memory: "It ended that way badly, or well, depending on what you wanted" (131). Just as one partner appears indistinguishable from another, so gang rape appears hard to tell apart from an orgy.

Yet it is Maria's intimacy with the "degenerate" BZ (162), the husband of her friend Helene, that reveals how deeply *Play It As It Lays* is committed to mediating the narrative of a purposeless existence through its most glaring emblem, a queer eroticism indistinct from violent exploitation. At one point the novel leads us to believe that BZ and Helene have made Maria an unwilling or at best an equivocal participant in a threesome. Part of what makes the factuality of this event hard to discern is that it is frequently unclear in *Play It As It Lays* whether lack of consent doesn't function for many of the novel's characters simply as a form of arousal. (One item on Maria's "list of things she would never do" is thus the ambiguous entry: "*do S.M. unless she wanted to*" [136].) Although most readers tend to characterize BZ as "bisexual," he is really a sort of equal-opportunity pervert. He swings from garden-variety infidelity to wife swapping to group sex to a procession of hustlers to a voyeurism that he nourishes via what Maria euphemistically calls "doing favors for people" (39). Even more pertinent to his degeneracy than this eclecticism, however, is the impresario-like way in which he manages to make Maria think she has consented when she does not recall exercising her volition as such.

Through such orchestrations and coercions, Didion makes it clear that, although Carter is the novel's resident "auteur" (138), the novel's sordid world of meaningless and perhaps nonconsensual sex is what Hollywood executives call a *producer's movie*. The climactic event of the novel, which concerns Maria's "Getting there," as BZ puts it, "where I am" (192), thus reads like a scene that BZ has arranged, a third act whose only possible finale is the suicide pact into which he invites her. Maria declines that invitation on terms that clarify by simplifying the novel's filigree of deviance, direction, and consent. Suicide by Seconal,

Maria tells BZ, is "a queen's way of doing it" (212). On this view of the matter, BZ's death by sleeping pills might be understood as a regicide, the founding act in the liberation of what Friedan calls the "sex-seekers." It is hard not to see Maria's refusal of BZ's invitation as a purgative rite of passage in which she learns to "live again" by unlearning the fatal habits of a life of sexual abandon.

Regarding her protagonist's star turn in *Angel Beach*, Didion tells us that "Maria preferred the studio's cut" of the film's ending (20), "a long dolly shot of Maria strolling across a campus," to her husband's version, "which ended with a shot of the motorcycle gang, as if they represented some reality not fully apprehended" (19). This is a preference worth considering in light of Maria's eventual "restoration" behind the asylum's walls. For the "definite knack for controlling her destiny" that Maria imagines of the character in the studio cut (20), projected through the "campus," becomes refigured for Maria through the lessons the asylum teaches, not the least of which is a newfound ability to differentiate right from wrong. One of the items to which she has to give a "yes or no" answer on the psychological test she takes is "A lot of people are guilty of bad sexual conduct" (4). And while Maria insists on a certain nihilism ("I know what 'nothing' means" [214], she tells us in the book's last chapter), it would not be inaccurate to see this "nothing" as a state of Zenlike clarity, a lucidity that reveals itself as a disillusionment with those tools (Rorschach tests, journal entries) designed to draw out explanations that she does not recognize or heed.

The asylum's ability to deliver to Maria the epiphany that its "business" (to "invent connections" [4]) is not *her* business, in other words, makes it a kind of safe house—a place that, by allowing her to disconnect from her past ("I have trouble with *as it was*" [7]), allows an absolution otherwise unavailable in a culture of proximate causes and guilt by association. Contained in the asylum, Maria acquires a steady concentration curatively at odds with the irresolute drifting that characterizes her actions throughout the novel. Seeking "nothing" instead of the phantom causalities that have long dogged her is the best thing to happen to her. By becoming an "agreeable player" in order to withdraw from the hospital's business (4), Maria appears to have absorbed the sensibility of a waning if not defeated cultural moment, that consensus of make-believe in which maturity of the sort prized in Didion's "The Women's Movement" was measured by the ability to pretend to a belief without giving in to it. Committed to the asylum, Maria acquires the Cold War liberal's "knack" for noncommitment.

Of course, the Neuropsychiatric Institute is a bit more posh than the public hospital in which Goffman did the bulk of his fieldwork for *Asylums*. Maria's detention comes with a swimming pool, an ocean view, and other amenities by no means typical of the average stint in a mental institution. But we would be remiss in counting these privileges *against* the redemptive work that the hospital does in Didion's novel. Indeed, compared to the filthy motels, the gaudy casinos, or the Encino tract house in the guestroom of which Maria has her abortion, the asylum is positively top drawer, an establishment that quells her "self-destructive" restlessness with a plan and a purpose (156), for it is in the asylum that Maria starts to rebuild the vision of a life with her daughter (who also happens to be in an institution): "*(1) get Kate, (2) live with Kate alone, (3) do some canning*" (210). Although her last thoughts in the novel turn on visions of "light" streaming through "filled Mason jars on a kitchen windowsill" (214), it would be inaccurate to infer from this reverie a desire to preserve domestic order. Rather, the asylum allows Maria to imagine a life reignited with a can-do spirit (implicit in the phrase "*do some canning*").

If this eccentric take on the institution has an oddly familiar ring to it, it may be because Maria's sun-kissed jars evoke the title of a more famous novel, Sylvia Plath's brittle 1963 bildungsroman *The Bell Jar*, which furnishes a template for Didion's construction of the asylum as an alternative to married life. In *The Bell Jar* as in *Play It As It Lays*, the asylum is a place of possibilities rather than their foreclosure, because Esther Greenwood's hospital stay appears to render her unmarriageable. Even more explicitly than Didion, Plath equates the mental hospital with the campus, finding in the asylum a means to redeem the promise of the school. Though it would be redundant at this date to spell out the ambivalence toward wedded life that Plath's writing exudes on almost every page, it is worth revisiting the special horror that marriage conjures for the heroine of her only novel. The threat of marriage focuses her mental illness in such a way as to make it seem that its only cure is for Esther to remain single.

Yet the prospect of a courtship, or at least a steady relationship, is also routinely couched in *The Bell Jar* in the discourse of the meritocracy. While she "didn't think" she "deserved" the mediocre "blind dates" she constantly faces (since her only vice is that she "studied too hard" and "didn't know when to stop"), Esther also thinks that if she could improve herself in other ways (if she had a more "shapely bone structure," or "could discuss politics," or "was a famous writer"), she might be found "interesting enough to sleep with."[25] This catalog of would-be improvements is interesting from the point of view of the meritocracy because it mixes things that cannot really be changed (bone structure) with plausible aspirations (becoming informed, becoming a writer). All the hard work in the world won't get you a new bone structure, but—here Plath borrows Susann's logic of deserved stardom—it might make you famous. Yet to put Plath's reflections on the meritocracy in these terms does not quite do them justice. For there is a strong sense running through *The Bell Jar* that a certain measure of luck is inevitable in the game of life, a sense that bone structure and fame are equally a function of some divine lottery that Esther is doomed not to win. "I just didn't have any luck" (65), she says of her blind dates.

The problem of luck absorbed political and social theorists in the decade following the publication of *The Bell Jar*. In *A Theory of Justice* (1971), John Rawls discounted defenses of inequality that "appeal to the notions of merit" by arguing that "persons with greater natural endowments" are merely beneficiaries of "luck in the natural lottery."[26] Taking this principle even further, Rawls's colleague Christopher Jencks argued in *Inequality* (1972) that "the effects of luck" more than any other factor determined one's position in the social pecking order. "In general," Jencks and his coauthors conclude, "we think luck has far more influence on income than successful people admit."[27] Jencks's goal was to "neutralize the effects of luck" in the interest of bringing about "equal results" rather than "equality of opportunity," under the presumption that status and income stratification—whether meritocratic, inherited, or (as Jencks construed it) largely random—can never be just.[28]

But *The Bell Jar* believes in equality of opportunity rather than outcome, and the salient form of luck in this novel thus consists in the chance to be admitted into settings where one might demonstrate one's mettle. A brief for the meritocracy, the novel explicitly refers Esther's nervous breakdown to an inability to prove herself. Her illness begins soon after she discovers that she has not been accepted to a summer writing class "with a famous writer" (119), the sort of writer she herself hopes to be. "Plath," argues Langdon Hammer, "conceived of the female professional as a kind of student."[29] I would adjust this claim by proposing that the asylum in *The Bell Jar* takes up the functions of vertical striving and self-renewal that Plath's world assigns to school culture. Finding her most ambitious self blocked by the impersonal machinery of the university, in the shape of a form letter that notifies her of her rejection from the summer class, Esther treats the mental hospital as the proving ground the school has failed to be. Thwarted by the "writer" who doesn't find Esther "good enough to be admitted into his class" (119), Esther gets admitted to the hospital instead.

It is worth noting in this regard Esther's disaffection from school culture at the novel's outset. College has become a place she fakes her way through, "escaping" a "semester of chemistry" (40) by convincing her dean that she is so devoted to the subject that she should get class credit without doing any work. Her studies and her ambitions no longer reflect or reinforce each other, and this disconnection leaves Esther in a vacuum of meaning that the asylum will come to fill, precisely on the college's terms. Hence *The Bell Jar*'s conclusion finds her in the "asylum library" (283) waiting to take an exam in which the hospital doctors "will ask . . . a few questions" in order to determine her sanity. Though the novel ends before we learn how Esther fares in the interview, the assumption is that she passes with flying colors. And part of why this assumption takes hold is that the face-to-face encounter in the boardroom of the hospital is structured as a reparation. It compensates for the "very small class" (119), the competitive workshop, from which Esther has been barred.[30]

Here we can measure Esther's progress by reference to a dialectic peculiar to the meritocracy: the interplay of impersonal effort (such as the application by manuscript submission to the writing class) and personal attention (such as one finds in the class itself). Her hospital stay helps Esther recover this dialectic, which has been compromised not only by rejection but also by her replacement of impersonal performance (academic labor) with the performance of *personality* (the masquerade of a studious grind) in which college life finds her engaged. No less than in the seminar will she be called upon to "defend herself" in the asylum's boardroom; only there her autocritique means the difference less between a draft and a rewrite than between freedom and confinement. It is an uncanny feature of *The Bell Jar*, however, that Esther tends to conceive of her new life precisely on the order of a *revision*. "There ought," she thinks as she waits outside the boardroom, "to be a ritual for being born twice—patched, retreaded, approved for the road" (284). As this metaphor suggests, Esther equates a writing career with a certain nonstop progress through the paces of writing's mechanics, as though a workshop were a body shop. Whereas the school's "requirements" have become *too* mechanical in their repetition, the asylum restores an element of the sacred to rote practices. For Maria Wyeth, the hospital carves out an opportunity-making disenchantment with the drills of inkblot and personality tests; for Esther, the hospital consecrates school culture anew.

Plath's novel is not unique in forging an affinity between the school and the asylum on the grounds of their shared interest in successful test taking as a metric of sanity. At the end of Joanne Greenberg's *I Never Promised You a Rose Garden* (1964), Deborah Blau's release from the institution that has housed her for three years parallels her taking the "high school equivalency examination."[31] And even though her passing the test "with enough points over" for "any college" (273) does not yet find her emancipated from the asylum, the novel's conclusion finds her opting to "hang with the world," a commitment "symbolized" (278) by the "schoolbooks" to which she pledges "her true allegiance" (277). The slightly obsessional behavior about which Esther betrays misgivings in *The Bell Jar*—studying "too hard," not knowing "when to stop"—proves Deborah's salvation; sanity is predicated on a life of perpetual examination. Plath and Greenberg oppose the school's labor, which proceeds incrementally and with an indefinite though lustrous object (more schooling), to the chore-wheel of wifehood or, in the case of *I Never Promised You a Rose Garden*, to the "occupational therapy" taken up by inmates in the mental hospital (215). Just as Deborah feels a somewhat ambiguous pity for her fellow patients' "imitation" labor ("make-work," she thinks, "of the most obvious kind" [215]), so Esther likewise "won't make anything in Occupational Therapy" (209) because she regards it as a degraded simulacrum of the work she wants to do.

At one point Esther muses over what "a dreary and wasted life" wifehood would be "for a girl with fifteen years of straight A's" (97). In this imagining, Esther confronts a version of the problem that Susann's characters face: the threat to getting ahead arises from having an unchanging audience. Adapting the glamour girl's dilemma to the college girl's, Plath suggests that the injustice in marriage is that it ties a woman to a single instructor. Even worse, it turns the straight-A overachiever into someone doomed forever to repeat the same grade. This analogy illuminates the issue both Plath and Greenberg raise in the invidious distinction they imply between the assembly-line toil of the mental patient and the career of the brain worker. In *I Never Promised You a Rose Garden* and *The Bell Jar*, school turns out to be valued less for the content it delivers than for the form its tuition assumes: a stepped scale that allows Deborah and Esther to imagine themselves always climbing upward. What they take away from the school is less its curriculum than its gradational logic, less a

round of knowledge than a crystal staircase by comparison to which the programs of therapeutic culture, twelve step or otherwise, are found inadequate
even if they serve both characters as stopgaps on the path to glory.

Hence, Buddy Willard's declining reputation in *The Bell Jar* is measurable
by the fact that, confined to a sanatorium for tuberculosis, he must interrupt
his medical school studies and, like Greenberg's occupational therapy patients,
devote his time to making "off-kilter clay pots" (105) and (what amounts to the
same thing) trying his hand at verse. Part of what makes Buddy's poem in
the "grey, thin magazine" so "dreadful" (107) to Esther is that, like the "painted,
but not glazed" ceramics (105) he's made, it is mere busywork, what Greenberg
calls "the illusion of satisfying labor" (215). Both poem and pot have a matte
drabness that compares unfavorably to the "thick book with a glossy cover,"
Thirty Best Stories of the Year, Esther receives from the staff of *Ladies Day* (55).
In *The Bell Jar*, "glossy" connotes the shining example that the meritocracy rewards, connotes a high (or first-place) finish in stark contrast with the dull
ceramics littering Buddy's bedside table.

Because it is just a way to spend down time rather than to take advantage of
it, busywork disallows the open-ended vista that Esther glimpses in the "eye
of the sky" (112) at the summit of a ski slope that she recalls in a flashback while
visiting Buddy at the sanatorium. Though her traversal of that slope is a headlong descent, its exhilarating momentum ("this is what it is like to be happy"
[113]) evokes the "climb to the top of Mount Everest" in *Valley of the Dolls*. For
Plath no less than Susann, vertical striving is crucial to what it means to have a
career, whose struggles indeed seem most meaningful when they include both
ups and downs. It is no doubt an ironic commentary on the gap between her
aspirations and achievements that Esther happens to break her leg in this particular downhill slalom. Esther mistakenly assumes she is launching herself into
"the sky," let us say, only to find herself bruised by her impact with the hard
ground of reality. But there is a further irony beyond this vaguely moralizing
lesson. For the phrase "break a leg," the line theater people use to wish good
luck to someone about to perform onstage, is itself a punning reminder of the
novel's deliberations on a gender meritocracy in which luck and performance
assume pride of place in the narrative of female potential.

The intervention Plath makes in this narrative is her novel's "discovery" that
the terms of the meritocracy do not neatly line up, that some things really are a
matter of luck. Yet *The Bell Jar* also undermines this conclusion by turning the

asylum into a kind of intensive schooling and by making it into the place where a husband cannot get to Esther because, or so Buddy suggests, the asylum has rendered her unable to get a husband. "I wonder who you'll marry now," he asks her when he visits her in the asylum, "now that you've been . . . here." It would be a mistake to see this question as enacting the "revenge" that Esther thinks Buddy intends (280), because by making Esther unavailable to any one man, the asylum increases her chances of gaining the recognition of many others. She gains the chance, that is, to earn the "mass love" Susann's characters acquire by bringing their show on the road.

In this respect, *The Bell Jar* inverts the role of the hospital in *Play It As It Lays*. Whereas the asylum focuses Maria, it mobilizes Esther, who considers herself a "retreaded" but street-legal vehicle by story's end. But we would be overstating their difference by insisting on the way each novel reverses the other's key figures. For both novels bear witness to a resurgent instrumentalism in the discourse of female merit, and both reflect on luck or chance as a limiting condition of performance. In *Play It As It Lays*, Maria comes to see the world as a state of sheer randomness in which there are no "correlations" and also to see that seeking correlations brings a kind of pain she can mitigate only by abandoning the search. In *The Bell Jar*, Esther imagines herself as having the bad luck of not getting the right dates or the right kinds of recognition; no matter how hard she tries, she is *not given a chance* to prove herself. Where *Play It As It Lays* ends with a return to the consensus liberal's opportunistic irony in the face of a world connected only by previously agreed-upon correlations, *The Bell Jar* reinvigorates the lessons of school culture by turning the asylum into the salvage site of the school's nearly bankrupted possibilities.

Encouraged by feminism's narration of its own past, we tend to think of mass-market blockbusters like *Valley of the Dolls* as the false consciousness of a sexual liberation that doesn't really liberate because it continues to take its directions from the playbook of masculine privilege. Parafeminism encourages women to become equal to men by becoming more pleasing to them. Yet *Play It As It Lays* and *The Bell Jar*, novels whose elite (or at least upper-middlebrow) credentials are above reproach, mount a stronger reclamation of the status quo ante than *Valley of the Dolls*, if by status quo we mean the opportunistic make-believe (in Didion) or school culture's veneration of incremental progress (in Plath) widely reviled by partisans of the New Social Movements. What makes these texts appear different in kind from a mere recapitulation of dominant culture is that both Didion and Plath write novels organized around a highly self-conscious symbolism, a kind of puzzle making that, by leading attentive readers through the gambling or rattlesnake imagery (in Didion) or the knife or mirror imagery (in Plath), encourages us in the assumption that we have arrived at a more intelligent design than can be found in *Valley of the Dolls*, a book wholly indifferent to (not to say incapable of) symbolic complexity. What makes the lessons of Didion or Plath significant is that they feel *earned*. It is by exerting ourselves on the text, industriously striving to assemble its symbolic parts, that we enjoy the dividend it pays out, the satisfaction of a job well done.

In the division of mental labor *The Bell Jar* constructs, reading a novel like *The Bell Jar* itself is an elevated because challenging mission, whereas reading *Valley of the Dolls* is just make-work. The relevant distinction is between *performing a reading* and *losing yourself* in a book. As if to confirm this opposition, Esther's breakdown coincides with her inability to get a handle on *Finnegans Wake*, and the most pronounced symptom of her deterioration is that "scandal sheet[s]" are "the only things I could read" (160). Such a distinction seems hard to sustain, since it has proved no more difficult to perform a reading on *Valley of the Dolls*, a kind of book-length "scandal sheet," than on *The Bell Jar*. But this is to miss the larger difference Plath is keen to draw between meaningful performance and just going through the motions. Like Susann, Plath sets great store by the meritocratic system and understands that performance pays only when the performer has an audience. What gives the "thick," "glossy" book of prize stories its luster is its public recognition, which appears as a form of nourishment, fattening the textual body on the sweet milk of attention. But only certain kinds of attention foster this increase. No upsurge of readers can grant the scandal sheet more than two dimensions. And what makes the scandal sheet an undesirable model of fame, a type of writing whose popularity is indistinct from an insurmountable flatness, is connected to the ever-present threat of declassing in *The Bell Jar*: such writing is unimprovable because it offers no way for its reader to improve herself.

The Impersonal Is Political: *Fear of Flying*

Plath shared with her fictional surrogate the most mixed of the meritocracy's blessings: the role of "scholarship" student, whose far-from-guaranteed presence in the ranks of the affluent is contingent on the nonstop delivery of a promised performance. Like Susann, Plath has a clear sense of what the right sort of performance can confer ("mass love" translated into literary reputation). But unlike Susann, Plath has a visceral sense of what the meritocracy saves the high achiever from: the degraded round of toil that makes wifehood indistinct in *The Bell Jar* from a job in the service economy. Buddy's confession that he has lost his virginity to "some slutty waitress" (80) marks Esther's decisive turn away from his proposals in the novel. In that admission, Esther begins to imagine how Buddy—and by extension all possible husbands—sees her: as a kind of unpaid server in the hospitality industry. (And not just potential husbands: "Buddy's mother had even arranged for me to be given a job as a waitress that summer in the TB sanatorium," Esther notes, "so Buddy wouldn't be lonely" [21].)

Unlike wives, of course, waitresses don't serve just one customer. Whatever liabilities we might attribute to her lack of career advancement, it is not her limited audience that holds the waitress back. It is the fact that however large the audience she has, each of its members can see the waitress only in that fixed part. But writers can have a versatility of roles no matter how large or small their audience. Like Plath, they can write novels as well as poetry; and that poetry itself can change from one book, or one "phase," to another. In terms of range, we might say, the writer has a certain obvious advantage over waitresses or wives, for whom any liberties they take with their assigned roles may be grounds for firing or divorce. The writer who departs from her role risks inconsistency; the wife who departs from her role risks losing her husband.

It is by talking up her range that a man makes a pass at Bettina Balser, the eponymous narrator of Sue Kaufman's *Diary of a Mad Housewife* (1967). Thus is the discourse of self-actualization reimagined as a pickup line. And while Bettina rejects the offer, the novel nonetheless insists on treating her "Secret Potential," as this would-be suitor puts it, as an outgrowth of the fact that, as a more successful suitor tells her, "in just a few minutes you've thawed, begun to come to life."[32] For Kaufman, as for the postwar medical establishment, frigidity is bound to unrealized potential, but that concept has accrued a different valence in this novel from what it meant to experts like Kroger and Freed. "Potential" names accession not to wifehood but to adultery, here conceived along the lines of what Plath would call a career. And just as Esther is relaunched on her own path with the help of the hospital, so it is strangely fitting that Bettina gets job counseling from, of all people, her analyst: "A college degree alone means nothing nowadays," he tells her. "You must have something . . . besides yourself you can sell" (29). Using the expansionist logic of Plath's and Green-berg's attraction to the school, Bettina notes that "the more you live up to your potential, the greater your potential becomes" (46).

This quality differs markedly from the "enthusiasm" that the working girls in Rona Jaffe's *The Best of Everything* (1958)—secretaries and editorial as-sistants in a down-market publishing house that specializes in the "scandal sheets" that Esther finds so degrading—are taught to see as "the most valuable commodity in business today."[33] To put it in class terms, we could say that the difference between potential and enthusiasm is the difference between brain work and service work, which amounts to the difference between education and what Jaffe calls "training" (160). Indeed, for service workers, training and enthusiasm go hand in hand. Enthusiasm is a quality that postwar managerial culture imagined as subject to a Method-style "self-prompting" that the soci-ologist Arlie Russell Hochschild calls "deep acting."[34] Jobs that "require face-to-face or voice-to-voice contact with the public," Hochschild argues in *The Managed Heart* (1983), not only "require the worker to produce an emotional state in another person" but also "allow the employer, through training and supervision, to exercise a degree of control over the emotional activities of employees."[35] Flight attendants, whom passengers see as "no more than glam-orous waitresses," represent the ultimate in "feeling management" placed at the service of the profit motive.[36]

We can gain a sense of how enthusiasm would be something of a career killer on Plath's or Kaufman's terms by glancing at a book about this particu-lar corner of the service industry. Appearing in 1967, *Coffee, Tea or Me?* was the bestselling memoir of two flight attendants, Rachel Jones and Trudy Baker, whose goal was to offer the world an "inside look" into the (then-sexy) airline industry. And while their situation would seem to remove them quite far from *The Bell Jar*'s version of the academically sanctioned meritocracy, Jones and Baker imagine their "flying careers" along the same lines as the writer's career envisioned by Plath.[37] Like Esther, the stewardess (the book never uses the term "flight attendant") finds herself having to go to school in order to get ahead. And though they pitch *Coffee, Tea or Me?* as an "uninhibited" tell-all, the point of Jones and Baker's book is really to deglamorize the stewardess by showing that despite the fairy-tale life she is alleged to lead, her job is just a lot of hard work. Such labor involves not only long hours serving passengers on planes at high altitudes but also cramming to pass the various certification tests required by the FAA and the airlines. The ideal "stew" (6) is something of a grind. In this respect she is a nightmare version of Esther's dream self, an Esther whose studying and hard work lead her no farther than up and down the aisle of a 727.

Baker and Jones lay the blame for their own disillusionment with the lush life of stewardesses at the feet of the school, which emerges in their memoir as a veritable nest of queer vipers. "The class was conducted by a faggy-looking man," they say of their course in (obviously) "hairstyle, makeup, and general grooming" (41). There thus emerges over the course of this lark of a book an all too recognizable alignment of the school with the deviant. The school both accredits the work of the stewardess, elevating it above waitressing, and serves as a source of deep suspicion, since it adds to its accrediting of flight attendance as skilled labor another pedagogy that it is not necessarily qualified to conduct: the skill set of feminine self-presentation. On the one hand, no one knows less about what a woman should be than a gay man who has no interest in her; on the other, no one is more expert about how to be a woman than the gay man whose most urgent desire is to impersonate her. Given this ambiguity, the value-added performance of femininity in flight, however charismatic and attractive it might appear, is always liable to be an imposture.

Cruising at a notably higher cultural altitude than Jones and Baker's tell-all, Erica Jong's *Fear of Flying* nonetheless shares with *Coffee, Tea or Me?* a dim view of what Jong sees as questionable pedagogies. Considerably less impressed with their counseling skills than Bettina or Esther, Isadora Wing finds herself on a charter flight to Vienna with 117 psychoanalysts, 6 of whom have treated her (and another of whom is her husband). As Isadora sees it, that treatment has been a "tribute" to "the shrinks' ineptitude," since—far from helping her reach her potential—it has consisted of attempts to get her to "ackzept being a vohman" on terms she does not consider legitimate.[38] "I don't *believe* what you believe" (24), she tells her last analyst before storming out of his office. In contrast to *The Bell Jar* or *I Never Promised You a Rose Garden*, where analysis is cognate with the self-study that was basic to the midcentury classroom, analysis in *Fear of Flying* is less emblematic of schooling than a betrayal of its promises.

Although Isadora may not "believe" what her analyst believes, such skepticism has not prevented her from becoming fluent in analytical "jargon" (13) nor from referring "every decision" to "the shrinking process" (12). She speaks the language of the school to voice her disenchantment with it. More to the point, Isadora's disenchantment with the school is the prerequisite for her enchantment with the meritocracy. Like Bettina Balser, Isadora breaks with the school in order to unleash her full potential on the assumption that accreditation begins rather than completes a career. In the "meritocracy," as Daniel Bell notes in *The Coming of Post-industrial Society* (1973), "credentials are mechanical at worst, or specify minimum achievement at best."[39] The goal of Jong's novel is to instill this realization in its wayward protagonist by pushing her beyond the diminishing returns of a performance that has become strictly *academic* into the upper atmosphere of a self-starting creativity.

Fear of Flying brings us full circle to the central claims I have been making throughout this book about the New Social Movements' ambivalent cathexis of postwar school culture. Whereas Plath sacralizes the college, Jong sexes it up. Isadora strives urgently "to stop being a schoolgirl" (419) because her identity, including her richly documented fantasy life, revolves around the classroom reimagined as a bedroom—an equivalence that, as befits the eighteenth-century libertinism to which *Fear of Flying* pays homage, turns the novel into a post-Sixties updating of Sade. During a "Proseminar in Eighteenth-Century English Lit.," Isadora dreams of "sucking off each male member (hah) of the class" and "fucking Professor Harrington Stanton" (264). This is to say nothing of her marriage to a fellow grad student, Brian Stollerman, an event that "ruined everything," by which Isadora means "four years of being lovers and best friends and Shakespearean scholars together" (263). Just as she asserts that "sex is all in the head" (49), so her head is all in the school. Her "nymphomania of the brain" (226) finds her accused (by her sister) of being "a grub and a grind" who spends her time "fucking around with creepy intellectuals" (62), as though promiscuity followed from studiousness.

If Isadora's arousal seems a reflex conditioned by the liberal arts or other dividends of her expensive education (her "heart" and "cunt . . . can be had" for "a couplet" or "a simile" [255]), the turn-ons of the school, as already noted, seem to have petered out by the commencement of her story. It is against this waning libidinal charge that Jong introduces her infamous fantasy of the "zipless fuck." What makes this an "absolutely pure" exchange, "free of ulterior motives," is that "no one is trying to prove anything" (21). Yet when its prospect is squarely facing Isadora as she rides the train out of Paris toward her estranged husband and must fend off a French conductor who tries "to grab me by the snatch" (416), it seems less like a meeting of equals "free of all remorse and guilt" (21) than like sexual assault. While this unwelcome overture debunks the zipless fuck on the presumption that a man and woman can never have the symmetrical exchange that marks the gay male economy of cruising (which, in its "brevity" and "anonymity" [18], the zipless fuck evokes), the threat of violence is not actually the deciding factor in Isadora's choice to keep the conductor out of her pants. For the zipless fuck is revealed as a fantasy of escape not so much from the obligations of conjugal fidelity as from the obligations of a life measured by the quality of its performances on a series of progressively grander stages. Though Jong presents the zipless fuck as a rebuke to heterosexual romance, in other words, she opposes it in a deeper sense to the culture of the school and its custom of predicting future earnings by past performances.

Thus, the train ride that finds her rejecting the zipless fuck as a false freedom (because it looks uncomfortably like rape) also finds Isadora in a debate with "a stuffy American professor" (417) about whether American education is too "permissive" or "democratic" for the polity's own good. Isadora argues in favor of both permissiveness and democracy, but she does not exactly disagree with the professor's reactionary view, which implicitly uses the subtext of student unrest as its own defense. Were it fleshed out, his argument would be John Searle's: the campuses are in disarray as a result of students whose loudly bruited discontent proves that they are not qualified to be there. Although Isadora has abandoned graduate school, she is quick to inform us that it has not abandoned her. Her dissatisfaction is a function of her being not under- but overqualified. In Isadora's version of events, extricating herself from the school is like extricating herself from a loveless marriage or an unhappy analysis: the men don't want her to go and either bribe or bully her to stay.

An element of coercion enters into her choice to go to graduate school in the first place: "I had allowed myself to be shunted into graduate school" (79), Isadora claims, deploying the passive voice to make this internment feel much more insidious than, under any circumstances, it could ever plausibly be. Isadora's "professors were always dangling fellowships before" her, even though she does little work and sleeps through her exams. All she need do is act the part of the "compulsive good girl." Graduate school is a "swindle" (79) because, like the gender masquerade that makes her professors favor her with a phallic belonging (another way to read a "dangling" fellowship), its lessons are too formulaic. For Isadora, uninterested in humorless monographs on Augustan satire, the thrill of the school is gone: "Criticism doesn't seem very satisfying somehow" (269). Graduate school seduces her into a life as restrictive as that of a wife or a secretary, a life in which she is meant to abandon her love for the great tradition in exchange for the dubious rewards of job security and a steady, albeit meager, wage.

Jong portrays Isadora's disillusion with the school as a falling out of love with it. She realizes the honeymoon is over when her major adviser and fantasy object, Professor Stanton, tells her that "literature is *work*, not fun" (269). For this reason the "permissiveness" of the school is an illusion: "too much bureaucratic disorganization," as she puts it, "masquerading as permissiveness." By forcing her to read criticism, it denies her the "independence" that "genuine permissiveness" affords (419). Isadora construes independence along the lines of a free market in creative labor whereby she will send her manuscripts out to impersonal editors who in turn will render their judgments on no other basis than the quality of the work itself. Like Esther Greenwood, Isadora grapples with the regnant meritocratic fantasy that one's work stands alone as confirmation (or disconfirmation) of one's personal quality. Graduate school means not the exciting possibility of being judged on her own terms but the dreary toil of genuflecting before and parroting other critics, so being judged on theirs.

Of far more interest than this dubious opposition between deference and originality is that the school should stand for Jong in the position of enemy rather than enabler of meritocracy by virtue of its infidelity to the contractual voluntarism that an earlier generation—the generation that taught Jong—privileged. The school as the laboratory for developing initiative, for producing the terms on which meaningful risks take shape, has been blocked in *Fear of Flying* by the interest bureaucracy has in perpetuating itself. In a novel that does not wear its political awareness lightly, Isadora's half-finished conversation with the pompous American chemistry professor on the train out of Paris is as close as the text gets to a discussion of the militancy of student unrest, or rather to the notion that there even *is* such unrest in Morningside Heights, where Isadora earns her bachelor of arts (at Barnard) and then her master's (at Columbia). One reason is that Jong is intent on portraying the school as a placid retreat, risk averse to the point of monasticism, a place that doesn't so much induce unrest as reveal to Isadora her own restless desire to withdraw from its suffocating embrace.

What Isadora wants is neither the episodic and chancy encounter of the zipless fuck nor the tedious and predictable slog reflected equally in bourgeois wifehood and in the "fellowship" of academics but a path that combines these two unacceptable alternatives into a meaningful third way: a life in which progress is both steady and open-ended, a stable chain of action punctuated by intervals of risk taking and its payout in accomplishment, intervals in which the striving writer can achieve her potential. The "stranger on a train" (417) who stars in the zipless fuck has become unappetizing to the degree that he has been supplanted if not sublimated by the richer, because more ecumenical, ambition central to Jong's version of meritocracy. Whereas Isadora begins the novel by thinking she wants a quickie on the train, she ends by realizing she wants a more sustained vehicle for advancement. Yet Jong's appeal to a new and improved meritocracy finds her rejecting the corporate ladder or schooling's ranked terraces in favor of what we might call the *unstructured structure* of the postindustrial economy.

This is not to deny that Jong shares with Plath or Susann the sense that potential is really intelligible only through a principle of hierarchy. Earlier I argued that Susann's characters work hard at being the best version of women they can be, striving to turn their ordinary lives into extraordinary ones. *Fear of Flying* meditates on the quest for extraordinariness from the opposite direction. Far from a desideratum, extraordinariness is the thankless fate ordained for Isadora by her mother, Jude, who has no harsher pejorative in her lexicon than "ordinary, . . . the worst insult she could find for anything" (202). But how Jude measures the extraordinary is somewhat telling, since everything about her, from her "odd clothes" to her "new decorating schemes" (205), is too idiosyncratic to be of any social value. Her efforts are "misplaced" because they are not really efforts at all (205). However much she prizes the extraordinary, "the humble doing of the thing means nothing to her," nor "the pleasure of the work" (207). To her daughter, Jude is thus less exceptional than embarrassing. If Jude has "a look of disdain" for anything "popular" (202), the novel reveals the error of this view by insisting that specialness can happily coexist with popularity or, more exactly, *cannot exist without it*. In this regard, *Fear of Flying*'s stature as an enduring international blockbuster recapitulates the novel's internal object of reconciling the discourse of the extraordinary with the quantifiable fact of popularity.

Jong's point is that if ordinariness is a default state, requiring no effort on our part, extraordinariness can never be merely the rejection of such passivity. It cannot on her novel's terms be chosen or asserted. It must be bestowed. And in *Fear of Flying*, that bestowal requires Isadora to shed the surface trappings of femininity (dressing, flirting, acting like a woman) in order to pursue the more lucrative rewards of an extraordinariness measured through prestige. Yet it would be more accurate to say not that femininity's surface trappings need to be discarded but that Isadora's attitude toward them needs correction. Isadora learns to valorize experience by renouncing matter, to prize the self's interior by demoting the superficial prizes of the surface world. Consciousness raising in Jong's novel is reminiscent of the preference for mind over matter that we find among characters in certain novels of Henry James, who set out to prove that no indulgence is more rarefied than the asceticism of the well-to-do. Among the many dividends of postwar prosperity, the "affluent society" democratizes the windfall of enlightenment from which James's characters profit when they renounce worldly trifles. If "it is the sheer *quantity* of goods" that occasions "freedom from using the brain,"[40] as Herbert Marcuse argues in *One-Dimensional Man*, then curbing the acquisitive appetite is the "generative principle," to quote Theodore Roszak on New Left politics, of "*consciousness consciousness*."[41]

The New Left's elevation of consciousness to an object of conspicuous consumption, in other words, resembles the invidious distinctions of characterological depth that novelists have been practicing for centuries. *Fear of Flying*'s spin on this practice is to measure the distance between a complex and a simple life by a culture- and a class-specific gauge: the difference between the poet and the secretary. Reuniting in Vienna with Dr. Happe, one of her many former analysts, Isadora receives permission to desert her husband for a trans-European adventure with Adrian Goodlove, the Laingian analyst whom Isadora finds irresistible. "You're not a secretary, you're a poet," Happe reminds her; "why do you expect your life to be uncomplicated?" (235). Just as Esther Greenwood steadfastly refuses to study the "shorthand" her mother urges her to "learn" (45), so Isadora excludes the secretary categorically from the open-ended path upon which she is launched, a narrative arc that construes personal development as a series of awakened if not achieved potentials. "The masochistic little secretary who reads *Cosmopolitan* and thinks herself a swinger" (111) is the novel's unredeemable object lesson. If her self-identification as a "swinger" were not enough to prove that she is stuck in place, her reading matter is a dead giveaway of her having missed the boat, given *Cosmopolitan*'s indelible link in the collective consciousness with its longtime editor Helen Gurley Brown. Whereas Brown's parafeminist rhetoric of striving takes secretaries as the baseline of female advancement, Plath and Jong understand the secretary as the meritocracy's foil. Content with a paycheck, she is both spared and deprived of Isadora's habit of "always wanting to be the greatest" (346).

Dedicated to charting its heroine's meritocratic *Bildung*, *Fear of Flying*'s version of consciousness raising finds Isadora bringing to the surface the feeling that "I *deserved* to spend the rest of my life immersed in [Brian's] madness" (389), that "I *deserved* to lose my life that way" (390). Soon after her confrontation with this inverted system of deserts, Isadora takes out her "notebook" and "began to be drawn into it as into a novel" (395). This marks the moment in *Fear of Flying* when consciousness raising's aim of lifting Isadora out of male-defined roles converges with the meritocracy's aim of lifting her out of a déclassé dependence on external approval and turning her into someone who can experience her labor's intrinsic rewards. Yet Isadora's awakening hardly conforms to the model of expressive authenticity found throughout Sixties liberationist discourse and its appeal to a self uncovered through painstaking autocritique. "Changing my life" (395), as Isadora puts it, in fact means taking up the "chaotic, almost illegible" compendium of notes, which has "no particular system" (394), and imposing an artificial one on it.

Newly capable of reading over her notes with an eye toward constructing them as a text, Isadora acquires a "loyalty to [her]self" (395). But that loyalty involves a commitment less to the politics of authenticity than to an agnosticism that teaches her to bracket beliefs and manage conventions regarding her own now suitably distanced and abstracted experience. "I didn't believe in systems" (174), Isadora declares early on in the novel, the remainder of which might be seen as providing a justification for this disbelief by way of the consensus liberal's attitude of choice. The chastening of her transference onto the school coincides with her adoption of school culture's strategic make-believe, which keeps her from becoming "trapped in [her] own book" (424). Isadora learns not to express but to edit herself. She learns specifically to be the kind of editor who can oversee the novel we have just read: a text that does not systematize the chaos of its protagonist's experience but shuttles between owning and disowning the various systems by which experience is ordered, from the seminar room to the analyst's couch.

In parsing Isadora's progress from her unbelieving state to her embrace of make-believe, we might take note of the difference between where Isadora finds herself and where her former husband ends up. Shortly after their marriage, Brian begins to suffer from messianic delusions: "He discovered he was Jesus Christ and underwent a conversion of character and belief" (261). Like Isadora, Brian has turned on the academy, having "dropped out of graduate school in a fit of fury with the establishment" (263). Unlike Isadora, he replaces his lapsed faith not with strategic make-believe but with the true believer's fundamentalist devotion to his star turn in a script not of his choosing. *Fear of Flying* equates Brian's mental breakdown with both a declassing and an erotic kink: Having been an undergraduate superstar at Columbia and a promising medievalist in its graduate program, Brian ends up "toiling away in a small market-research firm" (263) (and so reduced to glorified clerical work) and scrawling lewd cartoons like the one he attaches to the bathroom mirror, which "depicted a short man with a halo and an enormous penis" and another man "about to blow him" (277).

We might see this homoerotic rendering as yet another instance of the theatrical toilet whose prominence in midcentury novels we observed in the last chapter. Unlike the panicked masturbation behind the closed bathroom door in *Portnoy's Complaint*, however, the point of Brian's drawing is less its being acted out (since it is only a rendition) than its maker's interest in being seen, even if that means being caught in an act he hasn't actually performed. In this regard, Brian resembles Isadora's mother, who also makes a spectacle of herself and who takes no interest in "effort." Although Isadora calls him "a genius, a genuine 200-plus IQ kid who arrived at Columbia with a record-breaking history of College Board scores" (254), Brian is actually more idiot savant: "He never appeared to spend any time studying" and is capable of producing, "in one sitting, an A paper" (256). Like Jude, Brian sets a poor example because, rather than following any, he wants only to be one. He is the bad version of the meritocracy, the student who does well on tests but refuses to apply himself. And just as Jude's outfits could benefit from what fashion consultants call a more careful "editing," a scrutiny she refuses to indulge, so Brian considers revision beneath him. Yet what finally makes Brian a failure is less "his frenzy to have a constant audience" (271) than the form this ambition takes. Whereas Brian needs the physical presence of observers to lend his act meaning, Isadora learns to become her own best audience.

Isadora's acquisition of self-discipline through self-spectatorship is not really surprising, for meritocratic success is frequently attested by the ability to deliver an impressive performance for an audience in front of which one doesn't actually appear. In *The Bell Jar* and *Fear of Flying*, the path to both mental health and professional acclaim is the embrace of the risks and rewards of indirect action. Plath and Jong bring their heroines around to the special kind of recognition entailed by what we might call "performance at a distance." In *The Bell Jar*, Esther must overcome her dread of rejection by disaffiliating from her products, by ceasing to identify wholeheartedly with any given performance, and by learning how to be a reviser rather than a nonstarter, someone who follows through on a project instead of abandoning it (her thesis and her novel both prove too unpromising to sustain her interest). Finally, Esther must divest her written performance of what Hochschild calls the "emotional labor" that the service economy extracts from its workers.[42] "I wanted to dictate my own thrilling letters" (87), she says when explaining why she won't take stenography. But the notion that a letter can be thrilling is a mistake. The point is not for Esther to make herself into someone who dictates letters rather than takes them but to withdraw altogether from such workplace scenarios.

From the beginning of the women's movement, such acts of withdrawal in feminist texts have faced criticism for their denial of social constraints or lived conditions and their embrace of a self-possession verging on narcissism. Such was the argument made by Jo Freeman in "The Tyranny of Structurelessness" (1971). Critiquing the women's movement for accepting "the idea of 'structurelessness' without realizing the limitations of its uses," Freeman argues that "there is nothing inherently bad about structure itself—only its excessive use."[43] Yet Jong and Plath do not foster what Freeman calls "prejudices about organization and structure" any more than they maintain an unqualified commitment to the personal.[44] Noting that Isadora likens her "liberated" state to "teetering on the edge of the Grand Canyon" (372), Maria Farland concludes that Seventies feminism turned away from social engagement toward a shapeless and politically unproductive sublime. "Surprisingly, for the generation that would insist that the personal is political," Farland writes, "it is frequently impersonal entities—heaven, nature, and space—that provide the linguistic register through which liberation can be imagined."[45] This is not actually a surprise, however, because the impersonal in Jong is not really equal to the transcendence of structure. Far from opting out of the social contract, Isadora shapes her fantasy of flight over the abyss with the aspirations of postindustrial meritocracy.

Jong neither enshrines the structurelessness against which Freeman cautions nor betrays a commitment to the personal politics of feminism with a surrender to the asocial sublime but in fact writes her novel as a paean to the unstructured structure that business theorists were coming to treat as the salve for a hobbled corporatism at the end of the 1960s. This was the retooled meritocracy heralded in Laurence Peter's *The Peter Principle* (1969), which argued that promotion up the ladder of an institutional hierarchy resulted in a top-heavy bureaucracy staffed by those who could not deliver the performance their new roles required. "The more ranks," Peter concluded, "the more incompetence."[46] Thus, the alternative: the independent contractor set free from corporate bondage. In *The Age of Discontinuity* (1969), Peter Drucker argued that "the most dangerous restrictions on mobility are not police stockades" but "restrictions that present themselves as benefits," the "'golden fetters'... with which we tie managers, professionals, and skilled people to a particular employer."[47] For Drucker, the remedy for such indentured servitude was a system that unblocked creativity by eliminating incentives to identify with the organization: "We talk today increasingly about the 'free-form' organization as alone appropriate to knowledge work.... What controls is not rank but the task" (259).

Placing "a new individualism" and "a new responsibility" ahead of loyalty (260), this innovative organization delivers on the promise that corporate culture makes with the larger society, what Drucker calls its commitment to "justification by performance" (211). Workers in "the knowledge economy" cannot rely on the corporate structure to provide for them, since in its revamped form that structure "imposes on the individual the burden of decisions" and "demands from him the price of freedom: responsibility" (249). When Isadora contemplates the "arrogant decision" of pregnancy (52), of taking "responsibility for a new life when you had no way of knowing what it would be like" (53), and then, on the book's last page, defines her "survival" as "being born over and over" (424), she dramatizes what Drucker sees as the aversion to and ultimate acceptance of the "'free-form' organization" among "the romantics of the New Left" (370). As though personifying what Drucker calls the "one institution that has to prove its right to survival again and again" (238), Isadora adopts a business model whereby renewal supplants the vertical climb of organizational culture. Instead of marking the paces of a pregiven system, Isadora becomes her own pacesetter—and her achievements, a series of rebirths.

Like Esther Greenwood, Isadora disciplines her attachments toward both school and work in such a way as to reduce the emotional performance mandated in the gender meritocracy at both the high end (the glamour fields) and the low (the pink-collar army). The most glaring symptom of her writer's block is her "fail[ure] to write letters concerning [her] work" in response to requests from editors, one of which "sat in a drawer for two years" while she "tried writing various drafts." She finally composes "a disgustingly submissive, meek, and apologetic letter to the editor in question," who writes back with "a notice of acceptance and a check" (231). Like Esther's vision of "thrilling letters," Isadora's equivocation over editorial correspondence mistakes the instrumental cover sheet for the genuine article, as though a bureaucratic epistle were other than a pretext for the manuscript, the only performance that matters. This would be like mistaking a secretary's labor (which consists in mastering the niceties of courteous form letters) for the work of her boss (who has what Drucker calls "the burden of decisions").

Jong withdraws her surrogate from bureaucracy's presentational rigor, which induces a crisis of confidence because it forces Isadora to put on a kind of affective drag. The problem with Isadora's letter to the editor is not only that it is "too personal" (231) but that the person it inscribes is a fake. But even worse, the compulsive rewriting of the letter to the editor is a misallocation of resources. Cover letters don't merit revision; manuscripts do. In rejecting the presentational performance of the clerical worker for the performance at a distance of the meritocracy, *Fear of Flying* not only dispatches the parafeminist's recommendation for "how to make it in a man's world," as Letty Pogrebin would say, but also puts its protagonist's fantasy of the zipless fuck in its proper place. That "absolutely pure" experience depends exclusively on first impressions, on an immediate connection that by definition precludes a callback—or, given the performance at a distance that matters to Jong, an invitation to revise and resubmit.

In the effort to think beyond gender norms, the signal texts of the women's movement find a valuable resource in Fifties school culture, even going so far as to engage that culture's signature moves. Treating both belief and performance as opportunistic, Plath, Didion, and Jong all gesture toward an abject queerness in which the homosexual is possessed of a faulty instrumentality, a performance style that is either too artificial to be credible or too much beyond the performer's control to be agential. In asserting the possibility of female self-assertion on the basis of a meritorious performance of extraordinary womanhood, Susann makes her protagonists contend with the dual specters of "faggots" and frigid women. In asserting the possibility of female self-assertion on the basis of a meritorious performance of impersonal labor (in Plath and Jong) or a performance of ironic make-believe (in Didion and Jong), these novelists also offer up a variety of queer foils and sacrifices: the suicidal BZ in *Play It As It Lays*; *The Bell Jar*'s Joan, who makes a pass at Esther before taking her own life; the homoerotic doodler Brian, abandoned to the busywork of occupational therapy, "pounding a piece of clay into one of the tabletops" on the occasion of Isadora's last visit (285).

Alongside their figuration of queerness as outside the bounds of institutional legitimation, such novels embrace another standby of the midcentury classroom: the notion that a student's best teacher is herself. For all its reputed salaciousness, *Fear of Flying* reads like an almost clinical essay on femaleness in which Isadora's perpetually naked body is more gynecological specimen than source of titillation. "Secretly," she confides in a moment typical of the book's body consciousness, "I know my Fallopian tubes are probably healing over with scar tissue and my ovaries are drying up" (318). The intimacy that *Fear of Flying* conspires to manufacture in its readers also sustains a concerted reflexivity; the novel's goal is not to put an end to experts—gynecologists and psychoanalysts and other authorities on the female malady—but to fashion the conditions in which one can become one's own analyst, one's own gynecologist. Let us note that *Fear of Flying* was published the same year as another enduring bestseller, *Our Bodies, Ourselves*, the landmark woman's health volume now in its eighth edition.

While the novel has long been treated as a flagship text in the rise of feminist identity politics, *Fear of Flying* is a thoroughgoing homage to antiessentialism—if it is not, by way of its embrace of opportunistic make-believe, an homage to the even more prestigious category of "strategic essentialism." This is true of both its politics of gender ascription and its embrace of unstructured structure. For Isadora, the alternative to "system" is not essence; the alternative to both system and essence is what Drucker calls "justification by performance." Yet *Fear of Flying* places its author in the vanguard less of gender politics per se than of that socioeconomic shift whose parameters Daniel Bell forecast in *The Coming of Post-industrial Society*. Among Bell's "preoccupations" is what he calls the "disjunction, in Western society, between the culture and the social structure, the one becoming increasingly anti-institutional and antinomian, the other oriented to functional rationality and meritocracy."[48] But this disjunction is really not so dire after all. The goal of consciousness raising was always to assert the primacy of the person over and above the institutions that would constrain her. Revolting against institutions for presuming to impose their authority from on high obliged feminists to see that, as the Redstockings' Kathie Sarachild put it, "experience in consciousness-raising can't be judged by expertise in any alleged methods but by expertise in getting results."[49] Alongside a Drucker-like commitment to "justification by performance," the women's movement granted considerable power to the reference group itself—what Richard Florida, in *The Rise of the Creative Class* (2002), calls "the chance to win the esteem and recognition of others in the know."[50] Or to cite Sarachild: "It is striking how many people in the right circumstances can suddenly become experts!"[51] Consciousness raising does not eschew so much as subsume expertise.

Such antinomian advances are wholly compatible with the exaltation of performance at a distance, since in both the counterculture and the postindustrial meritocracy the goal is to put as much space as possible between persons and the reward system of traditional hierarchies like the school. In Florida's decidedly Whiggish view of the creative class's triumph, meritocratic strivers stand beyond class distinctions (or even in opposition to them) to achieve their privileges the hard way: by earning them. On the one hand, creative types are uninterested in "money" ("creativity" is a matter of "intrinsic rewards" [86]), and, on the other, "creativity" is "the great leveler": it "cannot be handed down, and it cannot be 'owned' in the traditional sense" (xiv). But what is most notable about the overlap between Bell's radicals and the new breed of brainworkers for whom Florida serves as tribune is that the meritocracy no less than the counterculture institutionalizes *unconventionality*. Here the older meritocratic principle of measurement by comparison gives way to what we might call measurement by nonconformity. This is what Florida has in mind when he says that "nonconformity to organizational norms may represent a new mainstream value" (78). In answer to the question, "Where could we turn for guidance?" (139), Isadora comes up with no one other than herself. Unlike her ex-husband and her mother, who reject exemplification outright, Isadora must become her own role model, a charge she takes up by announcing, "People don't complete us. We complete ourselves" (412).

Epilogue

In describing the overlap of the women's movement, New Left consciousness raising, and meritocratic striving, the previous chapter owes an obvious debt to work like Thomas Frank's *The Conquest of Cool* (1997), which traces the relays through which the Sixties counterculture and the corporate establishment co-opted each other. Frank's book inaugurated a healthy countertrend to the often self-congratulatory chronicles of the Sixties written by many of its participants. *Camp Sites* partakes of this revisionist impulse, but I have not been especially concerned, as many revisionist accounts are, with treating the New Social Movements as the "origin" of our contemporary situation. Rather than ask how we got here (twenty-first-century neoliberalism) from there (Sixties radicalism), I have been interested in how the Sixties got to be where they were from the vantage of a school culture that became all but hegemonic after 1945. The social style that developed in the college opened onto an array of concerns beyond the curriculum of any given discipline: from performance to identity to the role of institutions in modern society.

That ramification certainly carried over into Sixties radicalism—for example, into the overwhelming focus on the school as an institution whose dominance the student radicals often conflated with *domination*. Why did Mario Savio see the plight of impoverished southern blacks as identical to the grievances of Berkeley college students? What made Tom Hayden declare in a 1966 essay that "students and poor people make each other feel real," and what made such authenticity count as a political virtue to begin with?[1] Capable of mobilizing a great number of people, such equations were not simply instances of poor judgment or bad faith. They derived from an understanding of the relation between individuals and social structures that assigned primacy to experience at the same time that it bred a disdain or rejection of systematization. However different the experience of blacks living under Jim Crow and that of students in a lecture hall at Berkeley, the same technocratic system voided both experiences of meaning.

In forging this claim, New Leftists adopted key precepts of the postwar school culture that they positioned as their antagonist. Here I do not mean the banal fact that students protested against an institution of which they were fundamentally a part, nor the more nuanced point David Riesman makes in *On Higher Education* (1980) when he says that "the protesting students were insisting that the university live up to the ideals some of its most eloquent leaders proclaimed."[2] I mean that the prestige conferred on experience, no less than the animus toward "system," already enjoyed an enthusiastic following among midcentury academics by the time the New Left arrived on the scene. When Kathie Sarachild describes consciousness raising as the "decision to test all generalizations and reading we did by our own experience," it is hard not to be reminded of the syllabus of experience that higher education made central to the postwar classroom on precisely these terms.[3] And just as experience was central to midcentury pedagogy, so every system was suspect (particularly a system other than your own).

Despite attending to the ways in which Sixties thought spirals back to a prerevolutionary moment that the New Social Movements actively disown, I have also been leery of melding the 1950s into the 1960s. There were important differences between what the syllabus of experience meant to the teachers of Amherst's English 1 or Harvard's Hum 6 and to radicals like Sarachild. Whereas the postwar classroom both elevated experience and insisted on its inaccessibility, the innovation of the New Social Movements was to retain the centrality of experience while rejecting any claim that it was not dispositive or transparent. "Consciousness raising is a way of forming a political analysis on information we can trust is true," Barbara Susan Kaminsky wrote in 1970. "That information is our experience."[4] In pursuing the "commitment to commitment," the student Left repudiated both the ambiguous language and noncommittal affect of the professoriat. This was no small distinction, and we risk serious misreading of Sixties radicalism if we do not register the degree to which its adherents imagined themselves reversing the instrumental reason of the Cold War consensus and its makers.

Throughout *Camp Sites* I have invoked "camp" as a general rubric for pushing the sensibility common to the varied disciplines of postwar school culture in the direction of its insistent queer "other." One question I have been asking throughout is, What is it about queers that makes them routinely stand in for the abject version of the academic style, the instrumental reason or ironic self-fashioning of the liberal intellectuals? Another question I have been asking is, How is it that the queers, so thoroughly reviled by the liberal establishment, could also find themselves so emphatically unwelcome at the revolution? In the early Cold War context, the queer represents the extreme version of academic hubris, whether this is Nabokov's tyrannically oversensitive Kinbote or Ellison's simultaneously knowing and clueless Emerson the Younger. In the New Social Movements by contrast, the queer becomes a cunning closet queen, thus an emblem of the duplicity and anonymity characteristic of the invisible government. For Cold War liberals, queers are too expressive; they have proved to be poor students of the school, which demands a certain abstract aloofness toward one's own personality, a reluctance to give oneself away. For radicals, queers are not expressive enough; they are too fluent in the school's customs of masking and inconsequence to profit from the political boon of authenticity or to embrace the virtues of commitment.

That the university can convey these lessons of impression management in the first place, that what it delivers beyond a bachelor of arts or doctorate is a way of being in the world, is both obvious and underappreciated. We are more likely to associate the levels of compulsory education—the primary and secondary school—with the task of ideological formation, precisely because those tiers are conscriptive and powerfully normative. But the fact that college is voluntary should not make us any less willing to credit it with a range of socializing functions, chief among which is the widely shared conviction that it is a place no one forces us to be. For an institution built on no stronger foundation than the consent of its participants, it has proved surprisingly impervious to the winds of change. Part of the reason for its staying power, I have argued, is that the postwar university conferred a massive advantage on change itself.

It may be naïve to imagine that an institution that has undergone as much upheaval in the last seventy years as the university could be said to retain over several generations a consistent social style. But this criticism mistakes the degree to which any institution thrives on projecting an imaginary opposition between its core functions and its supposedly ephemeral or superficial attributes. *Camp Sites* has used the concept of style in both a historical and a polemical sense as a way of recovering an often belittled dimension of social life in general and an important dimension of postwar culture in particular. That culture venerated style over substance for the reasons that I have given throughout the book. And its anxiety about such a preference is readily apparent in the frequency with which camp, the style that coincides with homosexuality, was derided as a false or abject version of the attitudinizing basic to Cold War policy makers. Social style roughly translates to Bourdieu's *habitus*, which describes a process of social positioning neither reducible to embodied persons nor to the material conditions of any given institution but inseparable from both. But this translation also involves a provocation, since unlike *habitus*, the term "style" captures the importance our culture attributes to the voluntary; because it appears changeable, style also appears under the auspices of our agency. Style is what D. A. Miller calls "an obvious personal project."[5] *Camp Sites* has insisted by contrast that insofar as it is governed by institutional constraints, style is more compulsory and less mutable than we imagine. More exactly, the "personal project" we take style to be is the outer lining of the largely impersonal set of operations characteristic of institutions.

To see *habitus* as a matter of social positioning is to take cognizance of the fact, for example, that women who want to succeed in academe must attain (if they do not yet have it) the dispassionate bearing of the Cold War critic. The feminist recovery of sentimental fiction, like the more recent turn to affect, would surely not seem so controversial were it not for the conviction prevalent among academics that there is something unseemly about the validation of genres and categories that flout the professoriat's implicitly masculinist norms of ironic detachment and impersonality. A *habitus* always exists in uneasy tension with the institution that fosters it, particularly when that institution undergoes change; but its effect is inertial, exercising on even the most dynamic institution a centripetal drag. This is the reason that "the same *habitus* which engenders a particular practice," Bourdieu writes, "can equally well engender the opposite."[6] As confirmation of this point, we need only observe that the ironic stance of contemporary humanists is pressed into service less in defense of the state (as it was for Cold War academics) than on behalf of a more or less articulated opposition to it. Richard Rorty typifies how the academic *habitus* persists over time even when its referents might shift according to what Bourdieu calls *habitus*'s "logic of dissimilation."[7] Whereas Cold War ironists were resolutely opposed to utopian politics, after all, Rorty advocates "a liberal utopia: one in which ironism in the relevant sense is universal."[8]

If such claims reek of cynicism, I plead not guilty to a charge that often follows from cynicism: an acquiescence to the world as we find it, on the assumption that any "real" change is illusory. Rather than quietist, my aim throughout this book has been in fact more quarrelsome than I may have let on. I seek not to undo the political work in which critics have felt themselves engaged but to demonstrate that the politicization of the academic endeavor, the widely held view that scholarship is politics by other means, has long been compatible with the power structure to which many academics imagine themselves opposed. Politicality is as basic to the academic *habitus* as voluntarity. These twin pennons of our style, which of course fit together (ours is a politics of voluntarism), are determined by our institutional circumstances. To be an academic is to be inscribed in a social field whose hold on us consists in the voluntarism it affords us. Lest this sound like warmed-over Foucault, I want to add that this cunning ruse of power is quite specific to the academic fold. If laypeople have sometimes been bewildered by the account of politics set forth in academic life, this is no doubt a function of how much bad press academics get in a society as resiliently anti-intellectual as our own. But the confusion has another source, less easily brushed aside. Nonacademics do not understand our politics because they do not share our *habitus*. Few people, after all, have access to the elective liberties that tenured faculty enjoy. And though fewer and fewer academics enjoy that access in the age of the adjunct, this does not change the fact that the privileges of academic life sometimes make solidarity across "interest groups" rather challenging. We have difficulty recognizing (or admitting) that ours is a class politics or that the readiness with which some commentators have sought to identify a "lumpen professoriat" is a callow and empty gesture at best.[9]

The politicized academic in the present combines two powerful lines of reasoning: the Cold War liberal's investment in knowing artifice (where the relevant choice is to act as if an institution matters regardless of one's private beliefs) and the Sixties radical's investment in expressive authenticity (where the relevant choice is to assert one's private beliefs regardless of institutional constraints or consequences). If we were seeking evidence that these ostensibly contrary outlooks on the world share deep commonalities, not least because they spring from a joint source in the school culture that produces them, we need look no further than queer theory, the field in which the present book is fitfully at home. Queer theory's revolt against normativity presupposes a freedom of choice that itself serves as the governing norm of liberal society. Thus, in her *In a Queer*

Time and Place (2005), Judith Halberstam can argue that "we should take over the prerogative of naming our experience and identifications," as though this usurpation were a challenge to—rather than an instance of—the "bourgeois investment in the economy of authenticity."[10] For the New Social Movements, authentic identity derived not from a fideistic account of the real, of the sort that Halberstam rightly rejects, but precisely from justifying one's identity by endlessly questioning it. Yet we need only look back to John Stuart Mill to see that such a procedure is the very definition of "bourgeois."[11] An important continuity between the radicals of the 1960s and those of the 1860s would be the belief that self-determination arises from perpetual autocritique. "There must be discussion," Mill writes, "to show how experience is to be interpreted."[12] "Freedom," as one SDS member put it in 1965, "is an endless meeting."[13]

Though most faculty of my acquaintance are less inclined than this SDS member to look with favor on the prospect of endless meetings, academics in general and queer theorists in particular nonetheless harbor a powerful commitment to the value of *endlessness.* Throughout *Cruising Utopia* (2009), his effort to reclaim a "queer utopian imagination," José Esteban Muñoz maintains "an insistence on potentiality," a concept whose importance to the postwar liberal compact we have confirmed.[14] For Muñoz, queerness is another name for "the not-yet-arrived" (160), for what (borrowing from Giorgio Agamben) he calls a "politics of a 'means without end'" (91), for "something else, something better, something dawning" (189). The fluidity of these terms is occasioned by Muñoz's unabashed rejection of "queerness" as "an identitarian marker" (87) and his embrace of a productive indefiniteness, a sort of hollow core at the heart of queerness where those "who are bent on the normative" seek the consolations of substance (189). What gives queerness "resonance" (87), in other words, is the principle that underlies the acoustics of any echo chamber: its amplification stands or falls on the quality of the framing device, the structure that surrounds the space of conceptualization. The less clutter within that space, the less obstructed and more intense the reverberations. Queerness is thus capable of sounding most deeply when shorn of the static of a content-driven politics, a politics that treats queerness as an "identitarian" thing rather than a powerfully hazy "something."[15]

A skeptic might say here that queerness speaks most loudly when it has the least to say. But this would be to mistake the force of Muñoz's argument and thus to miss how that argument resonates into a much longer genealogy of academic thought. The point Muñoz insists upon is not that queerness is an empty signifier but that its emptiness permits activists to *fill in the blank* in ways that resist or subvert received definitions. Yet given the powerful incentive to choose our definitions afforded by a prior recognition that signifieds are only contingently aligned with their signifiers, and thus that referents themselves are an area of political contest, it is strange that Muñoz objects so fiercely to what he calls "pragmatic politics" (31). Muñoz uses this term in its "vernacular" sense; he is not assailing "the philosophical tradition . . . of Charles Peirce, William James, or John Dewey" (21). But these meanings are less far apart than he acknowledges. Pragmatism, as both another name for opportunism and a philosophical standpoint, blankets the university in the postwar world, from those critics who evolved the syllabus of experience in and around midcentury humanism (Richard Poirier chief among them) to those social scientists who evolved symbolic interactionism in and around midcentury sociology (Erving Goffman chief among them).

Like Muñoz, all these figures exploited a studied and provocative vagueness, from Poirier's view of reading as "the art of not arriving" to Goffman's stubbornly elusive definition of the "individual" as "a something that takes up a position somewhere between identification with an organization and opposition to it."[16] And like Muñoz, all these figures venerated "potentiality." Indeed, from Dewey onward, that concept was the promise of school culture. Moreover, like Muñoz, these figures understood potentiality as accessible through a means-oriented instrumentalism. "Means and ends are two names for the same reality," Dewey asserted in *Human Nature and Conduct* (1922), close to a century before Agamben sought to reorient our telos-driven epistemology.[17] Yet it is just here, where Dewey and his institutional legacy rear up in our sight line, that the analogy between Muñoz and the pragmatists appears to break down. For the tradition of pragmatism is not only a line of philosophical descent but also, in an important sense, a method powerfully invested in *tradition* itself. For this reason Rorty characterizes the act of "redescription" he places at the center of his political vision as "like refurnishing a house" (45). Since "contemporary liberal society already contains the institutions for its own improvement" (61), what is needed is a sprucing up rather than a teardown.

When presented in the form of Rorty's *Achieving Our Country* (1999), which indicts politicized academics for their nihilistic refusal to work within existing structures, pragmatism can look not only conservative but unforgivably nostalgic (the title of Rorty's polemic alone is a sentimental minefield). If it is not what Muñoz has in mind when he charges "the hamstrung pragmatic gay agenda" (10) with "antiutopian thought" (31), philosophical pragmatism, with its ongoing commitment to institutional life, cannot exactly be said to lend itself to "a forward-dawning futurity" (87), much less the "wave of potentiality" that Muñoz envisions "crashing" over the breakers of establishment culture (185). But this is only to say that for pragmatists, potentiality names an essentially liberal politics, whereas for Muñoz it names a "new mode of radicalism" (172). More precisely, for the school culture that arises out of American pragmatism, potentiality is itself *normative*. What makes Muñoz insist on identifying potentiality, then, with the utopian dream of upheaval?

In answer to this question, we could say that Muñoz rallies the key talking points of school culture, from its instrumentalist pedagogy of "means without an end" to its practiced veneration of the "not-yet-arrived," in the service of a politics that school culture has always entertained just short of execution. School culture projects a vision of indefinite possibility apparently at odds with its gradualist practices. Here again Rorty is of some help. Insofar as his vision of liberal utopia involves not radical leaps and reversals but what he calls "gradual, tacit substitutions of a new vocabulary for an old one" (77), "the gradual, trial-and-error creation of a new . . . vocabulary" (12), Rorty's "reformist political culture" (64) is in several ways beholden to the campus. From the well-paced turnover of its student body to the pride it takes in its own contingency to the plurality of its disciplines, the university epitomizes the "story of progress" Rorty wants to tell (55): a slowly simmering evolutionary advance, a Kuhnian paradigm shift tempered by methodical transitions. Muñoz's rejection of "the dominant academic culture," with its "dismissal of political idealism" (10), follows from an impatience with this slow tempo, not least because it helps secure an account of "legitimate" succession he refuses to endorse (46). Legitimacy is complicit in "the temporal stranglehold" of what, following Halberstam, Muñoz calls "straight time" (32) or, alternatively, "capitalism's naturalizing temporal logic" (87). The scare quotes he uses to mark legitimacy as a false idol would be for Rorty signs of the covenant made by people in "liberal societies . . . to recognize the contingency of the vocabulary in which they state their highest hopes" while remaining "faithful" to them (46).

Rorty brings us full circle to one of this book's running themes: the ascendance in postwar America of what I have called the consensus of make-believe.

"Camp," too, let us recall, "sees everything in quotation marks."[18] It is thus somewhat startling to find Muñoz describing the politics he favors, "a politics of sincerity that connote[s] transformative potential," as "the opposite of camp" (46). We have observed that when not merely true believers who act out according to scripts they always take too far, camp followers are emblematic of cynical reason, devotees of the normative by default because they comply with a social order whose arrangements, however unfair, they can do no more than ironize. For Muñoz by contrast, the "transformative" imagination depends on what looks like a dramatic, because counterintuitive, attitude adjustment, a dislocation of "romances of the negative" (11) by "idealism" (10).

Far from counterintuitive, many assumptions driving Muñoz's argument—including the notion that to change an attitude is to change a social arrangement—are native to the *habitus* of *Homo academicus* in postwar America. Even the "associative mode of analysis" and the reliance on "personal experience" (3) that Muñoz enlists as rebuffs to hermeneutic conventions would have been recognizable to any freshman enrolled in Hum 6 or English 1 in 1954. It is of course unlikely that said freshman would have recognized, much less appreciated, Muñoz's use of experience and association as "another way to ground historical queer sites with lived queer experience" (3). It is inconceivable that in pre-Stonewall America any such reference would have gone over too well in or out of the classroom. Yet this confirms not so much the radicalism of Muñoz's queerness as the resilience and flexibility of the institution that underwrites his account of it. We would be mistaken to see that account as in any relevant sense separable from school culture. Much more completely than Muñoz's queer utopianism, though by the same refusal of "ontological certitude" (11), school culture has presented itself as "a horizon imbued with potentiality" (1). The postwar campus was and remains at the bleeding edge of echo-chamber design.

Of course, this has an obvious drawback with respect to academic politics, queer or otherwise. The resonances of the campus tend also to be self-contained. There is undeniable value in politically engaging one another as academics. I am merely pointing out that with vanishingly rare exceptions, such political engagement does not move over the invisible fence marking off the territory of the campus. While it is a mistake to view the academy as outside or detached from the surrounding culture, it is an even greater mistake to see the academy as indistinguishable from the surrounding culture. As I have already suggested, the right name for the invisible fence between the campus and the social order it serves is simply class privilege. Despite its ample helpings of Frankfurt school Marxism, *Cruising Utopia* is remarkably tight-lipped on the subject of class relations. Queer theory, however utopian its aspirations, is no more able to face the need for a "transformative" view of class inequality than any of the Sixties movements from which it departs. Poor people and students make each other feel real, according to Tom Hayden. If academics have been justly reluctant to concede a politics based on such figmentary realness, they have exercised that reluctance at the cost of any serious engagement with poor people, actual or imagined.

This sort of claim is easily confused with that academic game of one-upmanship in which, as in prime time, the clear winner is the biggest loser. Yet my aim is not to deprecate Muñoz's focus on queers of color rather than the poor. Muñoz is well aware that in our society, where class inequality is structured on racial and gender inequality, these social identities do not often differ much. The point I want to stress is this: However academics choose to pursue the politics of representation within their scholarship—by whatever means they construct what we now call intersectionality, whether across racial or gender or erotic lines—that politics seems stubbornly unmindful of the institutional and material roadblocks thrown up at the intersection. If "over the last two decades," as Heather Love notes, "a queer coalition of outsiders has failed to materialize," I would say that this failure has less to do with the "false universalism" of queerness than with the fact that the queer academics leading the charge for such a coalition are only outsiders by courtesy.[19] The cause of our failure is not a lack of imagination regarding a truly queer "universal" but an all too material reality: the difference between the circumstances of academics and the circumstances of those who swim outside the tenure stream.

Primary among the divergences between academics and laypeople, I would hazard, is the radically different way that those of us in academic life mark time. Firm believers in the meritocracy, we tend also to have a Plath-like faith in open-endedness, the specific kind of progress that accompanies the rhythms of school time. Recently, queer theory has seen a flurry of work that questions what Elizabeth Freeman calls "chrononormativity," what Lee Edelman calls "reproductive futurism," what Judith Halberstam calls "repro-time."[20] Though its theoretical groundings range from Freud to Heidegger to Agamben, I suspect this critical interest in coercive temporality has just as much to do with the fact that, as academics used to wiping the slate clean every June, we are quite comfortable with the possibility of alternatives to heteronormative continuity precisely because we enjoy all the benefits of resetting our schedules with few of the costs. This hunch does not undermine the work being done in recent queer theory. It merely seeks to frame such work by way of the academic calendar from which it cannot finally be separated. "We have been cast out of straight time's rhythm" (182), Muñoz claims. But the "ecstatic time" he seeks, the "temporal disorganization" (87) that would "resist the stifling temporality and time that is not ours" (187), is hidden in plain sight in the organization to which he undeniably belongs. School culture flaunts the episodic and praises the dynamic, indeed insists that no one can make it through the college who doesn't at least pretend to embrace its policy of perpetual difference. School culture routinizes alterity.

In my view it would make queer work more rather than less interesting were we to admit that our favorite category, the antinormative, is most comfortable in the institution that houses us, even if we are reluctant to call it home. This is a position that, as befits the academic *habitus* with which this book has dealt, we might call pragmatist. While Muñoz differentiates between the "vernacular" meaning of pragmatism and the "philosophical tradition," it is worth recalling that for many critics both senses of this term are pejorative. Pragmatism maintains that we cannot stand outside our practice in order to judge it. As Rorty claims, "There will be no way to rise above the language, culture, institutions, and practices one has adopted and view all these as on a par with all the others" (50). Many critics have interpreted this claim as reactionary, since it appears to imply that we cannot transcend our contexts. This is a mistake. The assumption that we are tethered to the contexts in which we find ourselves does not mean that we cannot change them. Indeed, it may just as well provide us with the incentive we need for bringing such change about.

Reference Matter

Notes

Introduction

1. Herman Kahn, *Thinking about the Unthinkable* (New York: Horizon, 1962), 164.

2. Susan Sontag, *Against Interpretation and Other Essays* (New York: Farrar, Straus and Giroux, 1966), 286. Hereafter cited in text.

3. Lawrence Frank, "Culture and Personality," in *John Dewey: Philosopher of Science and Freedom: A Symposium*, ed. Sidney Hook (New York: Dial, 1950), 104, 88.

4. David Johnson, *The Lavender Scare: The Cold War Persecution of Lesbians and Gays in the Federal Government* (Chicago: University of Chicago Press, 2004).

5. Charles Taylor, *A Secular Age* (Cambridge, Mass.: Harvard University Press, 2007), 825.

6. Robert McCloskey, "American Political Thought and the Study of Politics," *American Political Science Review* 51.1 (1957): 126.

7. Ibid., 120.

8. William James, *Writings 1902–1910* (New York: Library of America, 1987), 571.

9. Ibid., 522.

10. Taylor, *A Secular Age*, 310, 497.

11. Ibid., 411.

12. John Dewey, *The Later Works, 1925–1953*, vol. 15, *1942–1948, Essays, Reviews, and Miscellany*, ed. Jo Ann Boydston (Carbondale: Southern Illinois University Press, 1989), 250.

13. Ibid.

14. Sidney Ratner, "Dewey's Contribution to Historical Theory," in Hook, *John Dewey*, 144, 148.

15. Sheldon Wolin, *Politics and Vision: Continuity and Innovation in Western Political Thought*, exp. ed. (Princeton, N.J.: Princeton University Press, 2004), 508.

16. Leo Strauss, *Liberalism Ancient and Modern* (Chicago: University of Chicago Press, 1995), 221.

17. F. W. Coker, "Some Present-Day Critics of Liberalism," *American Political Science Review* 47.1 (1953): 24, 25.

18. Philip Core, "Camp: The Lie That Tells the Truth," in *Camp: Queer Aesthetics and the Performing Subject: A Reader*, ed. Fabio Cleto (Ann Arbor: University of Michigan Press, 1999), 80. Cleto, *Camp*, is hereafter cited in text as *C*.

19. R. E. L. Masters, *The Homosexual Revolution* (New York: Julian, 1962), 226. Hereafter cited in text.

20. Harold Beaver, "Homosexual Signs (In Memory of Roland Barthes)," *Critical Inquiry* 8.1 (1981): 103.

21. Donald Webster Cory, *The Homosexual in America: A Subjective Approach* (New York: Greenberg, 1951), 123. Hereafter cited in text.

22. Milton Konvitz, "Dewey's Revision of Jefferson," in Hook, *John Dewey*, 170.

23. Alfred Gross, *Strangers in Our Midst: Problems of the Homosexual in American Society* (Washington, D.C.: Public Affairs, 1962), 130. Hereafter cited in text.

24. William S. Burroughs, *Letters: 1945–1959*, ed. Oliver Harris (New York: Penguin, 2009), 233.

25. Andrew Hacker, Liberalism and Social Control," *American Political Science Review* 51.4 (1957): 1021, 1020.

26. Ibid., 1021.

27. W. H. Auden, *Selected Poems*, ed. Edward Mendelson (New York: Vintage, 2007), 89.

Chapter 1

1. Irving Janis, *Air War and Emotional Stress* (New York: McGraw-Hill, 1951), 220.

2. Department of Defense, Federal Civil Defense Administration, and National Security Resources Board, *Project East River Part IX: Information and Training for Civil Defense* (New York: Associated Universities, 1952), 59.

3. Ibid., 62.

4. Sharon Ghamari-Tabrizi, *The Worlds of Herman Kahn: The Intuitive Science of Thermonuclear War* (Cambridge, Mass.: Harvard University Press, 2005), 143. Hereafter cited in text.

5. Bruce Kuklick, *Blind Oracles: Intellectuals and War from Kennan to Kissinger* (Princeton, N.J.: Princeton University Press, 2006), 87.

6. I borrow the term "emotion management" from Andrew Grossman, who describes the federal Civil Defense Administration's effort to build "its national policy planning on a general theory of emotion management or 'crisis mastery'" (*Neither Dead nor Red: Civilian Defense and American Political Development during the Early Cold War* [New York: Routledge, 2001], 2).

7. By calling the academic style "political," I mean to highlight a different concern from the collusion between research method and government power that found not a few postwar academics recruited to the various agencies of US intelligence. Robin Winks chronicles the partnership of the (mainly Ivy League) academy with first the OSS and then the CIA in *Cloak and Gown: Scholars in America's Secret War* (London: Harvill Press, 1987). Following Winks's lead, William Epstein reveals that the "alliance of textual politics between traditional (non-Marxist) humanist scholarship and the New Criticism" was crucial to "shaping the world-view that enabled and abetted the Cold War" ("Counter-Intelligence: Cold War Criticism and Eighteenth-Century Studies," *ELH* 57.1 [1990]: 80). Both Winks and Epstein characterize the Cold War academic's complicity

with statecraft as a *covert* operation. Yet regardless of the silence shrouding the pipeline from New Haven to Quantico, we need hardly dig beneath the surface of the era's academic discourse to notice the often *overt* self-identifications of Cold War professors as defenders of American statecraft.

8. Don DeLillo, *White Noise* (New York: Penguin, 1996), 204.

9. Theodore Caplow and Reece Jerome McGee, *The Academic Marketplace* (New York: Basic, 1958), 4.

10. Pierre Bourdieu, *Outline of a Theory of Practice*, trans. Richard Nice (Cambridge: Cambridge University Press, 1977), 72.

11. Pierre Bourdieu, *Homo Academicus*, trans. Peter Collier (Stanford: Stanford University Press, 1988), xiii.

12. Ibid.

13. Pierre Bourdieu, *Rules of Art: Genesis and Structure of the Literary Field*, trans. Susan Emanuel (Stanford: Stanford University Press, 1996), 147.

14. John Guillory, *Cultural Capital: The Problem of Literary Canon Formation* (Chicago: University of Chicago Press, 1992), vii.

15. Cleanth Brooks, *The Well-Wrought Urn: Studies in the Structure of Poetry* (New York: Harcourt, 1947), 253.

16. Ibid., 256, 257.

17. Grossman, *Neither Dead nor Red*, 5.

18. Gayatri Chakravorty Spivak, *Outside in the Teaching Machine* (New York: Routledge, 1993), 13.

19. Richard Ohmann, "English and the Cold War," in *The Cold War and the University: Toward an Intellectual History of the Postwar Years*, ed. Noam Chomsky et al. (New York: New Press, 1997), 73.

20. Daniel Bell, *The End of Ideology: On the Exhaustion of Political Ideas in the Fifties* (Glencoe, Ill.: Free Press, 1960), 16.

21. Howard Mumford Jones, "The Social Responsibility of Scholarship," *PMLA* 64.1 (1949): 43.

22. Hayward Keniston, "We Accept Our Responsibility for Professional Leadership," *PMLA* 68.1 (1953): 23.

23. Bayard Quincy Morgan, "Unrecognized Disarmament," *PMLA* 68.1 (1953): 42.

24. Ibid., 41.

25. Leslie Fiedler, *An End to Innocence: Essays on Culture and Politics* (Boston: Beacon, 1955), ix.

26. Reinhold Niebuhr, *The Irony of American History* (Chicago: University of Chicago Press, 2008), 34. Hereafter cited in text.

27. Reinhold Niebuhr, *Self and the Dramas of History* (New York: Scribner, 1955), 163.

28. Clark Kerr, *The Uses of the University* (Cambridge, Mass.: Harvard University Press, 1963), 72. Hereafter cited in text.

29. Alvin Gouldner, "Cosmopolitans and Locals: Toward an Analysis of Latent Social Roles—II," *Administrative Science Quarterly* 2.4 (1958): 449.

30. John Dewey, "I Believe," in Boydston, *The Later Works, 1925–1953*, vol. 14, *1939–1941, Essays, Reviews, Miscellany*, 92.

31. Seymour Lipset, *Political Man: The Social Bases of Politics* (Garden City, N.Y.: Doubleday, 1960), 67.

32. William K. Wimsatt and Monroe C. Beardsley, "The Intentional Fallacy," in Wimsatt, *The Verbal Icon* (Lexington: University Press of Kentucky, 1948), 5, 7. Hereafter cited in text.

33. Wolin, *Politics and Vision*, 520.

34. Ellen Schrecker, *No Ivory Tower: McCarthyism and the Universities* (New York: Oxford University Press, 1986), 105.

35. John Guillory, "The Sokal Affair and the History of Criticism," *Critical Inquiry* 28 (Winter 2002): 482.

36. Richard Rovere, *The Eisenhower Years: Affairs of State* (New York: Farrar, Straus and Cudahy, 1956), 11.

37. Suzanne Clark, *Cold Warriors: Manliness on Trial in the Rhetoric of the West* (Carbondale: Southern Illinois University Press, 2000), 26.

38. Charles Frankel, *The Democratic Prospect* (New York: Harper and Row, 1962), 80.

39. Lipset, *Political Man*, 416.

40. Eric Larrabee, *The Self-Conscious Society* (Garden City, N.Y.: Doubleday, 1960), 28.

41. Edgar N. Johnson, "The Background of the University Tradition," in *Freedom and the University: The Responsibility for the Maintenance of Freedom in the American Way of Life*, ed. Johnson Robert D. Calkins, Eugene V. Rostow, Joseph L. Lilienthal Jr., J. Robert Oppenheimer, and Edward C. Kirkland (Ithaca, N.Y.: Cornell University Press, 1950), 7.

42. Here my argument overlaps with a discussion of belief in Amy Hungerford's *Postmodern Belief* (Princeton, N.J.: Princeton University Press, 2010), which explores what Hungerford calls the postwar "dogma of no dogma" (16).

43. Arthur M. Schlesinger Jr., *The Vital Center: The Politics of Freedom* (Boston: Houghton Mifflin, 1949), 245.

44. Jacques Barzun, *The Teacher in America* (Boston: Little, Brown, 1945), 25, 33.

45. Paul Goodman, *The Community of Scholars* (New York: Random House, 1962), 159.

46. Paul Goodman, *Growing Up Absurd* (New York: Vintage, 1956), 134, 144, 143, 125. Hereafter cited in text.

47. Eric Hoffer, *The True Believer: Thoughts on the Nature of Mass Movements* (New York: Harper and Row, 1951), 82. Hereafter cited in text.

48. Robert Lindner, *Must You Conform?* (New York: Grove, 1956), 80.

49. Ibid., 124.

50. Alex Abella, *Soldiers of Reason: The RAND Corporation and the Rise of the American Empire* (New York: Houghton Mifflin, 2008), 33.

51. Herman Kahn, *On Thermonuclear War* (Princeton, N.J.: Princeton University Press, 1960), 162.

52. Richard Barringer, with Barton Whaley, "The MIT Political-Military Gaming Experience," *Orbis* 9.2 (1965): 444.

53. Abella, *Soldiers*, 59.

54. N. C. Dalkey, *Command and Control: A Glance at the Future* (Santa Monica, Calif.: RAND, 1962), 12, 8.

55. Ibid., 3.

56. Norman Dalkey and Olaf Helmer, "An Experimental Application of the Delphi Method to the Use of Experts," *Management Science* 9.3 (1963): 458. Hereafter cited in text.

57. William Egginton, *How the World Became a Stage: Presence, Theatricality, and the Question of Modernity* (Albany, N.Y.: SUNY Press, 2003), 7.

58. Cushing Strout, "The Twentieth-Century Enlightenment," *American Political Science Review* 49.2 (1955): 339.

59. Henri Peyre, "The Need for Language Study in America Today," *Modern Language Journal* 40.6 (1956): 328.

60. Betty Friedan, *The Feminine Mystique* (New York: Norton, 2001), 265, 270, 281. Hereafter cited in text.

61. Marcuse writes: "The irresistible output[s] of the entertainment and information industry carry with them . . . certain intellectual and emotional reactions which bind the consumers more or less pleasantly to the producers and, through the latter, to the whole" (*One-Dimensional Man: Studies in the Ideology of Advanced Industrial Society* [Boston: Beacon, 1964], 12).

62. Ralph Ellison, *Invisible Man* (New York: Vintage, 1995), 443. Hereafter cited in text.

63. Ralph Ellison, *The Collected Essays of Ralph Ellison* (New York: Modern Library, 2003), 458. Hereafter cited in text as *CE*.

64. Alvin Toffler, *Future Shock* (New York: Bantam, 1971), 220, 226. Hereafter cited in text.

65. The indispensable study of historically black colleges is Henry Drewry and Humphrey Doermann, *Stand and Prosper: Private Black Colleges and Their Students* (Princeton, N.J.: Princeton University Press, 2001), from which this outline of Tuskegee is drawn.

66. J. Saunders Redding, *Stranger and Alone* (New York: Harper and Row, 1969), 111. Hereafter cited in text.

67. Ralph Ellison, "Collaborator with His Own Enemy," *New York Times Book Review*, February 9, 1950, 4.

68. Ibid.

69. Redding's review is cited in Lawrence Jackson, *Ralph Ellison: The Emergence of Genius* (New York: Wiley, 2002), 437.

70. J. Saunders Redding, *No Day of Triumph* (New York: Harper, 1942), 42. Hereafter cited in text.

71. Faith Berry, "Introduction," in *A Scholar's Conscience: Selected Writings of J. Saunders Redding, 1942–1977* (Lexington: University Press of Kentucky, 1977), 5.

72. We might say that Redding meets Wimbush's politics of detachment with a politics of resentment. "Perhaps to a proportion greater than any single one of his contemporaries," Lawrence Jackson notes in a shrewd appraisal of Redding's career, he "resented his situation as a black American who came of age in the late 1930s" ("Irredeemable Promise: J. Saunders Redding and New Negro Liberalism," *American Literary History* 19.3 [2007]: 714).

73. Jackson, *Ralph Ellison*, 411.

74. Daniel Boorstin, *The Genius of American Politics* (Chicago: University of Chicago Press, 1953), 170. Hereafter cited in text.

75. Schlesinger, *Vital Center*, 256.

76. Daniel Kim, "Invisible Desires: Homoerotic Racism and Its Homophobic Critique in Ralph Ellison's *Invisible Man*," *Novel: A Forum on Fiction* 30.3 (1997): 309.

77. "Come Back to the Raft Ag'in, Huck Honey!" in Fiedler, *An End to Innocence*, 188.

78. Bell, *The End of Ideology*, 16.

79. Stringfellow Barr, *Purely Academic* (New York: Simon and Schuster, 1958), 5.

80. John Aldridge, *The Party at Cranton* (New York: David McKay, 1960), 6.

81. Pamela Hansford Johnson, *Night and Silence, Who Is Here?* (New York: Scribner, 1963), 27.

82. Fiedler, *An End to Innocence*, 143.

83. Leslie Fiedler, "The Jig Is Up!," in *Waiting for the End* (New York: Stein and Day, 1964), 124.

84. Fiedler, *An End to Innocence*, 143.

85. Louis Kampf, "The Scandal of Literary Scholarship," *Harper's*, December 1967, 87. Hereafter cited in text.

86. Sontag, *Against Interpretation*, 290 .

87. Ibid., 283.

88. Mike Zweig, *The Radical in the Academic World* (Ann Arbor, Mich.: Conference on Radicals in the Profession), 1.

89. As Armstrong writes in *Satchmo: My Life in New Orleans* (New York: Prentice-Hall, 1954), "At the corner of the street where I lived was the famous Funky Butt hall, where I first heard Buddy Bolden play. He was blowing up a storm" (22).

Chapter 2

1. Mary McCarthy, "The Vassar Girl," in *On the Contrary* (New York: Farrar, Straus and Cudahy, 1961), 207. Hereafter cited in text as *OC*.

2. Mark McGurl, *The Program Era: Postwar Fiction and the Rise of Creative Writing* (Cambridge, Mass.: Harvard University Press, 2009), 111.

3. Leslie Fiedler, "The War against the Academy," *Wisconsin Studies in Contemporary Literature* 5.1 (1964): 5. Hereafter cited in text.

4. In Malcolm Bradbury's 1965 novel *Stepping Westward* (London: Picador, 2000), the visionary president of the Podunk Benedict Arnold University sees his campus as

being "more scholarly than Harvard, better built than Yale, more socially attractive than Princeton, and with better parking facilities than all of them" (5).

5. John Barth, *The End of the Road* (Garden City, N.Y.: Doubleday, 1958), 3, 90, 99.

6. B. F. Skinner, *Walden Two* (Indianapolis, Ind.: Hackett, 2005), 6, 5. Hereafter cited in text.

7. Harvard University Committee on the Objectives of a General Education in a Free Society, *General Education in a Free Society* (Cambridge, Mass.: Harvard University Press, 1945), 93. Hereafter cited in text.

8. George Kateb, *Utopia and Its Enemies* (Glencoe, Ill.: Free Press, 1963), 149. Hereafter cited in text.

9. John Dewey, *Experience and Education* (New York: Free Press, 1997), 29.

10. Ibid., 75.

11. John Dewey, *Human Nature and Conduct: An Introduction to Social Psychology* (New York: Henry Holt, 1922), 225.

12. Reuben Brower and Richard Poirier, eds., *In Defense of Reading: A Reader's Approach to Literary Criticism* (New York: Dutton, 1962), vii. Hereafter cited in text.

13. Richard Poirier, *The Performing Self: Compositions and Decompositions in the Languages of Contemporary Life* (New York: Oxford University Press, 1971), 66.

14. Paul de Man, *The Resistance to Theory* (Minneapolis: University of Minnesota Press, 1986), 23. Hereafter cited in text.

15. Richard Poirier, "The Example of Hum 6," in *Poetry and Pragmatism* (Cambridge, Mass.: Harvard University Press, 1992), 175. Hereafter cited in text.

16. Kenneth Burke, *The Philosophy of Literary Form: Studies in Symbolic Action* (Berkeley: University of California Press, 1974), 89, 77.

17. Ibid., 89.

18. John Dewey, "The Need for a Recovery of Philosophy," in *Creative Intelligence: Essays in the Pragmatic Attitude*, by John Dewey et al. (New York: Henry Holt, 1917), 7.

19. Walker Gibson, "Theodore Baird," in *Traditions of Inquiry*, ed. John Brereton (New York: Oxford University Press, 1982), 137.

20. Theodore Baird, cited in Robin Varnum, *Fencing with Words: A History of Writing Instruction at Amherst College during the Era of Theodore Baird, 1938–1966* (Urbana, Ill.: NCTE Press, 1996), 250. Hereafter cited in text as *FW*.

21. William Pritchard, *Playing It by Ear: Literary Essays and Reviews* (Amherst: University of Massachusetts Press, 1994), 3.

22. Cited in Gibson, "Theodore Baird," 145.

23. Alison Lurie, *Love and Friendship* (New York: Henry Holt, 1997), 18. Hereafter cited in text.

24. Cited in Gibson, "Theodore Baird," 140.

25. Ibid., 139.

26. Louise Rosenblatt, *Literature as Exploration* (New York: Appleton-Century, 1938), 56. Hereafter cited in text.

27. National Council of Teachers of English, *English Language Arts* (New York: Appleton-Century-Crofts, 1952), 153. Hereafter cited in text.

28. Bernard Malamud, *A New Life* (New York: Farrar, Straus and Cudahy, 1961), 230.

29. Mary McCarthy, "The Fact in Fiction," in *A Bolt from the Blue and Other Essays*, ed. A. O. Scott (New York: New York Review Books, 2002), 196. Hereafter cited in text as *BB*.

30. Mary McCarthy, *The Groves of Academe* (New York: Mariner, 2002), 5. Hereafter cited in text.

31. Hannah Arendt, *Essays in Understanding*, ed. Jerome Kohn (New York: Harcourt, 1994), 294. Deborah Nelson contrasts Arendt's critique of "pure logic" with her preference for "common sense": "Arendtian common sense is not self-evident but self-altering. [It] requires individuals to engage with others in the act of perception, sharing the world in a way that corrects and amends subjective insight" ("The Virtues of Heartlessness: Mary McCarthy, Hannah Arendt, and the Anesthetics of Empathy," *American Literary History* 18.1 [2006]: 91).

32. Vladimir Nabokov, *Strong Opinions* (New York: Vintage, 1990), 95.

33. Reuben Brower, Anne Ferry, and David Kalstone, eds., *Beginning with Poems: An Anthology* (New York: Norton, 1966), 12.

34. Vladimir Nabokov, *Bend Sinister* (New York: Vintage, 1990), 73. Hereafter cited in text.

35. Michael Wood, *The Magician's Doubts: Nabokov and the Risks of Fiction* (Princeton, N.J.: Princeton University Press, 1997), 60.

36. Richard Rorty, *Contingency, Irony, and Solidarity* (Cambridge: Cambridge University Press, 1989), 163. Hereafter cited in text.

37. Eric Naiman, in *Nabokov, Perversely* (Ithaca, N.Y.: Cornell University Press, 2010), likewise considers the "torture of Krug by David's death" as an "instance of poetic justice" (62).

38. Rorty, *Contingency*, 158.

39. Nabokov, Strong Opinions, 178. Hereafter cited in text as *SO*.

40. Vladimir Nabokov, *Lectures on Literature* (New York: Mariner, 2002), 377. Hereafter cited in text as *LL*.

41. Vladimir Nabokov, *Pale Fire* (New York: Vintage, 1989), 79. Hereafter cited in text.

42. Brian Boyd, *Nabokov's "Pale Fire": The Magic of Artistic Discovery* (Princeton, N.J.: Princeton University Press, 2001), 69. Hereafter cited in text.

43. Brooks, *Well-Wrought Urn*, 490. "Eliot's exaltation of the so-called mythic method," Poirier writes, "had a profoundly damaging effect . . . on the reading of literature" ("Example," 187).

44. Catherine Gallagher and Stephen Greenblatt, *Practicing New Historicism* (Chicago: University of Chicago Press, 2001), 1.

45. Brower and Poirier, *In Defense of Reading*, 4.

46. Dewey, *Human Nature*, 209.

47. Wimsatt, *The Verbal Icon*, 50.

48. Steven Belletto argues that Nabokov conceives of a "patterned universe" of "meaningful coincidence" that serves as an invidious contrast to Kinbote's contrived design ("The Zemblan Who Came In from the Cold, or, Nabokov's *Pale Fire*, Chance, and the Cold War," *ELH* 73.3 [2006]: 780, 772). I claim that Nabokov asserts through Shade the creative writer's ability to engender something like an authentically random world immune to meaning making.

49. Vladimir Nabokov, *The Stories of Vladimir Nabokov* (New York: Vintage, 1997), 600.

Chapter 3

1. Huey P. Newton, *Revolutionary Suicide* (New York: Penguin, 2010), 183. Hereafter cited in text.

2. As Sean McCann and Michael Szalay have noted, the New Left's favorite metaphor for naming its opaque and impersonal enemy was "the system," a "hazy rubric" that "seemed both disturbingly alive and resistant to ready definition" ("Introduction: Paul Potter and the Cultural Turn," *Yale Journal of Criticism* 18.2 [2005]: 211).

3. Mark Rudd, "Symbols of the Revolution," in *Up against the Ivy Wall: A History of the Columbia Crisis*, by Jerry Avorn, with Andrew Crane et al. (New York: Athenaeum, 1969), 297.

4. David Bazelon, *The Paper Economy* (New York: Random House, 1963), 362. Hereafter cited in text.

5. Johnson, *The Lavender Scare*, 112.

6. Van Gosse, *Rethinking the New Left: An Interpretative History* (New York: Palgrave Macmillan, 2005), 173.

7. Tom Hayden, "The Trial," in *"Takin' It to the Streets": A Sixties Reader*, ed. Alexander Bloom and Wini Breines (New York: Oxford University Press, 1995), 444. Hereafter cited in text as *TS*.

8. Rudd, "Symbols," 292, 293.

9. Bernardine Dohrn, Bill Ayers, and Jeff Jones, eds., *Sing a Battle Song: The Revolutionary Poetry, Statements, and Communiqués of the Weather Underground, 1970–1974* (New York: Seven Stories, 2006), 239.

10. Tom Hayden, *The Port Huron Statement: The Visionary Call of the 1960s Revolution* (New York: Thunder's Mouth, 2005), 49.

11. Ibid., 149.

12. Robert Kaufman and Michael Folsom, "FSM: An Interpretive Essay," in *FSM: The Free Speech Movement at Berkeley* (San Francisco: W. E. B. Du Bois Club, 1965), 33, 29.

13. Hayden, *The Port Huron Statement*, 51.

14. Theodore Roszak, *The Making of a Counter-Culture* (Berkeley: University of California Press, 1995), 15, 21, 16.

15. David Wise and Thomas Ross, *The Invisible Government* (New York: Random House, 1964), 5. Hereafter cited in text.

16. Mario Savio, "Introduction," in *Berkeley: The New Student Revolt*, by Hal Draper (New York: Grove, 1965), 2.

17. Ibid., 3.

18. Neal Blumenfeld, "Human Dignity and the Multiversity," in *We Want a University*, by The Free Speech Movement (Berkeley: The Free Speech Movement, 1965), 4.

19. Michael Nelken, "My Mind Is Not Property," *Berkeley Graduate Student Journal* 4 (1965): 33.

20. Free Speech Movement, *We Want a University*, 9, 6.

21. Nelken, "My Mind," 33.

22. Michael Rossman, *The Wedding within the War* (Garden City, N.Y.: Doubleday, 1971), 130. Hereafter cited in text.

23. John Searle, *The Campus War: A Sympathetic Look at the Campus in Agony* (New York: World, 1972), 40. Hereafter cited in text.

24. Roszak, *Making of a Counter-Culture*, 79.

25. Allen Ginsberg, *Deliberate Prose: Selected Essays, 1952–1995* (New York: Harper-Collins, 2000), 4.

26. Ibid., 5.

27. Allen Ginsberg, with Allen Young, *Gay Sunshine Interview* (Bolinas, Calif.: Grey Fox, 1974), 34.

28. Hungerford, *Postmodern Belief*, 44.

29. Ginsberg, *Gay Sunshine Interview*, 34.

30. Jerry Rubin, *Do It! Scenarios of the Revolution* (New York: Simon and Schuster, 1970), 17, 37. Hereafter cited in text.

31. Abbie Hoffman, *Steal This Book* (New York: Da Capo, 2002), 76.

32. Jerry Farber, *The Student as Nigger: Essays and Stories* (New York: Pocket, 1970), 22. Hereafter cited in text.

33. Kaufman and Folsom, "FSM," 37.

34. Savio, "Berkeley Fall," 17.

35. Cited in Johnson, *The Lavender Scare*, 112.

36. Robert Dean, *Imperial Brotherhood: Gender and the Making of Cold War Foreign Policy* (Amherst: University of Massachusetts Press, 2001), 155.

37. Ginsberg, *Gay Sunshine*, 34.

38. Thomas Schelling, *Arms and Influence* (New Haven, Conn.: Yale University Press, 1966), 35. Hereafter cited in text.

39. Sontag, *Against Interpretation*, 7, 8.

40. John Rechy, *City of Night* (New York: Grove, 1984), 58, 59, 63.

41. Sontag, *Against Interpretation*, 14.

42. Thomas Pynchon, *The Crying of Lot 49* (Philadelphia: Lippincott, 1966), 73, 65. Hereafter cited in text.

43. Thomas Pynchon, *Gravity's Rainbow* (New York: Penguin, 2006), 525. Hereafter cited in text.

44. Terence Kissack, "Freaking Fag Revolutionaries: New York's Gay Liberation Front, 1969–1971," *Radical History Review* 62 (1995): 111.

45. Theodor Adorno, *Critical Models: Interventions and Catchwords*, trans. Henry Pickford (New York: Columbia University Press, 1998), 79.

46. For an account of the SDS gay baiting that led to Calvert's ostracism, see Douglas Rossinow, *The Politics of Authenticity: Liberalism, Christianity, and the New Left in America* (New York: Columbia University Press, 1998), 306.

47. Eldridge Cleaver, *Soul on Ice* (New York: Dell, 1968), 212.

48. Jim Fouratt, cited in Dudley Clendinen and Adam Nagourney, *Out for Good: The Struggle to Build a Gay Rights Movement in America* (New York: Simon and Schuster, 1999), 28.

49. Cited in Jeremy Varon, *Bringing the War Home: The Weather Underground, the Red Army Faction, and Revolutionary Violence in the Sixties and Seventies* (Berkeley: University of California Press, 2004), 88.

50. Craig Alfred Hanson, "The Fairy Princess Exposed," in *Out of the Closets: Voices of Gay Liberation*, ed. Karla Jay and Allen Young (New York: New York University Press, 1992), 269, 266. Hereafter cited in text as *VG*.

51. Gay Activists Alliance, "Preamble," in *Speaking for Our Lives: Historic Speeches and Rhetoric for Gay and Lesbian Lives*, ed. Robert B. Ridinger (New York: Routledge, 1999), 148.

52. Frank Kameny, "Does Research into Homosexuality Matter?," in *We Are Everywhere: A Historical Sourcebook of Gay and Lesbian Politics*, ed. Mark Blasius and Shane Phelan (New York: Routledge, 1997), 336. Hereafter cited in text as *WA*.

53. Justin Suran, "Coming Out against the War: Antimilitarism and the Politicization of Homosexuality in the Era of Vietnam," *American Quarterly* 53.3 (2001): 463.

54. Rossinow, *Politics*, 16, 15.

55. Bobby Seale, *Seize the Time: The Story of the Black Panther Party and Huey P. Newton* (New York: Random House, 1970), 267.

56. Kissack, "Freaking Fag Revolutionaries," 115.

57. Norman Mailer, *The Prisoner of Sex* (Boston: Little, Brown, 1971), 165, 170. Hereafter cited in text as *PS*.

58. Norman Mailer, *The Armies of the Night: History as a Novel, the Novel as History* (New York: Plume, 1994), 24. Hereafter cited in text.

59. *Armies of the Night* takes a strategically obtuse view of Goodman. Mailer considers Goodman's "damnable tolerance" no more than a "form of super-hygiene," bleaching sex of "sin" and leaving "nothing dirty in the damn stuff" (24). But in "Being Queer" (1969), Goodman writes: "A happy property of sexual acts, and perhaps especially of homosexual acts, is that they are dirty." In this essay, Goodman confesses that he "cannot . . . take seriously . . . ideological liberation movements" and finds "Gay Liberation" in particular marked by "the usual fanaticism" (Taylor Stoehr, ed., *Crazy Hope and Finite Experience: Final Essays of Paul Goodman* [San Francisco: Josey-Bass, 1994], 113, 109).

60. Noting Mailer's "enthusiasm for marital fidelity" in *Armies of the Night,* Sean McCann writes: "Through much of the cultural expression that responded to the Vietnam War . . . marriage serves as the prime metaphor for the obligations of citizenship" (*A Pinnacle of Feeling: American Literature and Presidential Government* [Princeton, N.J.: Princeton University Press, 2008], 146).

61. E. L. Doctorow, *The Book of Daniel* (New York: Random House, 2002), 42. Hereafter cited in text.

Chapter 4

1. Draper, *Berkeley,* 54.

2. Lewis Feuer, *The Conflict of Generations: The Character and Significance of Student Movements* (New York: Basic Books, 1969), 412.

3. David Riesman, "The Academic Career: Notes on Recruitment and Colleagueship," *Daedalus* 88.1 (1959): 163. Hereafter cited in text as "AC."

4. David Riesman, "Permissiveness and Sex Roles," *Marriage and Family Living* 21.3 (1959): 214. Hereafter cited in text as "PSR."

5. David Riesman and Christopher Jencks, *The Academic Revolution* (Garden City, N.Y.: Doubleday, 1968), 37. Hereafter cited in text.

6. Feuer, *Conflict,* 397.

7. Nathan Glazer, *Remembering the Answers: Essays on the American Student Revolt* (New York: Basic Books, 1970), 47. Hereafter cited in text.

8. David Riesman, "Education and Exploitation," *School Review* 68.1 (1960): 32.

9. Mario Savio, "An End to History," in Bloom and Breines, *"Takin' It to the Streets,"* 114.

10. Erving Goffman, *Asylums: Essays on the Social Situation of Mental Patients and Other Inmates* (Chicago: Aldine, 1962), 12. Hereafter cited in text as *A.*

11. Marx, "Role Models," 658.

12. It bears mentioning that Goffman was the sort of Berkeley professor who tended, as Yves Winkins observes, to "avoid teaching whenever possible" ("Erving Goffman: What Is a Life? The Uneasy Making of Intellectual Biography," in *Goffman and Social Organization: Studies in a Sociological Legacy,* ed. Greg Smith [London: Routledge, 1999], 28).

13. R. D. Laing, *The Politics of Experience* (New York: Pantheon, 1967), 84. Hereafter cited in text.

14. Erving Goffman, *Stigma: Notes on the Management of Spoiled Identity* (New York: Simon and Schuster, 1986), 18. Hereafter cited in text as *S.*

15. David Riesman, "Some Questions about the Study of American Character in the Twentieth Century," *Annals of the American Academy of Political and Social Science* 370 (March 1967): 32.

16. Erving Goffman, *The Presentation of Self in Everyday Life* (Garden City, N.Y.: Doubleday, 1959), 56. Hereafter cited in text as *EL.*

17. David Riesman, with Reuel Denny and Nathan Glazer, *The Lonely Crowd: A Study of the Changing American Character* (New Haven, Conn.: Yale University Press, 1950), 22. Hereafter cited in text as *LC*.

18. Herbert Blumer, *Symbolic Interactionism: Perspective and Method* (Berkeley: University of California Press, 1986), 8, 10.

19. Erving Goffman, *Interaction Ritual: Essays in Face-to-Face Behavior* (New Brunswick, N.J.: Transaction, 2005), 21. Hereafter cited in text as *IR*.

20. Mary Esteve notes that the ideal of autonomy informs both Riesman's original 1950 edition of *The Lonely Crowd* and its 1960s reissues, where Riesman's prefaces offer a pointed counterargument to the New Social Movements' equation of autonomy and authenticity ("Shipwreck and Autonomy: Rawls, Riesman, and Oppen in the 1960s," *Yale Journal of Criticism* 18.2 [2005]: 323–349).

21. David Riesman, "Some Observations on Changes in Leisure Attitudes," *Antioch Review* 12.1 (1952): 418.

22. Roland Barthes, *Mythologies*, trans. Annette Laver (New York: Hill and Wang, 1972), 26, 27. Hereafter cited in text.

23. Constantin Stanislavski, *My Life in Art*, trans. Elizabeth Hapgood (New York: Routledge, 1987), 344.

24. Stella Adler, *The Art of Acting*, ed. Howard Kissel (New York: Applause, 2000), 30. Hereafter cited in text.

25. Constantin Stanislavski, *An Actor Prepares*, trans. Elizabeth Hapgood (New York: Routledge, 1989), 177. Hereafter cited in text.

26. Robert H. Hethmon, ed., *Strasberg at the Actors Studio: The Tape-Recorded Sessions* (New York: Theatre Communications Group, 1991), 80.

27. Paul Gray, "Stanislavski and America: A Critical Chronology," *Tulane Drama Review* 9.2 (1964): 35. Hereafter cited in text as "SA."

28. Foster Hirsch, *A Method to Their Madness: A History of the Actors Studio* (New York: Norton, 1984), 108.

29. Richard Schechner, "Stanislavski at School," *Tulane Drama Review* 9.2 (1964): 89. Hereafter cited in text.

30. Skinner, *Walden Two*, 112 .

31. Ibid., 5.

32. Charles McGaw, *Acting Is Believing: A Basic Method for Beginners* (New York: Rinehart, 1955), 5.

33. Joseph Roach, *The Player's Passion: Studies in the Science of Acting* (Newark: University of Delaware Press, 1985), 195–217.

34. B. F. Skinner, *Science and Human Behavior* (New York: Free Press, 1953), 447.

35. Ibid., 166.

36. Robert Lewis, *Method—or Madness?* (New York: Samuel French, 1958), 90.

37. Sanford Meisner and Dennis Longwell, *Sanford Meisner on Acting* (New York: Vintage, 1987), 66.

38. Skinner, *Science and Human Behavior*, 62.

39. David Savran, *Communists, Cowboys, and Queers: The Politics of Masculinity in the Work of Arthur Miller and Tennessee Williams* (Minneapolis: University of Minnesota Press, 1992), 33.

40. Hirsch, *A Method*, 136, 138.

41. Marvin Carlson, "The Resistance to Theatricality," *SubStance* 31.2/3 (2002): 238.

42. Ibid., 241.

43. Patricia Highsmith, *Little Tales of Misogyny* (New York: Norton, 2002), 45. Hereafter cited in text.

44. Marijane Meaker, *Highsmith: A Romance of the 1950s* (San Francisco: Cleis, 2003), 199.

45. Andrew Wilson, *Beautiful Shadow: A Life of Patricia Highsmith* (New York: Bloomsbury, 2004), 299.

46. Patricia Highsmith, *Plotting and Writing Suspense Fiction* (Boston: The Writer, 1966), 146. Hereafter cited in text as *PW*.

47. Patricia Highsmith, *Strangers on a Train* (New York: Norton, 2001), 60.

48. Chris Straayer, "The Talented Post-structuralist: Heteromasculinity, Gay Artifice, and Class Passing," in *Masculinity: Bodies, Movies, Culture*, ed. Peter Lehman (New York: Routledge, 2001), 127.

49. George Haggerty, *Queer Gothic* (Urbana: University of Illinois Press, 2006), 163.

50. Patricia Highsmith, *The Talented Mr. Ripley* (New York: Vintage, 1992), 201. Hereafter cited in text.

51. That he expects to pass as Dickie with his intimates by ventriloquizing his voice on the phone does not alter the fact that Tom's neglect of the subjunctive ought to be secondary to the problem of having to imitate Dickie's voice (a mimicry he has at any rate perfected). What counts as real, and hence requires all of Tom's adroitness, is less the sound of Dickie's larynx than the far less tangible gestures, including solecisms, that constitute his *habitus*.

52. Larrabee, *The Self-Conscious Society*, 28.

53. Leo Braudy, *The Frenzy of Renown: Fame and Its History* (New York: Oxford University Press, 1986), 555.

54. William Wordsworth, "Daffodils," in *Romanticism: An Anthology*, ed. Duncan Wu (Oxford: Blackwell, 2012), 558.

55. Dickie might be said to borrow the approach to solitude, identified by Frances Ferguson in some Romantic writing, in which "individuation" manifests as "a terror of being included in a social induction"—that is, of being cast as indistinct from a "type" (*Solitude and the Sublime: Romanticism and the Aesthetics of Individuation* [New York: Routledge, 1992], 32, 31).

56. Charles Taylor, *The Ethic of Authenticity* (Cambridge, Mass.: Harvard University Press, 1991), 29.

57. Eve Kosofsky Sedgwick, *Epistemology of the Closet* (Berkeley: University of California Press, 1990), 67.

58. Ibid., 225.

59. James Baldwin, *Giovanni's Room* (New York: Dell, 2000), 31, 27. Hereafter cited in text.

60. Judith Butler, *Bodies That Matter: On the Discursive Limits of "Sex"* (New York: Routledge, 1993), 2, 3.

61. Ibid., 169.

62. Wilson, *Beautiful Shadow*, 441.

63. Ibid., 442.

64. Meaker, *Highsmith*, 58.

65. Patricia Highsmith, *Ripley under Ground* (New York: Norton, 2008), 161.

Chapter 5

1. Goffman, *Stigma*, 140.

2. Gayle Rubin, "Studying Sexual Subcultures: Excavating the Ethnography of Gay Communities in Urban North America," in *Out in Theory: The Emergence of Lesbian and Gay Anthropology*, ed. Ellen Lewin and William Leap (Urbana: University of Illinois Press, 2002), 26.

3. Howard Becker, "Whose Side Are We On?," *Social Problems* 14.3 (1967): 247.

4. Ibid., 243.

5. Mary McIntosh, "The Homosexual Role," *Social Problems* 16.2 (1968): 182, 183. Hereafter cited in text.

6. Gay Liberation Front, "Statement of Purpose," in Bloom and Breines, *"Takin' It to the Streets,"* 171.

7. Martha Shelley, "Gay Is Good," in Jay and Young, *Out of the Closets*, 33. Hereafter cited in text.

8. Laud Humphreys, *Tearoom Trade: Impersonal Sex in Public Places* (New York: Aldine, 1975), 27, 29. Hereafter cited in text.

9. Goffman, *Presentation*, 235.

10. Pynchon, *The Crying of Lot 49*, 52. Hereafter cited in text.

11. Saul Bellow, *Herzog* (New York: Viking, 1964), 227.

12. Philip Roth, *Portnoy's Complaint* (New York: Random House, 1969), 20. Hereafter cited in text.

13. James Baldwin, *Notes of a Native Son* (Boston: Beacon, 1955), 14. Hereafter cited in text.

14. Lionel Trilling, "The Kinsey Report," in *The Moral Obligation to Be Intelligent: Selected Essays*, ed. Leon Wieseltier (New York: Farrar, Straus and Giroux, 2000), 122. Hereafter cited in text.

15. Kurt Vonnegut, *Slaughterhouse Five* (New York: Dial, 2005), 25. Hereafter cited in text.

16. Goffman, *Presentation*, 52, 90.

17. Becker, "Whose Side?," 240.

18. Ibid.

19. Goffman, *Stigma*, 5.

20. Esther Newton, *Mother Camp: Female Impersonators in America* (Chicago: University of Chicago Press, 1979), 35. Hereafter cited in text.

21. Esther Newton, *Margaret Mead Made Me Gay: Personal Essays, Public Ideas* (Durham, N.C.: Duke University Press, 2001), 197.

22. Judith Butler, "Performative Acts and Gender Constitution: An Essay in Phenomenology and Feminist Theory," *Theatre Journal* 40.4 (1988): 528.

23. Erving Goffman, *Gender Advertisements* (New York: HarperCollins, 1979), 7.

24. Goffman appears once in a footnote in Butler's *Frames of War: When Is Life Grievable?* (London: Verso, 2009), where his *Frame Analysis* is listed among the sources for her "reading of the frame" (8).

25. Butler, *Bodies That Matter*, 178.

26. Butler, "Performative Acts," 526.

27. Heather Love, "Close but Not Deep: Literary Ethics and the Descriptive Turn," *New Literary History* 41.2 (2010): 381. Also see Abigail Cheever, *Real Phonies: Cultures of Authenticity in Post–World War II America* (Athens: University of Georgia Press, 2010): "What Goffman seeks to avoid is establishing some sort of authentic self against whom any individual performance might be judged" (211).

28. Goffman, *Gender Advertisements*, 9.

29. See the posthumously published "Felicity's Condition," *American Journal of Sociology* 89.1 (1983): 1–53, as well as the essays in *Forms of Talk* (Philadelphia: University of Pennsylvania Press, 1981), which touch very briefly on speech act theory.

30. Eliot Freidson, "Celebrating Erving Goffman," *Contemporary Sociology* 12.4 (1983): 362.

31. Dell Hymes, "On Erving Goffman," *Theory and Society* 13.5 (1984): 629.

32. Goffman, *Gender Advertisements*, 7.

33. Love, "Close but Not Deep," 376.

34. Michael Schudson, "Embarrassment and Goffman's Idea of Human Nature," *Theory and Society* 13.5 (1984): 637.

35. Goffman, *Presentation*, 254.

36. "To claim that all gender is like drag," Butler writes, "is to suggest that 'imitation' is at the heart of the *heterosexual* project" and "that hegemonic heterosexuality is itself a constant and repeated effort to imitate its own idealizations" (*Bodies That Matter*, 125).

37. Judith Butler, *Gender Trouble: Feminism and the Subversion of Identity* (New York: Routledge, 1990), 147.

38. Judith Butler, "Merely Cultural," *New Left Review* 227 (Jan.–Feb. 1998): 34.

39. Hayden, *The Port Huron Statement*, 153.

40. Judith Butler, *Undoing Gender* (New York: Routledge, 2004), 218.

41. Ibid., 219.

42. Butler, *Gender Trouble*, xi.

43. Butler, *Bodies That Matter*, 237.

44. Cited in Gary Marx, "Role Distance and Role Models: A Remembrance of Erving Goffman," *Theory and Society* 13.5 (1984): 658.

45. Sontag, *Against Interpretation*, 282. Hereafter cited in text.

46. F. William Howton, "Filming Andy Warhol's *Trash*: An Interview with Director Paul Morrissey," *Filmmakers Newsletter* 5.8 (1972): 25.

47. Jon Davies, *Trash: A Queer Film Classic* (Vancouver, Canada: Arsenal Pulp, 2009), 18.

48. Michael Moon and Eve Kosofsky Sedgwick, "Divinity: A Dossier, a Performance Piece, a Little-Understood Emotion," in *Tendencies*, by Sedgwick (Durham, N.C.: Duke University Press, 1993), 217.

49. John Waters, *Hairspray, Female Trouble, and Multiple Maniacs: Three More Screenplays* (New York: Thunder's Mouth, 2005), 219.

50. Frank O'Hara, *Collected Poems*, ed. Donald Allen (Berkeley: University of California Press, 1995), 197.

51. Gary Snyder, "Energy Is Eternal Delight," *New York Times*, January 12, 1972, 43.

52. Roderick Nash, *The Rights of Nature: A History of Environmental Ethics* (Madison: University of Wisconsin Press, 1989), 3.

53. John Waters, *Shock Value: A Tasteful Book about Bad Taste* (New York: Thunder's Mouth, 2005), 62.

54. Richard Bach, *Jonathan Livingston Seagull* (New York: Macmillan, 1970), 60.

55. Gore Vidal, *Myra Breckinridge* (Boston: Little, Brown, 1968), 14. Hereafter cited in text.

56. Where Myra finds the "films of the forties" unsurpassed in their relevance, Vidal saw them as "so many dinosaur droppings" ("The Ashes of Hollywood I: The Bottom Four of the Top Ten," *New York Review of Books*, May 17, 1973, 24).

57. Leo Bersani, *The Culture of Redemption* (Cambridge, Mass.: Harvard University Press, 1990).

58. John Waters, *Pink Flamingos and Other Filth: Three Screenplays* (New York: Thunder's Mouth, 2005), 63.

59. Waters, *Shock Value*, 62.

Chapter 6

1. Vonnegut, *Slaughterhouse Five*, 111.

2. Cited in Barbara Seaman, *Lovely Me: The Life of Jacqueline Susann* (New York: Seven Stories, 1996), 390.

3. Ibid., 226, 139.

4. Sara Davidson, "Jacqueline Susann: The Writing Machine," *Harper's*, October 1969, 65.

5. Jacqueline Susann, *Valley of the Dolls* (New York: Grove, 1997), 299. Hereafter cited in text.

6. William S. Kroger and S. Charles Freed, "Psychosomatic Aspects of Frigidity," *Journal of the American Medical Association* 143.6 (1950): 527. Hereafter cited in text.

7. Edmund Bergler, "The Problem of Frigidity," *Psychiatric Quarterly* 18.3 (1944): 390.

8. Clark Vincent, "Sources of Symptomatic Frigidity," *Marriage and Family Living* 18.4 (1956): 359. Hereafter cited in text.

9. Lena Levine and David Goldsmith Loth, *The Frigid Wife* (New York: Julian Messner, 1962), 117. Hereafter cited in text.

10. Helen Gurley Brown, *Sex and the Single Girl* (New York: Bernard Geis, 1962), 5, 6. Hereafter cited in text.

11. On the conflict between testing for "native intelligence" and testing for "achievement," see Nicholas Lemann, *The Big Test: The Secret History of the American Meritocracy* (New York: Farrar, Straus and Giroux, 2000), 27–41.

12. Cited in Seaman, *Lovely Me*, 288.

13. Letty Cottin Pogrebin, *How to Make It in a Man's World* (Garden City, N.Y.: Doubleday, 1970), 182, 40. Hereafter cited in text.

14. Abraham H. Maslow, *Toward a Psychology of Being*, 3rd ed. (New York: Wiley, 1998), 147. Hereafter cited in text.

15. Abraham H. Maslow, *The Maslow Business Reader*, ed. Deborah Stephens (New York: Wiley, 2000), 15.

16. Douglas McGregor, "An Uneasy Look at Performance Appraisal," *Harvard Business Review* 35.3 (1957): 92.

17. Douglas McGregor, *The Human Side of Enterprise* (New York: McGraw-Hill, 2005), 354.

18. Michael Fried, *Absorption and Theatricality: Painting and Beholder in the Age of Diderot* (Chicago: University of Chicago Press, 1980).

19. Maslow, *Maslow Business Reader*, 15.

20. Letty Cottin Pogrebin, *Getting Yours: How to Make the System Work for the Working Woman* (New York: David McKay, 1975), 8.

21. Ibid., 101.

22. Joan Didion, *Play It As It Lays* (New York: Farrar, Straus and Giroux, 2005), 23. Hereafter cited in text.

23. Friedan, *The Feminine Mystique*, 121. Hereafter cited in text.

24. Joan Didion, *The White Album* (New York: Farrar, Straus and Giroux, 1990), 118.

25. Sylvia Plath, *The Bell Jar* (New York: HarperCollins, 2009), 63, 64, 95. Hereafter cited in text.

26. John Rawls, *A Theory of Justice* (Cambridge, Mass.: Harvard University Press, 1971), 7, 74, 75.

27. Christopher Jencks, Marshall Smith, Henry Acland, Mary Jo Bane, David Cohen, Herbert Gintis, Barbara Heyns, and Stephanie Michelson, *Inequality: A Reassessment of the Effect of Family and Schooling in America* (New York: Basic Books, 1972), 227.

28. Ibid., 9, 3.

29. Langdon Hammer, "Plath's Lives," *Representations* 75 (2001): 66.

30. In "Sylvia Plath's Anti-psychiatry" (*Minnesota Review*, n.s., 55–57 [2002]: 245–

256), Maria Farland argues that *The Bell Jar*'s veneration of the "newly-privatized" (248) mental hospital shares in the antipsychiatric movement's effort to discredit state institutions. In my view Plath's hierarchy of institutions suggests less a critique of the welfare state than a plea for the meritocracy; the novel's private hospital, with its "exclusivity" (247) and its system of "privileges" (252), functions, after all, like a selective college.

31. Joanne Greenberg, *I Never Promised You a Rose Garden* (New York: Holt, 2009), 271. Hereafter cited in text.

32. Sue Kaufman, *Diary of a Mad Housewife* (New York: Thunder's Mouth, 2005), 245, 136. Hereafter cited in text.

33. Rona Jaffe, *The Best of Everything* (New York: Penguin, 2005), 45. Hereafter cited in text.

34. Arlie Russell Hochschild, *The Managed Heart: Commercialization of Human Feeling* (Berkeley: University of California Press, 1983), 53.

35. Ibid., 147.

36. Ibid., 91, 19.

37. Trudy Baker and Rachel Jones, *Coffee, Tea or Me? The Uninhibited Memoirs of Two Airline Stewardesses* (New York: Penguin, 2003), 200. Hereafter cited in text.

38. Erica Jong, *Fear of Flying* (New York: New American Library, 2003), 5, 7. Hereafter cited in text.

39. Daniel Bell, *The Coming of Post-industrial Society: A Venture in Social Forecasting* (New York: Basic Books, 1973), 453.

40. Marcuse, *One-Dimensional Man*, 242, 24.

41. Roszak, *Making of a Counter-Culture*, 62.

42. Hochschild, *The Managed Heart*, 5.

43. Jo Freeman, "The Tyranny of Structurelessness," in *Women in Politics*, ed. Jane S. Jaquette (New York: Wiley, 1974), 202, 213.

44. Ibid., 213.

45. Maria Farland, "'Total System, Total Solution, and Total Apocalypse': Sex Oppression, Systems of Property, and 1970s Women's Liberation Fiction," *Yale Journal of Criticism* 18.2 (2005): 402.

46. Laurence Peter and Raymond Hull, *The Peter Principle: Why Things Always Go Wrong* (New York: Harper, 2009), 63.

47. Peter F. Drucker, *The Age of Discontinuity: Guidelines to Our Changing Society* (New Brunswick, N.J.: Transaction, 2000), 253. Hereafter cited in text.

48. Bell, *Coming of Post-industrial Society*, 68.

49. Kathie Sarachild, "Consciousness-Raising: A Radical Weapon," in *Feminist Revolution*, ed. Redstockings (New York: Basic Books, 1978), 145.

50. Richard Florida, *The Rise of the Creative Class: And How It's Transforming Work, Leisure, and Everyday Life* (New York: Basic Books, 2004), 92. Hereafter cited in text.

51. Sarachild, "Consciousness-Raising," 145.

Epilogue

1. Tom Hayden, "The Politics of 'the Movement,'" in *The Politics of the Powerless*, ed. Robert Binstock and Katherine Ely (Cambridge, Mass.: Winthrop, 1971), 310.

2. David Riesman, *On Higher Education: The Academic Enterprise in an Era of Rising Student Consumerism* (New Brunswick, N.J.: Transaction, 1998), 68.

3. Kathie Sarachild, "Consciousness-Raising," 145.

4. Barbara Susan Kaminsky, "About My Consciousness Raising," in *Voices from Women's Liberation*, ed. Leslie Tanner (New York: New American Library, 1970), 242.

5. D. A. Miller, *Jane Austen, or the Secret of Style* (Princeton, N.J.: Princeton University Press, 2003), 96.

6. Bourdieu, *Outline*, 35.

7. Ibid.

8. Rorty, *Contingency*, xv. Hereafter cited in text.

9. Cary Nelson and Steven Watt, *Academic Keywords: A Devil's Dictionary for Higher Education* (New York: Routledge, 1999), 208. The phrase "lumpen professoriat" (145) also appears in John Searle's *The Campus War*, though Searle uses it not as a rallying cry but as an insult.

10. Judith Halberstam, *In a Queer Time and Place* (New York: New York University Press, 2005), 53, 70.

11. "The beliefs which we have most warrant for," Mill writes in *On Liberty* (1859), "have no safeguard to rest on, but a standing invitation to the whole world to prove them unfounded" (J. S. Mill, *On Liberty and Other Writings*, ed. Stefan Collini [Cambridge: Cambridge University Press, 1989], 24).

12. Ibid., 23.

13. Cited in Francesca Polletta, *Freedom Is an Endless Meeting: Democracy in American Social Movements* (Chicago: University of Chicago Press, 2004), 1.

14. José Esteban Muñoz, *Cruising Utopia: The Then and There of Queer Futurity* (New York: New York University Press, 2009), 1. Hereafter cited in text.

15. For an argument that treats "something" explicitly as another name for political possibility, see Lauren Berlant, "68, or Something," *Critical Inquiry* 21.1 (1994): 124–155.

16. Poirier, *Poetry and Pragmatism*, 182; Goffman, *Asylums*, 320.

17. Dewey, *Human Nature*, 36.

18. Sontag, *Against Interpretation*, 285.

19. Heather Love, "Queers _____ This," in *After Sex? On Writing since Queer Theory*, ed. Janet Halley and Andrew Parker (Durham, N.C.: Duke University Press, 2011), 183.

20. Elizabeth Freeman, *Time Binds: Queer Temporalities, Queer Histories* (Durham, N.C.: Duke University Press, 2010), 3; Lee Edelman, *No Future: Queer Theory and the Death Drive* (Durham, N.C.: Duke University Press, 2004), 26; Halberstam, *In a Queer Time*, 5.

Index